The
Italian
1 0 0

The
Italian
1 0 0

---

*A Ranking of the
Most Influential
Cultural, Scientific,
and Political Figures,
Past and Present*

Stephen J. Spignesi

*Ranking Compiled in Consultation
with Michael Vena, Ph.D.*

A Citadel Press Book
Published by Carol Publishing Group

A Citadel Press Book
Published by Carol Publishing Group
Citadel Press is a registered trademark of Carol Communications, Inc.

Editorial, sales and distribution, rights and permissions inquiries should be addressed to Carol Publishing Group, 120 Enterprise Avenue, Secaucus, N.J. 07094

In Canada: Canadian Manda Group, One Atlantic Avenue, Suite 105, Toronto, Ontario M6K 3E7

Carol Publishing Group books may be purchased in bulk at special discounts for sales promotion, fund-raising, or educational purposes. Special editions can be created to specifications. For details, contact Special Sales Department, 120 Enterprise Avenue, Secaucus, N.J. 07094

Designed by Andrew B. Gardner

Manufactured in the United States of America

10 9 8 7 6 5 4 3 2 1

Library of Congress Cataloging-in-Publication Data

Spignesi, Stephen J.
      The Italian 100 : a ranking of the most influential cultural, scientific, and
   political figures, past and present / Stephen J. Spignesi ; ranking compiled
   in consultation with Michael Vena.
         p.   cm.
      "A Citadel Press book."
      Includes bibliographical references and index.
      ISBN 0-8065-1821-9 (hc)
      1. Italy—Biography.   2. Celebrities—Italy—Biography.   I. Vena, Michael.
   II. Title.
   CT1124.S65   1997
   920.045—dc21   96-51799
      [B]   CIP

To my mother and father

A man who has not been in Italy is always conscious of an inferiority from his not having seen what it is expected a man should see . . . all our religion, almost all our law, almost all our arts, almost all that sets us above savages, has come to us from the shores of the Mediterranean.

—JAMES BOSWELL
The Life of Samuel Johnson

CONTENTS

ACKNOWLEDGMENTS

I received assistance for *The Italian 100* from a great many people and institutions, both in the United States and in Italy, and for their help, I am extremely grateful.

First, I'd like to thank my wife, Pam, for letting me lock myself away with people ranging from St. Francis of Assisi to Madonna without thinking it the least bit strange.

I would also like to especially acknowledge Italian scholar and writer Dr. Michael Vena of Southern Connecticut State University for his participation, valuable contributions, and astute insights; also, Mauro Spignesi in Sardinia, Italy, for his E-mailed suggestions and encouragement, as well as his frequent packages of research materials and books; my friend Joe Jarmie at Yale University and Yale's Beineke Rare Book and Manuscript Library; the University of New Haven for its exhaustive stacks and extremely helpful staff; the Hagaman Memorial Library; the James Blackstone Library; the Bettmann Archive; Photofest; John White; John Amore; Dante Fasano; Joseph Parcella; and my friend George Beahm for his cheering and encouragement from the sidelines.

And finally, special thanks to my editors Jonathan Erway and Juli Barbato and my publisher Steven Schragis, three *fantastico paesani* who were all exceptionally helpful and supportive during the writing of *The Italian 100*. Their suggestions and advice made the book better than I could have made it alone. Also, a special thanks to Phil Koslow for his inspired help with this book.

Molto grazia to one and all.

Stephen J. Spignesi
New Haven, Connecticut

INTRODUCTION

The traveller who has gone to Italy to study the tactile values of
Giotto, or the corruption of the Papacy, may return remember-
ing nothing but the blue sky and the men and women under it.
            —E. M. FORSTER
            A Room With a View

Luigi Barzini, in his book *The Italians* declares, "There is no denying that all her geniuses made Italy great . . ."; and Barzini is, of
course, correct. Italy and its people *are* great: Italians and Italian
Americans have contributed as much to the worlds of art, science,
music, and cuisine as any other group that has ever existed on this
planet—if not more.

I am very proud to be of Italian descent: The American
branch of my personal family tree only goes back two generations;
before that, all my ancestors are from the "old country." My dear
cousin, *mia cugino* Mauro Spignesi, a respected journalist on the isle
of Sardinia who helped with my research for this book via the
Internet, tells me that there are still many Spignesis in Italy; some
of them are related to me by blood, but I have never met or even
corresponded with most of them.

But they are still *mia famiglia* and thus are special to me.

And that may be the true essence of being Italian: the importance of blood; of being *connected,* over the years and the miles, and
by a common, proud heritage.

You will find in this volume biographical profiles of one hundred of the most influential Italians and Italian Americans in world
history. The areas of influence of these remarkable men and
women range from science (the subject with the highest represen-
tation) in all its configurations to the fields of exploration, politics,

xiii

religion, sports, and, of course, art in all its myriad forms.

In short, Italians have given the world much more than *mani-cotti* and Gucci shoes. In addition to the fields named herein, many aspects of everyday life—from banking to religious worship to cosmetic surgery to taking heart medication to playing the piano—have been influenced and enriched by the inspired work of Italians. Their stories are told in the pages that follow.

THE RANKING

The Italian historical figures profiled in *The Italian 100* lived and worked in the sixteen hundred years from the fourth through the twentieth centuries. Ancient Rome and its people have not been included because they warrant a book of their own; also, we felt that people who lived after the fall of Rome have had a more enduring impact on the world as we know it than figures from antiquity.

As would be expected, a great many names—thirty-four—are from the three centuries of the Italian Renaissance, the period that extends from the birth of Petrarch in 1304 through the death of Titian in 1576; those historical milestones are often taken as the beginning and ending of that unprecedented epoch.

The reader will find that scientists and inventors comprise a large part of the top half of the list. These men and women are the ones who have had the most direct impact on humankind: Many of them achieved medical breakthroughs of monumental importance (Morgagni, Golgi, Porta, Sobrero, Cerletti, and Bini); many invented something that changed the way we live for all time (Galileo, Marconi, Fermi, Volta, Torricelli); while others were courageous explorers who helped define the world as we know it today (Columbus, Polo, Cabot, Verrazano).

The people who have made life more interesting and *enjoyable*—composers, painters, sculptors, writers, and performers—are also represented in force. The list of Italian artists is awe inspiring. When choosing an artist to include in this ranking, I tried to concentrate on those whose work is likely to be eternal (Michelangelo, da Vinci, Dante, Verdi) and also those who redefined their field and changed the way art was created by those who followed them (Guido of Arezzo, Cimabue, Masaccio, Donatello).

Notorious and controversial characters have also been included here, since "influence" does not necessarily mean "good" influence. Benito Mussolini, Lucky Luciano, and Al Capone are profiled, as are Sacco and Vanzetti, the Italian immigrants whose execution greatly changed the perception of Italians in the United States.

Twentieth-century figures are also represented in all their glory, ranging from "Joltin' Joe" DiMaggio to Lee Iacocca to that lightning rod of controversy, Madonna. Though these individuals have been able to exert their influence for a relatively brief period in world history; the shrinking of the world through technology and mass communications have allowed them to have as widespread an impact as those whose influence has come down through the centuries.

The
Italian
1 0 0

Galileo Galilei
1564–1642

Having been admonished by this Holy Office entirely to abandon the false opinion that the Sun was the center of the universe and immovable, and that the Earth was not the center of
the same and that it moved . . . I have been . . . suspected of
heresy, that is, of having held and believed that the Sun is the
center of the universe and immovable, and that the Earth is
not the center of the same and that it does move . . . I abjure
with a sincere heart and unfeigned faith, I curse and detest the
said errors and heresies, and generally all and every error and
sect contrary to the Holy Catholic Church.
> — GALILEO GALILEI's recantation of his sup-
> port of Copernicus's heliocentric theory

Eppur si muove. And yet it moves.
> — GALILEO GALILEI's muttered remark after
> his recantation

Galileo was born in Pisa, Italy, on February 15, 1564. He has been ranked as the most influential Italian of all time in this volume primarily because he developed the scientific method, which has transformed modern life in ways too numerous to calculate. He is also honored here for his groundbreaking contributions to the sciences of physics, astronomy, mechanics, mathematics, timekeeping, entomology, hydrodynamics, and cartography.

The scientific method can be briefly defined as a process that uses experiments to show what *does* happen, not what *should* happen. Galileo redefined the parameters of science with his unwavering insistence on the experimental proof of any theory that attempted to explain a natural phenomenon. The *American Heritage Dictionary* today defines science as "the observation, identification, description, experimental investigation, and theoretical explanation of natural phenomena." This is essentially Galileo's scientific method, a paradigm for all serious explorations of the natural world as experienced by humans.

Galileo's first major contributions to science were in the field of mechanics. As a young man, Galileo questioned Aristotle's long-honored theory that heavier objects fall faster than lighter objects, and he went on to conduct experiments proving that they indeed did not. In 1592, when Galileo was twenty-eight, his deductions about falling objects caused such an uproar among his colleagues at the University of Pisa that he left the school and moved to the University of Padua, where he remained for eighteen years as a lecturer in mathematics.

Galileo also discovered the law of inertia, which the British scientist Isaac Newton later restated as his First Law of Motion: If friction is removed from a moving object, the object will continue to move indefinitely.

Galileo's other accomplishments vividly illustrate the ferocious power of his intellect and lead one to wonder what he might have achieved had he been born into a more technologically advanced age in which he had available to him computers, high-tech communications, and unlimited access to information. Here is just a sampling of his actual accomplishments:

● Galileo discovered, at the age of nineteen, the timekeeping properties of the pendulum, thereby establishing the rudimentary foundation for the invention of the pendulum clock (which was constructed in 1641, when Galileo's son devised a pendulum clock using his father's writings).

- In 1590, Galileo published *On Motion*, a work that completely refuted Aristotelian geocentricism, the theory that the sun and all the planets revolve around Earth.

- In 1592, Galileo "reinvented" the thermoscope (the forerunner of the modern thermometer, which had originally been conceived by Ctesibus in the third century B.C.); he also did experiments with water pumped from a well, which led to Evangelista Torricelli's development of the barometer and hence made important contributions to the study of weather patterns (see chapter 7).

- In 1597, Galileo invented the sector, a measuring and calculating device similar to what is now known as the compass. This tool will continue to be used for years to come.

- In 1609, Galileo heard about the invention in Holland (by Hans Lippershey) of a rudimentary device "by the aid of which visible objects, although at a great distance from the eye to the observer, were seen distinctly as if near." From this description, Galileo was able to construct a perfectly designed telescope (3 power, which eventually he improved to 30 power). With this instrument he determined that the Milky Way was composed of individual stars, described the surface of the moon, saw four of Jupiter's moons, and observed the phases of the planet Venus. In 1610, Galileo wrote the following in *The Sidereal Messenger:*

    > [W]e have a notable and splendid argument to remove the scruples of those who can tolerate the revolution of the planets round the Sun in the Copernican system, yet are so disturbed by the motion of one Moon about the Earth, while both accomplish an orbit of a year's length about the Sun, that they consider this theory of the universe must be upset as impossible; for now we have not one planet only revolving about another, while both traverse a vast orbit about the Sun, but our sense of sight presents to us four satellites circling about Jupiter, like our Moon about the Earth, while the whole system travels over a mighty orbit about the Sun in the space of twelve years.

- In 1610, Galileo used a microscope to study insect anatomy. Also in this year he published *Siderius Nuncius*, which described the surface of the moon.

- In 1613, Galileo published *Letters on the Solar Spots*, in which he publicly endorsed Copernican heliocentric theory.

● In 1632, Galileo published *Dialogue on the Two Great World Systems*, a book he wrote in Italian, not Latin, so that it would reach a wide-ranging, nonscientific audience. In this work, Galileo staunchly—and with deliberate scientific precision—again defended Copernican heliocentrism. This book so angered the Catholic church that the following year Galileo, then sixty-nine, was brought to trial before the Inquisition and charged with heresy. He publicly recanted his beliefs (although he did have the last word) and was sentenced to house arrest at Arcetri for the rest of his life. He died there in 1642. During this last decade of Galileo's life, the great English poet John Milton visited him at Arcetri. Milton described Galileo as "a prisoner to the Inquisition for thinking in astronomy otherwise than the Franciscan and Dominican licensers thought." In 1992, the Church—at the urging of Pope John Paul II—exonerated Galileo by repealing the prohibition against teaching the theories of Copernicus. Galileo's legacy as a great scientist and a daring, independent thinker remains dramatically alive.

Christopher Columbus
1451–1506

After all had rendered thanks to Our Lord, kneeling on the ground and kissing it with tears of joy for His great favor to them, the Admiral arose and gave this island the name San Salvador. Then, in the presence of the many natives assembled there, he took possession of it in the name of the Catholic Sovereigns with appropriate ceremony and words.
                    —FERNANDO COLÓN, *The Life of the Admiral*
                    Christopher Columbus by His Son

It is true that explorers as a group usually do not have the kind of overwhelming global and historical impact that scientists and inventors do, but in the case of Christopher Columbus, generalizations like that simply do not apply. The European exploration of the Americas ranks as one of the most significant developments in history.

Cristoforo Colombo was born in Genoa in 1451. Although the exact date of his birth is unknown, historians place it sometime between August 26 and October 31. It is known that he was a pirate when he was in his twenties and that he fought in the sea battle of Cape Saint Vincent when he was twenty-five. Christopher Columbus believed that it was divine prophecy that he should go on a quest of discovery, although at the time he believed he was destined to find a route to the Orient.

Ten years after his pivotal 1492 sea journey, in a 1502 letter to King Ferdinand and Queen Isabella, the great mariner told the monarchs, "In the carrying out of this enterprise of the Indies, neither reason nor mathematics nor maps were any use to me: fully accomplished were the words of Isaiah." The passage he was referring to, Isaiah 11: 10–12, concerns the regathering of the scattered peoples of Israel. Perhaps it was an interpretive stretch for Columbus to read a divine edict into this Old Testament passage, but such was his belief, and for close to a decade he strove to find the financing for what he believed would be his ultimate mission.

Columbus first proposed his venture—which ultimately resulted in the opening up of the Western Hemisphere to European colonization—to Portugal's king João II in 1484, but the king turned him down. On May 1, 1486, King Ferdinand and Queen Isabella of Spain provisionally accepted Columbus's exploration plans and set up a commission of "learned men and mariners" to review his planned journey. Four years later, the commission rejected Columbus's proposal—and not because they imagined that the world was flat but because they believed—correctly—that the Orient was much farther from Spain than Columbus estimated. Only in 1492, with the urging of friar-astronomer Antonio de Marchena and ship's pilot Martín Alonso Pinzón, did the king and queen reconsider their decision and agree to fund the trip.

Almost five centuries earlier, Vikings (most notably, Leif and Thorfinn Eriksson) had explored the North American coast but were completely unsuccessful at establishing viable colonies or commercially exploiting their discoveries. Prior to Columbus's momentous journeys, European exploration had mainly consisted of a few Portuguese expeditions to Africa and the Azores, and Italian explorer Niccolò Conti's 1440 journeys to Indonesia and Malaya.

Christopher Columbus set out from Palos, Spain, on August 3, 1492, hoping to find the aforementioned westward sea route to the Orient. Maps of the time had considerable errors, and Columbus did not even know of the existence of North America when he left

Spain with his three small ships, the forty-ton *Niña* (with eighteen men and commanded by thirty-two-year-old Vincente Yañez Pizon), the fifty-ton *Pinta* (with eighteen men and commanded by fifty-two-year-old Martín Alonso Pinzón), and his own one hundred-ton flagship, the *Marigalante*, rechristened the *Santa María* when Columbus took command (with fifty-two men).

Basing his voyage distance calculations on passages from the Second Book of Esdras in the Protestant Apocryphra, Columbus determined that "India" was just under 4,000 miles from Spain. On most of the maps of the age (primarily the works of cartographers Paolo dal Pozzo Toscanelli and Martin Behaim), the Earth's circumference was reduced by 25 percent, and the width of Europe and Asia was shown to be 180 degrees instead of 126 degrees. These miscalculations not only gave Columbus no way of knowing of the existence of North America, they also caused him to greatly underestimate the duration of the journey.

On August 6, 1492, Columbus stopped briefly at the Canary Islands, leaving there on September 6, 1492, to continue his westward journey. (He landed in the Canaries at Tenerife because the *Pinta* had lost her rudder and the ship needed refitting.)

On October 12, he sighted land. Columbus made landfall in the Bahamas on an island he christened San Salvador and stayed through the winter. He and his crew were met by large numbers of natives they called "Indians" (believing they had reached the Indies) and were received warmly. These individuals were amazed by articles made of steel (especially swords, which they unwittingly grabbed by the blade, cutting themselves) and treated anything given to them as holy objects since, as Columbus's son Ferdinand wrote, "[T]hey were convinced our men had come from heaven, and therefore they wished to have some relic of them." Columbus and his men went on to explore the other islands in the area [and stayed through the winter]. He returned to Spain in March 1493 and made three subsequent sea voyages trying to find the westward route to the Orient.

Columbus discovered many new foods in the New World, including corn, sweet potatoes, peppers, allspice, plantains, pineapples, and turtle meat. There also seems to be evidence that Columbus brought something else *less* appealing back to Europe: syphilis.

As promised, Queen Isabella made Columbus viceroy of the Indies he had discovered, but he was such an inept administrator that he was ultimately dismissed and returned to Spain in chains.

Columbus always wrote in Spanish, never Italian, and made subsequent exploratory journeys (one against direct royal orders) during his life. In his final years, he yearned for the glory and riches he had achieved as a young explorer, but his rewards were few, and he suffered from increasingly poor health.

There has been a great deal of speculation in recent years about Columbus's true ethnic heritage. Historical revisionists have attempted to prove that Columbus was not of Italian origin and have claimed that he was Portuguese, French, German, English, Irish, Greek, Russian, and even Native American. There exists, however, incontrovertible historical evidence (including writings by Columbus's own son Ferdinand) that Columbus was, indeed, born in Genoa, Italy. Columbus himself once wrote, "Being as I was born in Genoa," and renowned historian Samuel Eliot Morison concluded in his book *The Great Explorers*, "There is no more reason to doubt that Christopher Columbus was a Genoa-born Catholic . . . than to doubt that Abraham Lincoln was born in Hardin, Kentucky, in 1809, of British stock." Morison dismisses all other theories as to Columbus's "true" heritage as "fantasies."

Columbus died on May 21, 1506, and today his remains lie in the cathedral of Santo Domingo in the Dominican Republic on the island of Hispaniola.

The legacy of Christopher Columbus is incalculable. By opening up the Western Hemisphere to European exploration, he changed the world for all time and acted as the catalyst for the creation of societies that now account for one-sixth of the world's population and much of the world's industrial might.

Guglielmo Marconi

1874–1937

"S"
— GUGLIELMO MARCONI, The first message ever
transmitted by radio, December 12, 1901

When Guglielmo Marconi died in Rome on July 20, 1937, at the age of sixty-seven, all the radio stations in the world broadcast nothing but silence for two full minutes in honor of the great Italian scientist's contributions to the technology of wireless communication. "Dead air" is the gravest sin a radio or television station can commit, and yet, on that day, stations went silent. Such was the depth of appreciation for Marconi's achievements. Wireless transmission paved the way for the invention of the television and ushered in an age of rapid dissemination of weather information, military and police communications, medical and scientific research data, and, of course, entertainment. As the Italian historian Arturo Barone put it, "Marconi . . . laid the foundations upon which the whole system of modern communications was built."

Guglielmo Marconi was born in Bologna, Italy, on April 25, 1874, to an Italian father and an Irish mother. It is a Marconi family legend that a gardener, upon seeing the infant Guglielmo for the first time, exclaimed, "What big ears he has!" to which his mother, Annie, replied, "With these ears he'll be able to hear the still, small voices of the air."

As a young man of twenty, Guglielmo heard about the experiments of German scientist Heinrich Hertz, which proved the existence of invisible electromagnetic waves. (The *hertz*, a unit of frequency equal to one cycle per second, was named after Hertz.) Hertz had shown that these unseen waves traveled at the speed of light, and Marconi was immediately intrigued by the possible use of these waves as a communications tool.

A year later, in 1895, at the age of twenty-one, Marconi, with the assistance of Russian physicist Aleksandr Popov, invented a signal-strengthening radio antenna, produced the first working radio device, and used this equipment to send a wireless message to his brother, who was standing some distance away behind a hill. The following year, Marconi acquired his first patent. (Interestingly, Marconi originally offered his wireless communications device to the Italian government, but in an astonishingly shortsighted decision they refused it.)

Marconi ultimately patented his device in London, where he also obtained financial backing (from his British relatives) for continued improvement and research. In November 1896, Marconi's Wireless Telegraph Company, Ltd., was established, and the first authentic permanent wireless installation was built at the Needles on the Isle of Wight in Hampshire, England.

In 1899, Marconi sent the first wireless messages across the English Channel, and on Thursday, December 12, 1901, he sent radio waves from England to Newfoundland, Canada (the letter *S*, in Morse code, picked up with a kite antenna), marking the invention of radio.

In 1902, Marconi built a radio station at Glace Bay, Nova Scotia, and on Monday, January 19, 1903, he assisted U.S. president Theodore Roosevelt in sending a wireless greeting to Great Britain's king Edward VII. Also that year, Marconi built four 250-foot wooden towers that were anchored in cement at South Wellfleet, Massachusetts, and, using electrical waves, sent a seventeen-word-a-minute message to his Glace Bay radio station.

In 1904, Marconi's company (now called Marconi International Communications) adopted the CQD distress signal. This was the "Stop Sending and Listen" message that was used in crisis situations until it was replaced by SOS in 1906. Marconi sent the first voice transmission via radio waves in 1906, and in 1910, he successfully sent radio messages from Ireland to Argentina, a distance of over six thousand miles. Marconi's pioneering work won worldwide recognition in 1909, when he and Karl Braun won the Nobel Prize for Physics. (In 1897, Braun had expanded on Marconi's work, inventing a cathode ray tube that paved the way for the invention of television.) In the same year, radio messages were for the first time used to rescue survivors of a scuttled ship, the *S. S. Republic.*

In September 1915 as World War I raged, the first military application of radio occurred. Marconi's lifelong friend and assistant, Luigi Solari, communicated with Marconi from the air as he flew in an Italian two-seater military biplane. Later in life, Marconi also did shortwave and microwave communication research.

The historian Michael Hart has stated that in the annals of communications, the invention of radio transmission occupies the highest rank: "It is plainly a more important invention than the telephone, since a message sent by telephone might be sent by radio instead, whereas radio messages can be sent to places that cannot be reached by telephone."

The advent of the cellular phone only confirms this statement because cellular phones use FM radio waves to transmit voice messages and are thus essentially portable wireless radios.

Guglielmo Marconi is ranked as the third most influential Italian in world history in recognition of the colossal importance of communications to mankind and his pivotal contributions to this field.

Enrico Fermi

1901–54

The Italian navigator has entered the New World.
  —Enrico Fermi, The message sent out from the University of Chicago to cryptically confirm Enrico Fermi's first successful creation of a nuclear chain reaction

Enrico Fermi is the one member of *The Italian 100* the world can hold responsible for two monumental scientific developments; one glorious, the other terrible.

Fermi's revolutionary achievements in physics, specifically his work on nuclear fission, marked the beginning of the atomic age and gave the world the benefits of nuclear power. His work also cursed humanity with the unimaginable terrors of the nuclear bomb. Fermi has an extremely high ranking in this book because of his work in unleashing the power of the atom. This event ushered in a new historical era and irrevocably altered the power equilibrium among nations.

Enrico Fermi was born in Rome on September 29, 1901. He received a doctorate in physics in 1922, at the extremely young age of 21, from the University of Pisa for his thesis on X rays. Fermi also studied at Göttingen, Germany; and Leiden, the Netherlands (1923–24); taught physics at Columbia University (1939–45) and the Universities of Florence (1924–26), Rome (1926–38), and Chicago (1946–54). Because of his work on the atomic particles known as neutrons, Fermi was awarded the Nobel Prize in Physics in 1938.

After accepting his Nobel Prize in Stockholm, Sweden, Fermi decided not to return to Italy. Instead, he boarded a ship bound for the United States with his wife and two children, Nella, 7, and Giulio, 2. Fermi's beloved homeland was under the oppressive rule of Benito Mussolini and his Fascists, and the government had recently implemented a number of severe anti-Semitic laws. Fermi's wife, the former Laura Capon (whom he had married in 1928), was Jewish. Fermi did not want to live under a regime in which his wife was considered an outcast because of her heritage and ethnic origin.

Fermi's work, beginning with his bombardment of uranium and other elements with neutrons in 1934, resulted in neutron-induced radiation. In 1942, working with Leo Szilard at the University of Chicago, Fermi built the first nuclear reactor based on the fission (or splitting) of uranium atoms. This was a momentous development that Fermi's fellow physicist Albert Einstein saw as both promising and perilous. In a 1939 letter to President Franklin D. Roosevelt, Einstein wrote:

> Some recent work by E. Fermi and L. Szilard which has been communicated to me in manuscript leads me to expect that the element uranium may be turned into a new and important source of energy in the near future. Certain aspects of the situation which has arisen seem to call for watchfulness and, if necessary, quick action on the part of the Administration. . . . In the course of the last four months it has been made almost certain . . . that it may become possible to set up a nuclear chain reaction in a large mass of uranium, by which vast amounts of power and large quantities of radium-like elements would be generated. . . . This new phenomenon would lead also to the construction of bombs.

Along with Einstein and other leading scientists, Fermi (whose code name was "Henry Farmer") worked on the Manhattan Project at Los Alamos, New Mexico, from 1942 to 1945. The end result of that top-secret effort was the development of the atomic bomb.

On August 6, 1945, the United States dropped an atomic bomb, code-named "Little Boy," on Hiroshima, Japan. This uranium-core bomb had the explosive force of 12,500 tons of TNT and instantly killed 130,000 people; and another 100,000 later died from burns and radiation poisoning. Three days later, a plutonium-core bomb code-named "Fat Man" was dropped on the Japanese port city of Nagasaki, immediately killing 75,000, with another 75,000 dying later.

For his work on the Manhattan Project, Fermi was awarded the Congressional Medal for Merit in 1946. In 1954, he received the first annual award of the Atomic Energy Commission, which he served as an adviser. Shortly afterward, on November 28, Enrico Fermi died in Chicago. His two-volume *Collected Papers* (1962–65) was published posthumously.

How did Enrico Fermi feel about his role in the creation of the atomic bomb? We know that some of the scientists involved in the Manhattan Project were so overwhelmed with guilt over what they had done that a group of them began immediately working to ban atomic weapons completely. A group of scientists at the University of Chicago began publishing *The Journal of the Atomic Scientists*, famous for the "Doomsday Clock" on the cover of every issue, its hands signifying how close the world was to nuclear war.

But Enrico Fermi apparently did not share those feelings.

In a 1994 interview, Fermi's oldest child, Nella, acknowledged that "a lot of scientists were in fact worried that this was not the weapon to end all weapons, but the weapon to end all mankind." She revealed, however, that her father was convinced that the bomb was the unavoidable result of studying the powers of the atom. Throughout the months prior to the dropping of the bombs on Hiroshima and Nagasaki, Fermi never revealed to his family what he was working on. Nella said she considered her father a hero and stressed the loyalty he felt to his adopted country. Fermi, according to his daughter, did what he believed was right for the United States—and for the world. "Most people," Nella Fermi said, "felt this was something that needed to be done."

Today, the Fermi National Accelerator Laboratory, located outside Chicago, carries on important research in nuclear physics. Scientific terms named after Fermi include the following:

- **Fermi-Dirac statistics:** In quantum mechanics, one of two possible ways in which a system of indistinguishable particles can be distributed among a set of energy states: Each of the available discrete states can be occupied by only one particle.

- **Fermi level:** A measure of the energy of the least tightly held electrons within a solid. The value of the Fermi level at absolute zero is called the Fermi energy and is a constant for each solid.

- **Fermi surface:** In solid-state physics, abstract boundary or interface useful for characterizing and predicting the thermal, electrical, magnetic, and optical properties of metals, semimetals, and semiconductors.

- **fermion:** Any number of a group of subatomic particles having odd half-integral angular momentum (spin 1/2, 3/2), named after the Fermi-Dirac statistics that describe its behavior.

- **fermium (Fm):** Synthetic chemical element, atomic number 100 in the periodic table of elements.

In the United States, the cities of Chicago, Toledo, Virginia Beach, Omaha, and Newark each generate between 45 and 75 percent of their electrical energy from nuclear power. Nuclear power releases no air pollutants or greenhouse gases, but it does generate harmful radioactive waste that can only be disposed of by burial in remote locations. The disastrous 1986 explosion of a nuclear reactor in Chernobyl, Ukraine, underscored these dangers—radioactivity from Chernobyl contaminated farmland throughout the region and was blamed for 25,000 premature deaths.

There can be no underestimating the significance of Enrico Fermi's scientific breakthroughs: If the problems of radioactive waste disposal are eventually solved, nuclear power may become the single most important energy source for an increasingly overcrowded and power-hungry planet. And with the first use of nuclear weapons in 1945, humans for the first time exhibited the power to make their own species extinct.

Such developments may someday ultimately be reckoned as the defining moments in the survival—or demise—of the human race.

5

Alessandro Volta

1745–1827

In trying to make something new, half the undertaking lies in discovering whether it can be done. Once it has been established that it can, duplication is inevitable.

—HELEN GAHAGAN DOUGLAS
A Full Life

Today, the average home is equipped with a variety of electrical devices that have their own internal energy source—the battery. These include remote controls, flashlights, calculators, clocks, power tools, radios, tape recorders, and telephones. Those who enjoy the convenience of these and other devices—and all those who drive automobiles as well—are indebted to Count Alessandro Volta, the man who invented the battery.

Alessandro Giuseppe Antonio Anastasio Volta—physicist,

chemist, physician, and inventor—was born on February 18, 1745, in Como, Italy, a town that had a long association with the mysterious force known as electricity. Como was also the birthplace of the Roman philosopher and encyclopedist known as Pliny the Elder. In A.D. 70, Pliny wrote about his own experiments with electrical charges that duplicated results obtained by Greek philosopher Thales of Miletus in 600 B.C. In Thales's experiments, he vigorously rubbed the fossil resin amber and noted that it then attracted feathers and other light materials. Pliny performed similar experiments (including receiving electric shocks from torpedo fish) and wrote about them in his only surviving book, *Natural History*.

Volta first began publishing his own findings on electricity when he was in his twenties and became professor of physics at Como Gymnasium in 1774, at the age of twenty-nine. In 1775, he invented the electrophorus, an instrument that could produce static electric charges. The electrophorus consisted of a disk that could be electrified negatively through friction and a metal plate that became electrically charged when placed on the disk.

In the two years between 1776 and 1778, Volta did work that resulted in the identification of methane gas, and in 1779, he was made professor of natural philosophy at Pavia, where he remained for twenty-five years.

Volta's most important contribution to science occurred on March 20, 1800. On that day, he built the first battery by placing different metals in piles between pads soaked with a salt solution. This "voltaic pile," as it is called, was the first device that could provide a continuous source of direct current electricity.

In 1801, Volta reported the results of his research and work to the Royal Society of London, which had elected him a fellow ten years earlier. His findings were published in the society's journal, *Philosophical Transactions*, and the society also awarded him its prestigious Copley Medal. Once Volta's groundbreaking findings were made available to other scientists, many advancements in the study of electricity occurred at a rapid pace, including the invention of the electromagnet.

At the invitation of French emperor Napoleon Bonaparte, Volta traveled to Paris, where he put on a demonstration of his battery before the Institut de France. Napoleon and the Institut were so impressed with Volta's achievements that they struck a gold coin in his honor and gave him a cash award of 6,000 francs. A commission of scientists and learned men was also created to repeat his remarkable experiments. At this time, Napoleon also made Volta a

count and a senator of the Kingdom of Lombardy. Volta later
received the Cross of the French Legion of Honor.

Count Alessandro Volta died in Como, Italy, on March 5, 1827.
In 1881, the volt, the defining unit of electromotive force, was
named in his honor. Volta's writings were published in seven volumes in the years 1918 through 1929. There is today in Como, Italy,
the Museo Alessandro Volta, a museum dedicated to Como's most
famous son.

6

Leonardo Fibonacci
(a.k.a. Leonardo Pisano and Leonard of Pisa)
1180?–1250

The nine Indian figures are: *9 8 7 6 5 4 3 2 1*. With these nine figures, and with the sign *0* . . . any number may be written, as is demonstrated below.
—LEONARDO FIBONACCI
The opening passage of *Liber Abaci*

A certain man put a pair of rabbits in a place surrounded on all sides by a wall. How many pairs of rabbits can be produced from that pair in a year if it is supposed that every month each pair begets a new pair which from the second month on becomes productive?
—LEONARDO FIBONACCI, The famous "Fibonacci sequence" problem from chapter 12 of *Liber Abaci**

The mathematician Leonardo Fibonacci, born sometime around 1180 in Pisa, Italy, has been described by historian Joseph Gies as "the greatest Western mathematician of the Middle Ages." Fibonacci

---

*See page 23 for the solution.

brought to Europe a system of mathematical notation originally known as Hindu-Arabic, but now simply called Arabic. This innovation changed mathematics and made a monumental contribution to the progress of science and technology.

Prior to the introduction of Arabic notation, Western Europe used Roman numerals for all mathematical calculations. The Roman system of numerical notation started with letters to denote numbers: I = 1; II = 2; III = 3; IIII = 4 (although eventually IV became common for 4); and then added V for 5; X for 10; L for 50; C for 100; D for 500; and M for 1,000. Letters placed to the left of another letter indicated subtraction; letters following another letter indicated addition, e.g., IX = 9; XVI = 16.

Roman notation was simple when it came to addition and subtraction. Multiplication and division, however, were essentially impossible, and so for those calculations, Italians and other Europeans turned to the abacus, a bead-and-string device, for complex "figuring." As one can imagine, the combination of paper calculation with Roman numerals and mechanical bead-movement on the abacus combined to make for a very clumsy system of managing business transactions, market sales, and other mathematical reckonings.

Fibonacci first learned the system of Arabic notation during a business trip to Bugia in North Africa. Arabic notation includes the concepts of "place value" and the all-important zero, critical elements in the construction of an easily accessible system of mathematical ordering. (Interestingly, the ubiquitous abacus *did* provide place value through its arranging of beads in columns indicating thousands, hundreds, tens, and single units, but there was no way to preserve complicated abacus calculations on paper.)

Leonardo's father, who had gone to Bugia to work as a customs official, had sent for him so that Leonardo could complete his business education "with a view to future usefulness." The young Leonardo immediately recognized the usefulness and importance of place value in mathematics and studied the Arabic system with (it is assumed) Arab businessmen and merchants. While still in his twenties, Leonardo left North Africa and, for several years, traveled around the Mediterranean, visiting Constantinople, Egypt, Sicily, Syria, and Provence.

In 1202, after several years of work, his handwritten book, *Liber abaci* (*The Book of the Abacus*), was published in Pisa. In 1228, he issued an expanded and revised edition, and it is that version of his magnum opus that has survived. The importance of Fibonacci's work and thus of Fibonacci himself is that he brought to Western Europe a system of mathematical notation that simplified the manipulation of numbers.

This eventually presented all types of advantages, giving even the lowliest merchant access to an accounting system that was simple to use, consistently accurate, and easily recordable. All branches of the sciences—medicine, astronomy, architecture, navigation, engineering, bookkeeping—ultimately benefited, expanded, and advanced thanks to Leonardo Fibonacci's writings and contribution to mathematics. (It took almost three centuries for Fibonacci's work to be implemented, though, such was the blasé attitude with which it was originally received as a result of the dominance of the Roman system of notation.)

Also, *Liber abaci* presented Leonardo's famous "rabbit" problem (see the respective epigraph), which delineated what came to be known as the "Fibonacci sequence" and is defined as a series of numbers of which each is the sum of the two previous numbers. This sequence illustrated what came to be known as the "golden section." This is a ratio—.618—that occurs when a geometrical figure is divided such that the smaller dimension is to the greater as the greater is to the whole. This perfectly proportional .618 ratio has been found in nature in snail shells, sunflowers, and elsewhere; it has been used for centuries in art and architecture by painters, builders, and sculptors to achieve a pleasing, symmetrical design.

Leonardo Fibonacci, who is now also known as Leonardo of Pisa and Leonardo Pisano, was ahead of his time. The value of his work was not recognized until three hundred years after his death, in 1250.

Solution to the Fibonacci Sequence "Rabbit" Problem:

At the beginning, the number of living pairs of rabbits is 1. At the end of the first month, there are 2 pairs: The first pair has produced a pair. At the end of the second month, there are 3 pairs: the first pair has produced a second pair. At the end of the third month, there are 5 pairs: The 2 pairs of the first month have produced 2 new pairs. This progression continues for 9 more months, producing the sequence 1, 2, 3, 5, 8, 13, 21, 34, 55, 89, 144, 233, 377. Thus, at the end of a year, there are 377 pairs of rabbits. This problem illustrates the first number sequence in Europe in which the relationship between two or more successive terms can be expressed in formula notation. The Fibonacci sequence can be expressed by the formula $U_n + 2 = U_n + 1 + U_n$, with *U* representing the terms, and the subscript its rank in the sequence.

Evangelista Torricelli
1608–47

We watched the ocean and the sky together,
Under the roof of blue Italian weather.
— PERCY BYSSHE SHELLEY
Letter to Maria Gisborne

Meteorology, the science of studying one of the most critical aspects of life on earth, the weather, took a giant leap forward in 1643 when Evangelista Torricelli invented a device for measuring the pressure of air. This device we now know as the barometer, an instrument critical to the accurate forecasting of weather patterns.

The modern barometer is a tube partially filled with mercury that is open to air on one end and has a vacuum on the other. The height of the mercury balances the column of air sitting above the open end of the tube and moves up and down as the air pressure changes. When the mercury falls (a "falling barometer") it means that the air pressure is falling, which usually signals an approaching storm. When the mercury rises (a "rising barometer") it means that the air pressure is increasing and a body of high pressure is approaching, usually bringing with it fair weather.

The invention of the barometer was an important development that greatly facilitated the rapid advancement of the science of meteorology, and Torricelli's invention contributed to and expedited subsequent work and progress by, among others, Isaac Newton, Blaise Pascal (who made great use of barometers in his study of air pressure), Edmund Halley, Robert Boyle, John Hadley, Jean Le Rond d'Alembert, Benjamin Franklin, John Dalton, and Luke Howard.

Evangelista Torricelli was born in the town of Faenza, in the Romagna region of Italy on October 15, 1608. Little is written of Torricelli's personal life. He had a round face and wore a mustache and a thin goatee but little else about his appearance is known. It seems as though Torricelli spent the majority of his short life working on his discoveries and his writings.

Prior to the seventeenth century, weather *forecasting* consisted mainly of weather *speculation* (much of it based on ancient writings, including Aristotle's *Meteorologica*, which was published in 340 B.C.). In 1640, when the great scientist GALILEO GALILEI (see GALILEO GALILEI [1]) was pumping out a well, he noticed that it was impossible to raise the column of water in the pipe higher than 10.3 meters. This was the result of the role air pressure played on the fluid; but at the time, Galileo did not recognize this phenomenon nor come to this conclusion.

That same year, thirty-two-year-old scientist Evangelista Torricelli (who had been greatly influenced by Galileo's writings), published *De motu gravium* (*Concerning Movement*), which applied Galileo's laws of motion to fluids. This work marked the birth of the science of hydrodynamics and so impressed Galileo that the following year he invited Torricelli to work as his secretary and assistant. Torricelli filled this post until the great scientist's death in 1642. Torricelli then assumed Galileo's position as philosopher and court mathematician to Grand Duke Ferdinando II of Tuscany, and he was also installed as professor of mathematics at the Florentine Academy, another of Galileo's positions. In 1640, Torricelli also succeeded in manually grinding telescope lenses with such precision that they came close to optical flawlessness.

At the age of thirty-five, in 1643, Torricelli came to believe that the earth's surface (including the seas) sat at the bottom of a huge ocean of air. He logically hypothesized that this "sea of air" had *pressure* and that it exerted a force on everything it touched. In an attempt to prove his theory, Torricelli filled a four-foot glass tube with mercury and inserted the tube upside down into a dish of liquid. He then observed that not all of the mercury flowed out of the tube and that the space above the mercury in the tube was a vacuum. He later concluded that the volume of this vacuum was directly related to atmospheric pressure and that this data could be quantified and recorded. (Later, in 1665, Englishman Robert Hooke added a needle to Torricelli's barometer, thereby allowing accurate readings of the differences in air pressure.)

A year after his invention of the barometer and his innovative contributions to hydrodynamics and meteorology, Torricelli published his findings about the cycloid. The cycloid is a curve that is generated by a point on the circumference of a circle as it is rolled along a straight line. Torricelli had determined methods of calculating the cycloid's range and constructing its tangent. (This discovery ultimately led to the development of integral calculus.) Later that year, Torricelli released *Opera Geometrica* (*Geometric Works*), in which he published his findings on the motion of fluids and also on the motion of projectiles.

Torricelli's work on fluid motion resulted in a mathematical statement now known as Torricelli's theorem (or Torricelli's law, principle, or equation). This equation—$v = \sqrt{2gh}$—states that the speed of a liquid flowing out of a pipe under the force of gravity (v) is proportional to the square root of the vertical distance (h) between the surface of the liquid and the center of the pipe's opening and to the square root of twice the acceleration ($2g$). This discovery added even more to the body of knowledge that was rapidly accumulating in Torricelli's new science of hydrodynamics.

Torricelli died in Florence, Italy, on October 25, 1647, at the age of thirty-nine. The writings, discoveries, and inventions he left behind made major contributions to several branches of science, including meteorology, hydrodynamics, and optics, and his legacy and influence are still remembered and being felt today. Torricelli is one of a handful of brilliant scientists (such as Volta) whose inventions became part of everyday modern life. It is proper and necessary, then, that he be ranked in the top ten of *The Italian 100*.

8

Filippo Mazzei
1730–1816

We hold these truths to be self-evident, that all men
are created equal . . .
—THE DECLARATION OF INDEPENDENCE

In the Declaration of Independence, there is no idea more powerful than the five words "all men are created equal." The phrase is
credited to Thomas Jefferson, the document's principal author.
Though the words are undeniably his, he borrowed the fundamental concept from an Italian, specifically his dear friend Filippo
Mazzei.

Filippo Mazzei was born on Christmas Day, 1730, in Poggio a
Caiano in the Tuscany region of Italy. As a young man, Mazzei studied medicine in Florence and then practiced in Turkey until he was
twenty-five. He then moved to London, where he established an
importing company for Italian olive oil, cheeses, and wines, and for
over twenty years his business prospered. Around 1770, he met
Benjamin Franklin, who ultimately persuaded Filippo to move to
Virginia in the American colonies and conduct a series of agricul-
tural experiments on American soil. Mazzei had been pursuing his
interest (transplanting cuttings) in England, and in 1773, he sailed
for America with a tailor, a party of Italian peasants who had
worked with him in England, and cuttings from vines, trees, and
plants that he had brought from Italy and transplanted in England.

In Virginia, Mazzei established a farm near Charlottesville on which he conducted his botanical experiments. His farm was right next door to Thomas Jefferson's estate, Monticello, and he soon became close friends with Jefferson.

Mazzei had always been sympathetic toward the American colonies and their efforts to gain independence from England. Living in Virginia stoked his passion to the point where he actually got involved in the colonists' fight for freedom. He began writing a series of essays for the *Virginia Gazette* under the pseudonymous byline of Furioso, which in Italian means "furious" or "raging." He wrote his impassioned tracts in Italian, and they were then translated into English by Jefferson, who spoke and wrote fluent Italian. Mazzei, in one of his articles, wrote the following:

> All men are by nature equally free and independent . . .
> each equality is necessary in order to create a free gov-
> ernment. All men must be equal to each other in natural
> law.

Jefferson was greatly impressed by the powerful simplicity of this idea: Shortly after the publication of Mazzei's essay, Jefferson used it verbatim in the Bill of Rights he wrote for the Virginia constitution. In 1776, however, Jefferson changed Mazzei's wording to "All men are created equal," and thus Mazzei's heartfelt defense of the unity of all mankind was incorporated into the American Declaration of Independence.

Mazzei was so impressed with this document that he later wrote, "[The Declaration of Independence is] a true affirmation of the principles necessary to preserve American liberty," and that "the surest mode to secure Republican systems of Government from lapsing into Tyranny, is by giving free and frequent information to the mass of people." Appropriately, Mazzei was later a part of a constitutional society organized by James Madison and James Monroe that had as its goal a free dissemination of information about the new government.

In 1779, three years after the adoption of the Declaration of Independence, Mazzei, then forty-nine, wanted to enlist in the colonial army and fight against the British. But he was persuaded by Patrick Henry, the governor of Virginia, to travel to Italy and try and persuade the Duke of Tuscany to lend money to the American freedom fighters. Mazzei made it to Europe but was stymied by Benjamin Franklin (then the American representative in France) in his attempts to represent the colonies; Franklin believed (probably correctly) that only the government should be allowed to borrow money in the name of the United States.

Mazzei returned to Europe in 1786 and later wrote a four-volume history of the formation of the thirteen American colonies and their conflict with England called *Historical and Political Enquiries.* Mazzei died in Pisa, Italy, on Tuesday, March 19, 1816, at the age of eighty-five.

In 1941, President Franklin Delano Roosevelt specifically praised Mazzei and his contribution to the Declaration of Independence, and in 1980, the U. S. Postal Service issued a forty-cent stamp in honor of the 250th anniversary of Mazzei's birth. Filippo Mazzei is remembered today as the enlightened Italian whose ideas became the cornerstone for the most important document in the history of the United States.

9

Michelangelo
(Michelangelo Buonarroti)
1475–1564

The *terribilità* of Michelangelo, the terrifying power of
the inspired artist, would leave its mark on the future
of the arts. The genius of Michelangelo inspired others
to make a fetish of genius.
— DANIEL J. BOORSTIN, *The Creators:*
A History of Heroes of the Imagination

*T*erribilità is the colorful Italian word used to describe a stormy
personality comprising impatience, temper, anger, insecurity, lead-
ership, passion, narrow-mindedness, and egotism (often bordering
on a God complex). *Terribilità* has survived through the ages as the

30

defining term for the great Michelangelo, revered in his own time as the greatest of sculptors *and* painters, and christened Il Divino (the Divine)—such was the timeless brilliance of his work.

Michelangelo's body of work encompasses magnificent sculptures (*The Pietà, David, The Dying Slave, Moses,* and the tomb of Giuliano de'Medici); breathtaking paintings (the frescoes on the ceiling of the Sistine Chapel, *The Last Judgment*); inspired architecture (St. Peter's Basilica in Rome); and lyrical writings (over 300 beautiful sonnets and poems, many published after his death).

Michelangelo was born Michelangelo di Lodovico Buonarroti Simoni on March 6, 1475, in Caprese, Florence, where his father was mayor. When he was thirteen, he agreed to a three-year artist's apprenticeship to Domenico Ghirlandaio but left after one year, complaining that he had nothing left to learn. After studying for a time under the patronage of Lorenzo de'Medici, Michelangelo returned home after de'Medici's death and, with the help of a supportive cleric, dissected corpses to learn human anatomy.

At the age of twenty-six, Michelangelo began sculpting what some consider to be the most famous statue in the world: *David.* The Florence Operari (the governing "Board of Works") had an irregularly shaped block of Carrera marble thirteen and a half feet high that had been lying around for a century. The Board offered Michelangelo the opportunity to chisel a statue from it—if he thought he could. Michelangelo consented, and on August 16, 1501, a contract was drawn up:

> [T]he worthy master Michelangelo . . . has been chosen to fashion, complete, and finish to perfection that male statue called *Il gigante* [The Giant], of nine cubits [about thirteen and a half feet] in height.

The contract also built in a possible bonus:

> [W]hen the statue is finished the Guild consuls and the Operari . . . shall estimate whether he deserve a larger recompense, and this shall be left to their consciences.

Sixteenth-century art historian Giorgio Vasari [62]—in his ten-volume *Lives of the Most Eminent Painters, Sculptors, and Architects*—tells the revealing story of how the great Michelangelo responded to an idiotic criticism of his *David.* An officious bureaucrat, upon seeing *David* for the first time, complained to Michelangelo that David's nose appeared to be too big. The artist complacently picked up a chisel and mounted a ladder, climbing to the top of the statue, where he proceeded to tap away at the nose. The assemblage below watched as marble dust slowly drifted down to the floor. When Michelangelo climbed down the ladder, the bureaucrat smugly announced that the sculpture was now acceptable and that it had been much improved. Michelangelo remained silent. The official did not know that Michelangelo had anticipated such a display of bombast and had hidden a quantity of marble dust in his hand. As the crowd watched him "chip away" at the statue, all he was really doing was lightly tapping the nose and releasing clouds of marble dust from his hand.

Michelangelo was ultimately paid 400 florins for his masterpiece. Today, that would come to approximately $6,000, for thirty months' work.

The frescoes on the ceiling of the Sistine Chapel (described by art historian H. W. Janson as a "huge organism" and "a masterpiece of truly epochal importance") were painted in the four years from 1508 to 1512. On May 10, 1508, Michelangelo signed a contract that read:

> I, Michelangelo, sculptor, have received from the Holiness of Our Lord, Pope Julius II, 500 ducats, on account of the painting of the vault of the Sistine Chapel, on which I begin to work.

There are over three hundred individual figures in the many scenes in the thirty-three panels of the ceiling. The central area of the almost 6,000-square-foot ceiling exhibits nine scenes from the Book of Genesis, beginning with the creation of the world, through the drunkenness of Noah (also included are the creation of Adam and the fall of man and the expulsion from the Garden of Eden). The interwoven themes of creation, downfall, and redemption are gloriously interpreted in Michelangelo's work, and it is clear that the drama and terror of such cosmic, divine concerns fired his imagination and stimulated his astonishing creative powers.

Work on the chapel ceiling consumed Michelangelo. He painted standing up (*not* lying down as legend has it) and worked ceaselessly to realize his vision. In a poem about the project he lamented:

> I've grown a goiter by dwelling in this den,
> My beard turns up to heaven,
> My nape falls in, fixed on my spine.
> My breastbone visibly grows like a harp;

> A rich embroidery bedews my face from brush
> > drops,
> thick and thin.

Twenty-two years after completing the Sistine Chapel ceiling, Michelangelo returned to paint *The Last Judgment* for the wall above the chapel's altar. This somber and frightening work includes Michelangelo's bleak and mocking commentary on man's (and his own) unworthiness and place in the universe: The face on the flayed skin held by St. Bartholomew in the painting is that of the artist himself, so well disguised that it went unrecognized in his own time.

Michelangelo became a wealthy man from his work. Yet rather than spend his later years in indolent repose, he continued exploring the possibilities of art until eight days before his death on February 18, 1564, at the age of eighty-nine. (He left a new *Pietà* unfinished at his death.)

Michelangelo's legacy is that of the singular genius: He redefined excellence in the fields of sculpture and painting and greatly influenced the visual arts for centuries to come. He was obsessed with the realization of his visions, and his art continues to transcend the fickle appetites of later centuries. His words speak to and inspire us, even today:

> If I was made for art from childhood,
> Given a prey for burning beauty to devour;
> I blame the mistress I was born to serve.

10

Leonardo da Vinci
1452–1519

Saper vedere.
Knowing how to see.
      — LEONARDO DA VINCI'S guiding principle

Men of genius do most when they work least.
      —LEONARDO DA VINCI'S response to questions
          as to why he would often sit and stare at
          the wall on which he was painting *The
          Last Supper* without painting a stroke

Leonardo da Vinci—painter, sculptor, scientist, inventor, writer, engineer—considered the human eye the most wondrous of God's creations. "Seeing," to Leonardo, was the singularly conclusive way of perceiving reality:

34

Do you not see that the eye encompasses the beauty of the whole world? . . . It has created architecture and perspective, and . . . the divine art of painting. O, thou most excellent of all God's creations! What hymns can do justice to thy nobility; what people, what tongues, sufficiently describe thine achievements?

It is true that Leonardo da Vinci often started projects and did not complete them, and that less than two dozen of his paintings actually survive. It is also true that Leonardo did not directly influence the actual invention of any of the wondrous devices he conceived, drew, and described in his acclaimed notebooks. The notebooks were not published until years after his death, and these inventions were brought into being by others without any influence from Leonardo's writing. Nevertheless, Leonardo's ideas included rudimentary designs for the airplane, the air conditioner, the oil lamp, the alarm clock, the printing press, the odometer, the pedometer, the magnetic compass, eyeglasses, the telescope, the differential transmission, the water turbine, the machine gun, the tank, an underwater diving suit, the life preserver, and the parachute ("If a man have a tent made of linen, of which the apertures have all been stopped up, and it be twelve cubits across and twelve in depth, he will be able to throw himself down from any great height without sustaining any injury").

Leonardo da Vinci is ranked in the top ten of *The Italian 100* because his surviving body of work—including his writings, anatomical drawings, and paintings—are, without question, a definitive manifestation of pure genius expressing itself artistically. (Michael Hart said of Leonardo, "It is possible that Leonardo da Vinci was the most talented person who ever lived. . . .")

Leonardo's sublime portrait *Mona Lisa* is without a doubt the most well-known painting of all time. And the second most famous painting in the world, *The Last Supper*, is also a product of Leonardo's hand. Moreover, Leonardo's defining thesis—"He who loses sight loses his view of the universe, and is like one interred alive who can still move about and breathe in his grave"—continues to influence the way artists perceive reality and how they define their interpretive role.

In addition to his skill as an artist, Leonardo was also a brilliant military strategist and weapons designer. In 1482, at the age of thirty, he wrote to Lodovico, regent of Milan, offering himself as military engineer to the city:

Most Illustrious Lord . . . in order to acquaint you with my secrets, thereafter offering myself at your pleasure effectually to demonstrate . . . all those matters which are in part recorded below.

1. I have plans for bridges, very light and strong. . . .

2. When a place is beseiged I know how to cut off water from the trenches. . . .

4. I have plans for making cannon, very convenient and easy of transport, with which to hurl small stones in the manner almost of hail. . . .

9. Where it is not possible to employ cannon, I can supply catapults, mangonels, traps, and other engines of wonderful efficacy. . . .

He concluded by offering Lodovico his additional services as an architect, a sculptor, and a painter; and essentially challenging the regent to demand evidence that he could, indeed, do all the things he described in what may be the world's most unique job application.

Leonardo was born on April 15, 1452, in Vinci, in the Tuscany region of Italy. He was born the illegitimate son of Caterina, a peasant woman, and Ser Piero d'Antonio, a Florentine landlord and notary. When he was fifteen, his father apprenticed him to the artist Andrea del Verrocchio, in whose workshop Leonardo learned the fundamentals of sculpture, painting, and the mechanical arts. He worked for the Duke of Milan from 1482 to 1499; in Florence from 1500 to 1506; in Milan again, from 1506 to 1513; in Rome, from 1513 to 1516; and in Cloux, France, from 1516 through May 2, 1519, when he died at the age of sixty-seven.

Leonardo was a vegetarian, an animal rights activist (he bought caged birds just so he could set them free), and he dressed elaborately and with great care. Historians and psychologists (including Sigmund Freud) have speculated about his sexual orientation, as he was known to have surrounded himself with young men (as students and models) throughout his life. Unquestionably, he was a man of unusual sensitivity. The historian Will Durant stated that Leonardo "understood well many phases of woman's nature; no one has surpassed him in representing virginal delicacy, motherly solicitude, or feminine subtlety."

Leonardo's legacy is that he was, as historian Will Durant

described him, "the fullest man" of the Renaissance. There were many who were more learned; but when Leonardo focused his magnificent mind on a subject, there were none who produced better work.

As the defining figure of the Renaissance, then, Leonardo da Vinci well deserves an exalted place in *The Italian 100*.

11

Giovanni Battista Morgagni
1682–1771

A physician takes his cue from Nature, who does things
step by step, never by leaps and bounds.

—GIOVANNI MORGAGNI

Giovanni Battista Morgagni—nobleman of Forli. In the year
1763 the townspeople of Forli erected a marble statue because
he distinguished himself for his country and all the people of
the world with his discoveries and excellent books. As learned
men sincerely believe, Morgagni is the foremost in the history
of the human race.

— INSCRIPTION ON A MARBLE MEDALLION BEARING
THE IMAGE OF MORGAGNI IN THE TOWN HALL OF
MORGAGNI'S BIRTHPLACE, FORLI, ITALY

Italian anatomist and pathologist Giovanni Battista Morgagni had a powerful impact on the practice of medicine. He was the first physician to determine that disease was caused by the malfunctioning of specific internal organs, rather than by something going wrong with one of the four "humors," bodily fluids that were thought to control the health of the human body. Imbalances of any or all of these fluids, or, in some cases, too much of them, were believed to cause all manner of illness and disease and thus, the need for painful and often deadly bloodletting. An ancient medical text (appropriately titled *On Ancient Medicine*) stated the Hippocratic belief that a perfect blend of the four humors was necessary for a human being to have perfect health. Dr. Sherwin B. Nuland, in *Doctors: The Biography of Medicine*, writes:

> [I]t was as though [Morgagni] had been placed on earth to carry out a mission for which the medical world had been preparing itself, and which needed only the appearance of a single unifying intellect to achieve. The mission was the bringing of a message. The message itself was a simple one: it is useless to seek the causes of disease among the foggy vapors of the four humors or any variations of such theories. Diseases are not general imbalances of an entire patient, but rather are quite specific derangements of particular structures within the body. Each disease, to state it another way, has a seat in some organ that has gone wrong. It is the job of the physician to identify that seat.

Morgagni believed that symptoms were "the cry of the suffering organs," and through autopsy, he was able to pinpoint the specific anatomical changes that caused first, disease, and if not treated, ultimately death. In 1761, after over fifty years of solid medical research that rendered his findings irrefutable, Morgagni published a book that was one of the most significant events in the history of medical science: *De sedibus et causis morborum per anatomem indagatis libri quinque* (*The Seats and Causes of Disease Investigated by Anatomy*). Anatomical study was the key to diagnosis, Morgagni proclaimed, essentially founding the science of pathological anatomy and defining the art and science of modern diagnosis. Morgagni's book detailed 700 autopsies and was immediately hailed as one of the most important and valuable books about medicine ever published.

Throughout his career, Morgagni did pioneering research on many human anatomical structures, including the "pockets" of the larynx, the urethra, the cervical muscles, the heart's arterial valves, the reproductive organs, and the corneas.

Human anatomical structures have often been named after the person who accurately identified them and defined their purpose. Examples are the fallopian tubes, named after Italian anatomist GABRIEL FALLOPIUS [12], and Bellini's tubes (the excretory tubes of the kidneys), named after Lorenzo BELLINI [60]. It has been said that Giovanni Morgagni discovered and described so many internal organs and structures of the human body that if they had named each one after him, over a third of the human anatomy would today bear his name.

Giovanni Morgagni was born on February 25, 1682, in Forli, a small town in northeastern Italy. Morgagni graduated from the University of Bologna in 1701 at the age of nineteen with degrees in medicine and philosophy and ultimately became professor of theoretical medicine in 1711 at the University of Padua. Four years later, at the age of thirty-three, he was named professor of anatomy at the university, the most prestigious position at the institution.

Morgagni had begun doing autopsies when he was in his twenties, noting the specific anatomical reasons why a person died. He correctly identified the site of a ruptured appendix in one autopsy but wrote "[I]n what manner the inflammation crept into the contiguous intestine, and other circumstances I have described, there is no chance to explain." Morgagni did not know *how* the gangrenous abscess invaded adjacent organs, but he was certain that they did, and he was certain of the pathological results. Appendicitis would not be correctly diagnosed for another one hundred and fifty years, but Morgagni had set the stage for an anatomical explanation of disease.

Morgagni and his wife, Paola, had eight daughters, all of whom left home in pairs to enter convents. Throughout his long and illustrious life, he treated many patients, believing himself to be a physician first. His patients included James Boswell, the renowned biographer of Samuel Johnson, who visited Morgagni for advice about his chronic gonorrhea. Morgagni advised him to stop syringing himself (Boswell was syringing his penis in an attempt to cure his chronic urethral inflammation) and allow the inflammation to heal by itself. Morgagni also told Boswell to live soberly and stop exercising. Morgagni considered Boswell a "fine, decent old man," and was able to converse fluently with him in the Italian language.

Morgagni died on December 5, 1771, at the age of eighty-nine, leaving behind a legacy of medical revelations and advancements that changed medical science for all time.

12

Gabriel Fallopius

1523–62

Diseases desperate grown,
By desperate appliances are relieved.
Or not at all.
— WILLIAM SHAKESPEARE,
Hamlet, Act IV Scene III

The renowned Italian anatomist Gabriel Fallopius was only thirty-nine years old when he died, but in his short life he made enormous and enduring contributions to the sciences of anatomy and contraception. Fallopius identified some of the most important organs and structures of the human body, including the narrow ducts in the female reproductive system that bear his name—the fallopian tubes.

In addition to discovering the fallopian tubes, which conduct the egg from the ovary to the uterus, Fallopius also identified and named the semicircular canals of the ear, the cochlea, the palate, the vagina, the clitoris, and the placenta.

Fallopius made his discoveries during anatomical research at Padua in the years prior to the publication of his treatise, *Observationes anatomicae* (*Anatomical Observations*), which was published in 1561, when the author was thirty-eight. Gabriel routinely dissected human cadavers and recorded what he found, and his work was hailed by physicians of the time for the new and valuable information it uncovered.

In addition to his work on human anatomy and his revelatory discoveries, Fallopius is also credited with the invention of the device that has often prevented sexually transmitted diseases and unwanted pregnancies during the past four hundred years—the condom.

Fallopius seems to have conceived the idea for the condom primarily as a means to prevent the spread of disease. Around 1550 or so, he designed a sheath made out of washed pig's intestine that originally fit only over the glans, or the head of the penis. Before long it became apparent that this device was also a very effective means of birth control. Soon, condoms were being handmade out of waxed linen, with a satin ribbon threaded through the base with which to secure the device.

The historian Arturo Barone translated from Latin the following passage from a sixteenth-century text on the effective use of condoms:

> Therefore every time [a man] has intercourse he should if possible wash his genitals or wipe them with a cloth; afterwards, he should have a small linen cloth made to fit over the glans which he should then put upon the glans drawing it forward over the prepuce. Although not essential, it would be useful to moisten it with saliva or with a good lotion.
>
> I myself have experimented this in hundreds, nay thousands of men, and as God is my witness, none of them caught any infection.

Gabriel Fallopius was born in Modena, Italy, just north of Bologna, sometime in 1523. (The exact date of his birth is unknown.) In the center of the town, about six blocks from the Piazza Dante Alighieri, is the avenue named for this great physician, the Via G. Fallopia.

As a young man, Gabriel was intent on becoming a priest and

spent years studying theology and serving as a canon at the Cathedral of Modena. He ultimately decided against a life in the church and left Modena to study medicine when he was in his teens. He pursued his studies at the University of Ferrara and ultimately received his medical degree there when he was in his early twenties. After teaching anatomy at Ferrara for a few years, he then took a position at the University of Pisa for the three years from 1548 through 1551. Finally, Fallopius settled at the University of Padua for the last eleven years of his life. At Padua he held the position of professor of surgery and anatomy. In this post, he continued his research into human anatomy and made all of his important discoveries.

Fallopius was very friendly with the noted Belgian anatomist Andreas Vesalius, a physician who was also doing postmortem dissections and compiling drawings of his findings. Like Fallopius, Vesalius was working to identify and correct errors in the writings of the legendary second-century Greek physician Galen, who, unlike Vesalius and Fallopius, had written anatomical texts without ever having seen a dissection of a human cadaver. All of Galen's dissections had been performed on animals. Nevertheless, Galen's ideas had dominated Western medicine for close to fifteen centuries and Vesalius's attacks on his work were not met with unanimous approval. (Galen did correctly recognize that urine was produced in the bladder and not the kidneys, and he also did important work on the human nervous system, but his writings suffered from the presumption that he alone knew the truth about the workings of the human body, and he thus altered his findings to fit what he believed rather than what actually was. This rejection of reality was one of the faults Galileo corrected with his development of the scientific method.)

Fallopius was a passionate supporter of Vesalius and his work. Together, the two researchers initiated what surgeon and writer Sherwin Nuland describes as a "reawakening" that directly led to the exponential growth of Renaissance medicine.

Gabriel Fallopius died in Padua on October 9, 1562, at the age of thirty-nine. His contributions to medicine and anatomy were critically important, and his invention of the condom was crucial to making easily accessible contraception available to the masses.

13

Girolamo Fabrizio
1537–1619

It has been shown by reason and experiment that blood by the beat of the ventricles flows through the lungs and heart and is pumped to the whole body. There it passes through pores in the flesh into the veins through which it returns from the periphery everywhere to the center, from the smaller veins into the larger one, finally coming to the vena cavae and right atrium. . . . It must therefore be concluded that the blood in the animal body moves around in a circle continuously, and that the action or function of the heart is to accomplish this by pumping. This is the only reason for the motion and beat of the heart.

> — WILLIAM HARVEY
> *De motu cordis (On the Motion of the Heart)*

All animals, even those that produce their young alive, including man himself, are evolved out of the egg.

> —WILLIAM HARVEY

The sixteenth century was an era of monumental change for the science of medicine. Prior to the work of Vesalius, Fallopius, Fabrizio, Malpighi, and Harvey, the overall workings of the human body and the specific functioning of individual organs and bodily systems was only vaguely understood, depending almost completely on the work of the second-century Greek physician Galen. Galen made some important strides by championing the importance of direct observation and in using the experimental method as a tool for medical investigation, but his religious and philosophical beliefs influenced his observations and caused him to draw conclusions that were resolutely unprovable and usually incorrect.

Unfortunately for many patients, Galen's conclusions ruled the art of medicine for centuries after his death. The seeds of change were planted with Andreas Vesalius, the sixteenth-century Belgian physician who debunked much of Galen's work. This wave of reform grew with FALLOPIUS [12], and then came to fruition when Fabrizio's student William Harvey delineated the circulation of blood in his seminal work *De moto cordu* in 1600.

Girolamo Fabrizio is remembered and acknowledged for several accomplishments throughout his life and career, not the least of which was continuing the work of his mentor Fallopius, who died when Fabrizio was twenty-five. (Fallopius is ranked higher than Fabrizio because Fallopius was the inspiring teacher; Fabrizio, his eager student.)

Fabrizio wrote two important treatises on blood circulation and fetal development, but he is most remembered for his influence on the great English physician William Harvey, the anatomist who discovered the exact nature of blood circulation and who also made enormous strides in our understanding of the heart's function as a pump for circulating blood throughout the body. Girolamo Fabrizio was William Harvey's most admired and beloved teacher at the University of Padua. Fabrizio did the groundbreaking work that led Harvey to his critically important findings.

Girolamo Fabrizio, who was also known as Fabricius ab Aquapendente, was born in Acquapendente, Italy, on May 20, 1537. After an unremarkable childhood, Fabrizio entered the University of Padua, where he was taught by Fallopius. After Fallopius's death, Fabrizio taught anatomy and medicine at the renowned school, which in the words of Sherwin Nuland "provided the most open atmosphere in Europe in which to study any of the classical four disciplines of law, theology, medicine, and philosophy." Fabrizio ultimately succeeded Fallopius as professor of anatomy and surgery, an august position he held for over fifty years, from 1562 through 1613.

In 1600, at the age of sixty-three, Fabrizio published his treatise *De formatu foetu* (On the Formation of the Fetus.) This work described in detail the development of a chick embryo, an important step toward the establishment of embryology as a branch of medicine. Fabrizio also gave a very specific and accurate description of the placenta (the vascular organ, identified by Fallopius, that unites the fetus to the uterus). This was the first time that the organ Fallopius had named had been studied in such detail.

In 1603, when Fabrizio was sixty-six, he published the work that would lead his student William Harvey to his important findings. *De venarum ostiolis* (*On the Valves of the Veins*) was the first description of the semilunar valves of the coronary arteries. The semilunar valves, two in number, are situated in the heart at the pulmonary artery (the pulmonary valve) and the beginning of the aorta (the aortic valve). Each valve is made up of three cusps (flaps of tissue). The semilunar valves are responsible for keeping the flow of blood moving in one direction, and one direction *only*.

De venarum ostiolis was a revelation to Harvey. Later in his life he credited his knowledge of this one-way blood flow as being crucial to the formulation (and verification) of his circular explanation of blood flow throughout the body, a critical breakthrough in medicine's understanding of countless body systems and diseases.

Other important medical contributions by Fabrizio included a complete and accurate description of the larynx and how it functions as an organ of speech. He also performed experiments demonstrating that the pupil of the eye changes size according to the amount of light that strikes it, as well as from physiological changes such as those caused by fear and sexual arousal.

Girolamo Fabrizio died at Padua, Italy, on May 21, 1619, one day after his eighty-second birthday. This great anatomist left behind a body of work (produced as part of a lifelong career in medicine) that is a tribute to his insight and devotion to the medical arts, and which also constituted one of the most important influences on the great William Harvey, whose work changed medicine for all time.

14

Marcello Malpighi
1628–94

It is a custom well known among artists, my learned colleagues, to refrain from gazing long and fondly at the designs for pictures they will later execute and at the first outlines sketched upon their tablets as soon as these escape from phantasy's maternal bosom, in order that they may not forthwith take final form; but they have them put out of sight to rest for a long time until the image of the unfinished offspring has been effaced from the mind of the maker; then after a while, giving it a hasty survey, they bring the work to conclusion. Some similar practice we should also follow in contemplating Nature's first portrayals; and, for me at least, I believe it both advantageous and necessary.

> —MARCELLO MALPIGHI
> *Repeated and Additional*
> *Observations on the Incubated Egg*

In the seed are enclosed all the parts of the body of the man that shall be formed.
> —SENECA

Before the advent of digital computerized scales to weigh gold and diamonds, people in the jewelry industry used a delicate balance scale that consisted of two brass bowls suspended on chains. These bowls were connected by a crossbar that rested gently on a pin, allowing the bowls to move up and down as gold or gemstones were placed in them. By placing a known quantity in one bowl (such as a 10-gram weight), the jeweler could then slowly add to the other bowl the material he was weighing until the two were perfectly even, seemingly suspended in midair, each flawlessly balancing the other.

In the long history of science and medicine, the analogy of the balance scale can be applied to two of the world's greatest scientists and most astute thinkers, Galileo Galilei (the Italian genius who reigns at the top of *The Italian 100*) and the subject of this chapter, the Italian physician and biologist Marcello Malpighi.

These two men "balanced" our view of the universe; Galileo providing the large picture, Malpighi, the small one. Galileo used the telescope to venture as far as he could into the *visible* reaches of our solar system; Malpighi focused his gaze in the other direction and used the microscope to study the tiny, *invisible* universe. Marcello Malpighi's findings and discoveries were so revolutionary (and thus, inflammatory), that his house was burned to the ground by those opposed to his views, with his books, papers, and manuscripts in it, and his all-important microscopes were smashed to pieces.

What was so frightening about Malpighi's discoveries and writings? Apparently, it was his rejection of the old teachings that so offended the people of the seventeenth century. Malpighi revealed, through his innovative work, the true structure of the human body and the microscopic functioning of human organs and circulatory processes.

Malpighi is the father of histology, which is the microscopic study of plant and animal tissue. In addition to his general advancement of the use of the microscope in medicine and research, Malpighi also discovered capillary circulation (filling in the missing link in William Harvey's discovery of blood circulation forty years earlier) and identified the taste buds, the optic nerve, and the red blood cells. He also described the microscopic structures of the brain, the liver, the spleen, the bones, the kidneys (specifically the renal glomeruli and urinary tubules), and the skin (the dermal papilae). The anatomical structures known as the malpighian body (the renal corpuscle) and the malpighian tubule were named after him.

In addition to his work with human anatomy and his research into the previously unseen functioning of the body, Malpighi also worked extensively with silkworms and chick embryos. In 1669, he published his findings on the silkworm, revealing that the insect did not have lungs but instead possessed a tracheal system that sent air throughout its body. Four years later, in 1673, he published his findings on the development of the chick embryo, making an enormous contribution to the science of embryology.

But Malpighi was not only interested in the physiology of humans, animals, and insects. In 1671, when he was forty-three, he founded the science of plant anatomy with writings that identified and described the stomata, one of the minute openings in the epidermis of a plant through which gaseous exchanges take place. He continued for the next decade to make detailed microscopic studies and drawings of plants.

Marcello Malpighi was born on March 10, 1628, in Crevalcore in the Papal States, Italy. His father had him study grammar as a child, and when he was eighteen, he entered the University of Bologna, where he studied medicine and philosophy. In 1653, at the age of twenty-five, Malpighi received doctorates in both disciplines, after which he decided to devote his time to studying human anatomy and medicine. He left Bologna in 1656 and became professor of theoretical medicine at the University of Pisa. He stayed in Pisa for only three years and returned to Bologna in 1659, mainly due to his own poor health. In Bologna he pursued his work with the microscope, and it was there, near the place where he was born, that the most violent opposition to him and his work surfaced. After enduring three years of continual hostility and jealousy from his neighbors and colleagues in Bologna, he decided he had had enough and accepted a position as professor of medicine at the University of Messina, on the island of Sicily, five hundred miles away from Bologna. For some unknown reason, Malpighi stayed in Messina for only four years, after which he returned once again to Bologna and went on with his studies.

On March 4, 1668, Malpighi, then forty, was named a fellow of the Royal Society in London, the group that had previously published some of his writings in their journal, *Philosophical Transactions*. (Malpighi was only the second Italian to be welcomed into this illustrious scientific organization. In January of that year, the society had admitted Count Carlo Ubaldini as a member, but no records survive to reveal Ubaldini's identity or the reason for his election.)

In 1684, ten years before Malpighi's death, the assault on his villa took place. To make up for this grievous insult, Pope Innocent XII appointed Malpighi as his personal physician; he was elected to the College of Doctors of Medicine, awarded the title of count, and entered into the Roman Patriciate Roll. Malpighi died in Rome on November 30, 1694, at the age of sixty-six.

Marcello Malpighi's legacy is one of critical importance to the sciences of physiology, embryology, botany, histology, anatomy, and pathology. His landmark discoveries and writings changed medicine for the better and served to illuminate previously unseen and unknown regions and functions of the human body. As is often the case with those ahead of their time, some people did not like what Malpighi's work revealed, and they lashed out at him because of their fears and superstitions. (These attitudes still thrive today, as evidenced by the creationists who insist that the biblical creation story be taught as science in public schools and that the principles of evolution be labeled as "guesswork," regardless of the documented scientific evidence backing them up.)

Regardless of the initial resistance to his work, Malpighi is unquestionably one of the most important names in the pantheon of the world's physicians and scientists, and he merits a high ranking in *The Italian 100*.

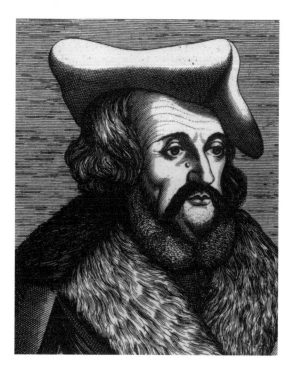

15

Girolamo Fracastoro
1483–1553

You must remember that nothing happens quite by chance. It's a question of accretion of information and experience . . . it's just chance that I happened to be here at this particular time when there was available and at my disposal the great experience of all the investigators who plodded along for a number of years.

> —JONAS SALK, on the discovery of the polio vaccine quoted in Richard Carter's *Breakthrough: The Saga of Jonas Salk*

Poetry is probably not the first thing that comes to people's minds in relation to the venereal disease syphilis, but it was the response of Girolamo Fracastoro, the sixteenth-century physician and poet, who was also the world's first epidemiologist.

Greek mythology tells the story of a lowly shepherd who refused to worship the gods in accordance with their demands, and instead chose to venerate his king. Apollo (god of the sun, prophecy, music, medicine, and poetry) was so outraged by this peasant's arrogance that he fouled the air around the shepherd with horrible, poisonous fumes that caused lesions and sores to break out all over his body. The shepherd's name was Syphilus, and this legend was Girolamo Fracastoro's inspiration when he gave the then widespread disease its modern name.

In 1521, Fracastoro published an epic poem called *Syphilis, sive de morbo Gallico* (Syphilis, or the French Disease), which detailed the specifics of the disease—completely *in rhyme*. Here is an excerpt from Girolamo's poem (rendered in English prose):

> [The infection] did not manifest itself at once, but remained latent for a certain time, sometimes for a month . . . even for four months. In the majority of cases small ulcers began to appear on the sexual organs. . . . Next, the skin broke out with encrusted pustules. . . . Then these ulcerated pustules ate away the skin, and . . . infected even the bones. . . . In some cases the lips or nose or eyes were eaten away, or, in others, the whole of the sexual organs.

Fracastoro's intent was to study that "fierce and rare sickness, never before seen for centuries past, which ravished all of Europe and the flourishing cities of Asia and Libya, and invaded Italy in that unfortunate war whence from the Gauls it has its name." Interestingly, Fracastoro did not believe that Christopher Columbus and his sailors had brought the disease back to Europe from the Americas as was the widely held opinion at the time. Fracastoro noted the outbreak of the disease in several European countries at the same time and determined that it was probably of European origin.

Girolamo Fracastoro was born in Verona, Italy, in 1483. When he was an infant, his mother was struck by lightning as she was holding him in her arms. Girolamo's mother died instantly, but her tiny young son was unhurt.

As a young man Girolamo studied at the University of Padua, where the great astronomer Copernicus was one of his classmates. In 1538 he wrote *A Single Center of the Universe*, which postulated that the earth revolved around the sun. This book was published a full *five years* before Copernicus's seminal work *De revolutionibus orbium coelestium,* which stated the same conviction. Copernicus refused to allow his book to be published until he was on his deathbed. It is not known if the two friends discussed heliocentrism, but Fracastoro's book *was* published first.

In addition to his work on venereal diseases and in astronomy, Fracastoro also studied many other diseases and their impact on civilizations, essentially founding the science of epidemiology.

Epidemics were of great interest to him, and in 1546 he wrote *De contagione et contagiosis morbis* (*On Contagion and Contagious Diseases*), which explained that all diseases were caused by individual germs that were transmitted from the infected to the uninfected. This was three hundred years before the work done by French scientist Louis Pasteur, and it set the stage for further developments in the study of the spread of diseases. In 1862 Pasteur published a paper in which he supported the germ theory of disease and later, in 1863, he developed the scientific process of pasteurization, a method of eliminating harmful organisms from foods and liquids. But Fracastoro anticipated Pasteur, and it is likely that Pasteur read Fracastoro and was inspired by his research and findings. Fracastoro's theory of germs as a cause of disease was the first recorded and accurate explanation of the disease process.

Fracastoro also described typhus in his *On Contagion* and postulated that *seminaria contagionum*—tiny life-forms that could duplicate themselves—were the means of spreading disease from one person to another.

Fracastoro was a highly respected and honored scientist during his time. He was made head physician of the Council of Trent in 1545, and his work was widely disseminated. In addition to his work in medicine and his poetry writing, he was also a geologist and an astronomer. A statue in his honor was erected in his home town of Verona, and Giovanni dal Cavino crafted a medallion with his likeness on it.

Girolamo Fracastoro died in Caffi, Italy, on August 8, 1553, at the age of seventy-five. His work changed the way disease was identified, evaluated, and treated; and he paved the way for many related scientific discoveries that occurred during the next three centuries.

16

Lazzaro Spallanzani
1729–99

The purpose of organ transplants and artificial organs is, of course, to replace parts of the body which have been damaged or which have become worn out before their time. A good deal of research, however, is now being dedicated to the question of why our bodies should wear out at all, and why they should not repair themselves more efficiently. Why is it that—unlike planarian worms and starfishes—we cannot regenerate severed parts? (Though recent work involving the placing of injured limbs in a very small-voltage electric field has shown that some regeneration of bone cells and even nerve cells is possible.) Why is it that our bodies grow gradually more decrepit until they grind to a halt? If we could find answers to these problems, we might be close to the most dramatic medical breakthrough of all.

—PETER NICHOLLS
The Science in Science Fiction

Beginning in 1767, Lazzaro Spallanzani began the biological work that would lead him into areas that no one had studied previously. He was keenly interested in biological regeneration and transplantation and worked with a number of different species, including amphibians, snails, and planarians (small aquatic worms).

Through his experiments, he documented three important findings:

1. The lower animals have greater regenerative powers than the higher animals.
2. Younger animals have greater regenerative powers than older animals.
3. In almost all cases except the simplest of life-forms, regeneration is limited to external limbs and surface parts, not internal organs.

Spallanzani's research in the field of cellular regeneration prodded him to go further and try to apply these new principles of biological regrowth to his transplantation studies. Around 1770, he successfully transplanted the head of one snail onto the body of another snail. This feat laid the groundwork for the widespread modern practice of transplantation, which currently includes tissues and organs such as the skin, corneas, blood vessels, heart valves, fascia, nerves, bone marrow, kidneys, heart, liver, lungs, and pancreas.

In addition to his work with tissue and organ regeneration and transplantation, Lazzaro Spallanzani made other breakthroughs that have contributed to the advancement of medicine and the improvement of the quality of life (as well as lay the groundwork for research done by Louis Pasteur and others).

In 1768, Lazzaro did experiments which once again disproved the theory of spontaneous generation (something Francesco Redi did over a hundred years earlier with his putrefying meat experiments (see REDI [25]). Using mutton broth as the test medium, Spallanzani, in a series of experiments similar in design to Redi's, proved that food could be protected from microorganisms by sealing the food so that air could not get at it. This proved that it was the microorganisms causing the rotting of the food, not a spontaneously generated process without any form of catalyst.

Spallanzani is also known for his work with ovulation and artificial insemination. He was the first scientist to theorize and then prove that spermatozoa was necessary for the fertilization of a mammal, thereby being one of the first to accurately define the reproductive process conclusively, and with supporting evidence to prove his research.

Spallanzani began his studies of fertilization by experimenting with frogs. Joseph Bellina and Josleen Wilson have described his ingenious technique in *The Fertility Handbook*:

> In 1775 he came up with a colorful experiment. Spallanzani dressed up a bevy of male frogs in little taffeta trousers. He then put the frogs together with female frogs. The male frogs clasped the females in amorous embrace and released their sperm. Instead of falling upon the female's deposit of eggs, the semen was caught and encased in the froggy pants. When eggs failed to produce tadpoles, the inventive Italian knew he was onto something. He collected some of the frog semen from the trousers and mixed it with female eggs. The eggs became fertilized.

In 1780, Spallanzani applied his findings about fertilization and spermatozoa to an experiment that was essentially the blueprint for a procedure that has now become common—he artificially inseminated a dog.

The son of a lawyer, Lazzaro Spallanzani was born in Modena, Italy, on January 12, 1729. He was educated by the Jesuits and was ordained a priest in 1757. It must be acknowledged that his religious training and vows tended to negatively influence his interpretation of scientific results. He would at times defer to religious dogma instead of scientific fact when evaluating a result that seemed to contradict his spiritual education.

Nonetheless, Spallanzani made some major breakthroughs that helped advance science and especially medicine. In addition to his work with tissue regeneration and insemination, he also was the first physiologist to accurately determine the pressure of blood as it flows through the body. He was also responsible for establishing the protocols for "sterile cultures," an experimental medium absolutely necessary for accurate test results.

Spallanzani was made a fellow of the Royal Society in 1768 at the age of thirty-nine. He also wrote books about his travels to Sicily and elsewhere. Early in his career, at the age of thirty-one, he was well versed enough in *The Iliad* to write an article condemning a new translation of Homer's epic.

Lazzaro Spallanzani died in 1799 in Pavia, Italy, at the age of seventy. His groundbreaking work has helped infertile couples and transplant patients for decades and must be considered an important contribution both to medicine and the science of fertility.

17

Camillo Golgi
1844–1926

Faith is the substance of things hoped for, the evidence of things not seen.
—HEBREWS, 11:1

Camillo Golgi is yet another of those critically important Italian scientists whose name has become part of their field's terminology. We are all familiar with his fellow countrymen likewise enshrined, including Antonio Scarpa (Scarpa's fascia, Scarpa's fluid, Scarpa's femoral triangle, Scarpa's membrane, and Scarpa's ganglion); Gabriel Fallopius (the fallopian tubes); Luigi Galvani (galvanism); Enrico Fermi (fermions); Leonardo Fibonacci (the Fibonacci sequence); and Alessandro Volta (the volt). Add to this list the Golgi tendon organ, a point where nerve fibers end in an intricate branching network; and the Golgi complex (or Golgi apparatus), a small network of cavities, fibers, and granules found in all cells except those of bacteria. Both were discovered and described by Golgi and are thus named for him.

Camillo Golgi's primary fields were cytology (the biology, structure, and function of cells), and medicine. Golgi developed the technique of staining nerve cells with silver nitrate, which allowed the physician or researcher to see clearly all the varied features of nerve elements. Bruno Zanobio has described Golgi's breakthrough method:

> In the second half of the nineteenth century considerable progress was made in the study of histology and microscopic anatomy; until the work of Golgi, however, little headway had been made in the study of the nervous system because of a lack of appropriate techniques; and theories on the function of nerve cells and their extensions were nebulous and conflicting. Golgi invented a completely original method based on the coloration of cells and nerve fibers by means of the prolonged immersion of samples, previously hardened with potassium bichromate or ammonium bichromate, in a 0.5 to 1 percent solution of silver nitrate.

This staining process allowed the membraneous network of vesicles in the nerve cells to be clearly seen for the first time, greatly advancing—with one stunning discovery—the sciences of medicine, neuroanatomy, histology, pathology, and cytology.

In addition to his clinical experimental work, Golgi also analyzed the blood of malaria patients. His research in this area led to the specific delineation of the three distinct forms of the disease as well as the sequential nature of the often debilitating fevers malaria patients experience. Golgi determined that the severity of the malaria attack was directly related to the quantity of protozoan parasites in the blood. His work with malaria led to improved diagnosis and treatment methods as well as improved survival rates. In his later years Golgi also studied the disease pellagra (which is caused by a deficiency of the B vitamin niacin); did extensive work on the structure of the kidney; and attempted to determine the origins of mental disease.

Camillo Golgi was born in Corteno in the Lombardy region of Italy on July 7, 1843. His father, Alessandro, was a doctor, and Camillo followed in his footsteps, attending the University of Padua and receiving his medical degree in 1865 at the age of twenty-three. Golgi then worked for a short period in a psychiatric clinic headed by Cesare Lombroso, while continuing to pursue his primary interest, histological research, which he carried out in the laboratories of the Italian histologist Giulio Bizzozero.

In 1871, Golgi taught a course on clinical microscopy, and in

1872, needing a steady income, he took the position of chief physician at the home for incurables in Abbiategrasso, Italy. He continued his research into the nervous system while working at the home. It was while working at the home in 1873 that Golgi, apparently using less-than-optimum equipment and facilities, perfected the silver nitrate cellular staining process for which he is known today. In the same year, he also described two types of nerve cells, which are today known as Golgi cells type I and II. In 1875, Golgi was offered a position as lecturer in Histology at the University of Pavia, which he gladly accepted.

In 1879, when Golgi was only thirty-six, he was given the chair of anatomy at the University of Siena but only stayed a year. In 1880, he returned to the University of Pavia as professor of both histology and general pathology. He taught until 1918, when he retired (as required by Italian law) at the age of seventy-five.

In recognition of his work, Golgi won the Nobel Prize for medicine or physiology in 1906, sharing the prestigious award with Santiago Ramón y Cajal. In addition to his medical and scientific work, Golgi also had an interest in politics and public service. In 1900, when he was president of the University of Pavia and dean of the faculty of medicine, he also became an Italian senator.

Throughout his life, Golgi published many notable scientific papers, all of which were published in a massive four-volume set titled *Opera omnia* (*The Complete Works*).

Golgi died in Pavia, January 21, 1926, at the age of eighty-two. Thanks to his discoveries, it is now possible to definitively study and evaluate the nerves and the nervous system, a development that has led to advancements in many of the branches of medical science.

18

Luigi Porta
1800–75

This living hand, now warm and capable
Of earnest grasping, would, if it were cold
And in the icy silence of the tomb,
So haunt thy days and chill thy dreaming nights
That wouldst wish mine own heart dry of blood
So in my veins red life might stream again,
And thus be conscience-calm'd—see here it is—
I hold it towards you.
                    —JOHN KEATS
                        Lines Supposed to have been
                        Addressed to Fanny Brawne

In the late eighteenth and early nineteenth centuries, the great Italian surgeon and anatomist Antonio Scarpa identified many important body parts and was also the first physician to correctly determine that arteriosclerosis consisted of thickened lesions lining the walls of arteries. As great a man of medicine as he was, though, Scarpa was surpassed by one of his students, Luigi Porta, the subject of this chapter. Because of Scarpa's definitive description of arteriosclerosis, Porta was able to greatly advance the foundational knowledge of arterial flow, ligation, and torsion and move forward to make the enormous contributions he is credited for: the development of modern vascular surgery. (Vascular surgery is surgery on the blood vessels—the veins, arteries, and capillaries—of the

60

human body.)

Porta also contributed to the development of modern lithotripsy, a procedure in which kidney stones are crushed in the bladder, after which the small fragments of stone can be safely removed through suction and irrigation. This procedure has saved countless numbers of people the agony of having to pass a kidney stone naturally, and Porta's invention—a piece of equipment that was a combination of a drill and pincers—greatly advanced the effectiveness of this valuable surgical technique.

Luigi Porta was born on January 4, 1800, in Pavia, Italy, a small town south of Milan. His parents were not well-to-do, and this situation was exacerbated by the death of his father at an early age. Luigi had to struggle and work very hard, therefore, to acquire an education, which he resolutely did; in 1822, at the age of twenty-two, he graduated from the University of Pavia with a degree in surgery. His mentor at the university, Antonio Scarpa, believed that Porta needed to gain maturity and sent the young man to Vienna for further study. Porta spent four years in Vienna studying medicine, and in 1826 he returned to Pavia. Later that year he was awarded a degree in medicine from the University of Pavia, and six years later, in 1832, at the age of thirty-two, Porta was given the position of professor of clinical surgery at the university.

Bruno Zanobio has described Porta's methodology and contributions:

> Porta's work lay in many surgical fields; that in which he was preeminent was experimental pathological surgery. By his research on the pathological changes caused to arteries by ligation and torsion he contributed to establishing the foundations of modern vascular surgery. Beginning in 1835 he made an extensive series of animal experiments on more than 270 animals of various species, including dogs, sheep, goats, horses, asses, oxen, and rabbits. He continued these investigations for nine years, and his results, coupled with his clinical observations, led him to significant discoveries concerning experimentally induced pathological changes of the arteries. Among these, his findings on the manner in which collateral circulation is established following the obliteration of parts of the arteries are of particular interest.

In addition to his pioneering work on arterial pathology, Porta was also a prolific writer. Throughout his career he wrote over fifty scientific treatises, including his two most important works: *Delle alterazioni patologiche delle arterie per legatura e la torsione. Esperienze ed osservazioni* (*The Pathological Changes of Arteries Through Ligation and Torsion, Experiments and Observations* [1845]), and *Della litotrizia di Luigi Porta* (*On the Lithotripsy of Luigi Porta* [1859]).

Porta was also interested in a great many other fields of medicine, including anesthesiology (the study of the administration and effect of anesthetics); thyroid pathology (the study of diseases of the thyroid); urology (the study of the urinary tract); traumatology (the branch of surgery that deals with wounds arising from injuries); and autoplasty (the replacement of tissue with a graft from the same body).

Luigi Porta lived a long and interesting life that was marked by painful episodes and adverse circumstances. The early death of his father made his pursuit of an education difficult, and he was also burdened throughout his life with the care of his mentally retarded sister. He never married, and his responsibility for his sister may have been one of the reasons for this. He was quite well known and respected during his life and received many awards and honors, including being named a senator of the Kingdom of Italy (during the reign of King Vittorio Emmanuele II) and head of the medical and surgical faculty of Pavia. He also founded an anatomical museum, which he willed to the University of Pavia, and he was responsible for an impressive collection of pathological samples.

Luigi Porta died in his hometown of Pavia on September 9, 1875, at the age of seventy-five. His many scientific contributions continue to this day to improve people's lives and further medical knowledge.

Salvador Edward Luria
1912–91

The single biggest threat to man's continued dominance on
the planet is the virus.

—NOBEL LAUREATE JOSHUA LEDERBERG

The Italian-born biologist Salvador Edward Luria literally "wrote
the book" on viruses. His college-level textbook, *General Virology*, is a
seminal work on the branch of molecular biology that deals with
viruses, viral self-replication, and bacteriophages (viruses that infect
bacteria). Luria, born in Turin on August 13, 1912, is also credited
with the development of the science of molecular biology, an
advancement that has greatly enhanced the studies of virus repro-
duction and mutation, as well as helping to move forward research

into the fields of DNA and genetic engineering. For these marked discoveries and his insightful research, Luria was awarded—along with his colleagues Max Delbrück and Alfred Day Hershey—the Nobel Prize for physiology or medicine in 1969.

Luria's work has been primarily in the field of bacteriophages, an area that holds promise for the fight against many deadly strains of virus. Bacteria are microscopic organisms that are present in everything: air, water, soil, the human mouth and digestive tract. They reproduce by binary fission, a biochemical process that occurs approximately every twenty minutes. Bacteria can be astonishingly fecund: a single bacterium is capable of generating 16 million copies of itself in a twenty-four-hour period. In 1942, Salvador Luria photographed bacteriophages with an electron microscope. This was the first time a virus—in this case, phage particles—had been seen as something other than a nondescript speck. Luria's electron microscope photograph of the bacteriophage confirmed earlier speculation that they were long, with round heads, and thin tails.

Luria did research into viruses and bacteriophages in Paris at the Pasteur Institute when he was in his twenties. He came to the United States in 1940 at the age of twenty-eight and met the German microbiologist Max Delbrück. At that time, there was an organization called the American Phage Group, an informal alliance of scientists and biologists who were all studying viruses. Working with this organization, Luria made his pioneering electron microscope photograph of the phage in 1942. Luria and Delbrück later published their findings in 1943.

In 1945, Luria and Alfred Day Hershey made an extraordinary advance in the study of these "anti-bacteria" viruses: They showed that bacteriophages mutate, adapting themselves to the changing DNA structure of evolving bacteria and new bacteria. This was a profound—and alarming—discovery. Luria and Hershey proved that viruses are capable of changing so as to remain lethal to a constantly changing "menu" of cells. Permanent mutation of a virus into a *new* virus was now confirmed as fact.

Recently, it has been suggested that because of this newly discovered ability of viruses to mutate in order to remain viable as an infectious agent, there was really no reasonable hope of a *cure* for any viral-based diseases. This theory is even more alarming when we factor in the 1986 finding that it is possible and probably likely that fully half of all known cancers could be caused by some kind of viral agent. One hopes the day will come when children are automatically vaccinated against all forms of cancer, and malignancies become as rare as a case of polio, but the complexity of the process and the possibility of a viral cause are truly daunting hurdles that medical science has so far not been able to successfully leap. French science writer Gerald Messadié has written on the nature of viruses:

> The existence in the living being of non-infectious proviruses, which only become infectious in conditions which are not yet established, through genetic recombinations, with the aim of organizing the DNA of the host cell to their advantage, indeed the possibility that unexpressed fragments of the human genetic capital might trigger the formation of viruses, and other indicators show that virology is closely identified with the study of the mechanisms of life itself.

In 1974, Salvador Luria became director of the Center for Cancer Research at MIT and won the National Book Award for his first nonacademic book, *Life: An Unfinished Experiment.* (He had been a member of the MIT faculty since 1959.) *Life* was translated into German, French, Italian, Spanish, and Japanese. Luria's discoveries in bacteriophage identification set science on the path of a possible definitive defense against the virus, and someday, perhaps a vaccine against cancer.

Throughout his life, Luria was passionate about causes he believed in. In 1958, the naturalized American told *Time* magazine, "I made up my mind that as a citizen I would be an active participant in American politics, taking advantage of the democratic opportunities that were not available to me in Italy." During the 1960s, he was resolutely opposed to U.S. policy during the Vietnam War.

In addition to his scientific work and his writing, Luria also sculpted and worked as a senior scientist for a biotechnology firm in Cambridge, Massachusetts.

Luria died on February 6, 1991, of a heart attack at his home. He was seventy-eight. His legacy was that of a scientific pioneer, and his work contributed to the development of such complex procedures as genetic engineering and recombinant DNA technology.

20

Rita Levi-Montalcini

1909–

If I had not been discriminated against or had not suffered
persecution, I would never have received the Nobel Prize.
—RITA LEVI-MONTALCINI

During World War II, Rita Levi-Montalcini, an Italian born in
Turin, Italy, to a Jewish mother and Christian father, had to go into
hiding in Florence because of her Jewish heritage. Ever the dedicated researcher, Levi-Montalcini set up a small laboratory in the
house where she was hiding and for two years continued her
research and experiments. Fortunately, she survived the war and
went on to do notable work with tumor and nerve-cell growth,
research that will someday lead to new techniques for battling cancer and regenerating damaged nerves. Ironically, these medical
breakthroughs might well save the life of patients descended from

the Nazis who would have shipped Levi-Montalcini off to a death camp if they had found her during the war.

Following the war, Levi-Montalcini served until 1947 as physician tending to the many uprooted by the conflict. She then accepted a post at Washington University in St. Louis, Missouri, where scientists and researchers under the zoologist Viktor Hamburger were working to identify what would come to be known as NGF—nerve growth factor.

In 1948, Levi-Montalcini and her colleagues made an important breakthrough. They discovered that a certain type of mouse tumor stimulated new nerve growth when the tumor was implanted into chick embryos. The suspicion arose that the growth was initiated in the living embryo through some process yet unknown. The scientists disproved this theory, however, by injecting the tumor cells into a live tissue culture kept in a petri dish in the laboratory. Nerve growth occurred even in this primitive culture as well.

This was an astonishing discovery: A tumor could spur new nerve growth. The researchers ultimately identified exactly how this happened: The tumor contained a factor—a protein later identified as NGF—that could be identified and isolated.

At this point the renowned scientist Stanley Cohen joined Levi-Montalcini at Washington University and began pursuing the actual growth factor in the tumor. He ultimately conclusively identified NGF, and this began the identification and cataloging of many other growth factors that could be found in the bodies of animals, including, of course, human beings.

The practical application of such a discovery will be to someday regenerate new nerve pathways in people who have suffered severed nerve damage through trauma. (A well-known recent case involved the actor Christopher Reeve, paralyzed from the shoulders down after crushing two spinal discs during a riding accident in 1995.) This finding also provided important information into the nature of tumors and may aid in the development of more effective treatments against cancers of all kinds.

Rita Levi-Montalcini was born on April 22, 1909. She spent her childhood in Turin and later attended the University of Turin, where she studied medicine and biochemistry, earned her medical degree, and began her research into nerve cell growth.

After coming to the United States, Levi-Montalcini remained at Washington University for fourteen years, from 1947 through 1961. She then returned to Italy and accepted a position at the Institute of Cell Biology in Rome, where she remained extremely active in nerve cell research until her retirement in 1978. In 1986 Rita Levi-Montalcini and Stanley Cohen received the Nobel Prize for physiology or medicine, for their work identifying the protein NGF.

When the call from Stockholm came informing her that she had won the Nobel, Levi-Montalcini was on the second-to-last page of an Agatha Christie novel—*Evil Under the Sun*. She postponed celebrating until she finished the book and learned the identity of the killer.

Two years later, in 1988, Levi-Montalcini made her own contribution to literature when her acclaimed autobiography, *In Search of Imperfection*, was published.

Now in her eighties, Levi-Montalcini lives in Rome with her sister. She is president of the Italian Multiple Sclerosis Association and was the first woman elected to the prestigious Pontifical Academy of Sciences. "I can do things that are very, very important, which I would never have been able to do if I did not receive [the Nobel]," she told *Scientific American*. "It has given me the possibility of helping a lot of people." She also has a laboratory at the Institute of Neurobiology in Rome and regularly mentors young students there, advising them about their education and talking to them about her own work.

Levi-Montalcini is now studying nerve growth factor in the immune and endocrine systems. "The neotrophic factor was just the tip of the iceberg," she told *Scientific American*. Vital and energetic, she feels that she still has the spirit and enthusiasm she had as a young woman. "At my old age," she said with a laugh, "I could have no more capacity. I believe I still have plenty."

Understanding and being able to control nerve cell growth in humans is one of the most important areas of medical research. Nerve cell growth has applications for use in almost every medical situation, from burns to cancer; from heart and brain surgery to spinal cord injuries. Levi-Montalcini's identification of the nerve-growth factor that exists in all bodies may someday lead to a time when paralysis is reversible and new, healthy nerves can be transplanted into injured bodies, the same way blood is transfused today. She and her colleague Stanley Cohen opened the door on a stunning new technology that has enormous ramifications for the future of medicine. Rita Levi-Montalcini is included as one of *The Italian 100* because she did the research and made the discoveries that have changed, and will continue to change, people's lives.

21

Renato Dulbecco

1914–

Anatomy is destiny.

—SIGMUND FREUD
Collected Writings

Cancer has been around for millennia. We have historical records from 1,500 years before the birth of Christ that mention cancer, and the disease (actually a number of diseases with similar characteristics) also appears in animals, birds, reptiles, and fish.

The problem with finding a universal cure for cancer is formidable: Because there is no universal *cause* for cancer, what works for one form of the disease does not work for another. Chemical poisoning, radiation, and myriad viruses are all believed to cause one or another form of cancer and thus, the single "magic bullet" anticarcinogenic agent has so far eluded us.

Italian-born virologist Renato Dulbecco is one of the scientists who spent their lives working toward eliminating cancer. Through his pioneering research, Dulbecco showed that the key to understanding and ultimately conquering cancer may lie in DNA research.

In the 1950s, Dulbecco and his colleague Marguerite Vogt grew animal viruses in cultures and then inserted these viruses into mice. They determined that certain viruses caused tumors in the rodents and they were then able to identify the process by which this occurred. They learned that one specific virus, the polyoma virus, causes a tumor by inserting its own DNA into the DNA of the host cell. This "invaded" cell then becomes a cancer cell that replicates itself as a normal cell would, but while so doing, also duplicates the "bad" DNA, thus forming a malignant growth that cleverly uses the host cell's own reproductive capabilities to clone itself over and over again. This discovery led to the discovery of the enzyme RNA transcriptase (by Dulbecco's students, Howard Temin and David Baltimore), a universal component of all cells.

From these findings, Dulbecco posited the theory that human cancers are formed in a similar manner, thus providing researchers with a critically important lead as to how to conquer cancer. Research into the genetic components of cancer cells continues to this day and ongoing breakthroughs have steadily improved cancer survival rates and cures.

Renato Dulbecco was born on Sunday, February 22, 1914, in Catanzaro, a small town just a few miles from the coast of the Ionian Sea in Italy's Calabria region. He earned his medical degree at the University of Turin in 1936, and from 1940 through 1947 he worked there as a researcher. He emigrated to the United States in 1947 and was naturalized as a citizen six years later.

In 1947, he worked as a bacteriologist at Indiana University for two years with his former Turin associate, SALVADOR LURIA [19]. In 1949, at the invitation of another former colleague, Max Delbrück, Dulbecco began teaching biology at the California Institute of Technology. (In the 1940s, Dulbecco had worked under Delbrück on research involving polioviruses which had led to the development of a polio vaccine.)

Dulbecco remained at the California Institute of Technology until 1963 when he joined the Salk Institute for Biological Studies, in La Jolla, California, where he worked until 1972. That year he relocated to London, England, to join the Imperial Cancer Research Fund, where he remained for five years. In 1977, he then returned to the United States, where he joined the faculty of the University of California as a professor of pathology and medicine. He also rejoined the staff of the Salk Institute and became president of that institution in 1988.

Dulbecco has been the recipient of many academic honors and awards during his distinguished career, the most notable being the 1975 Nobel Prize for physiology or medicine for his research into cancer replication. He was also named London's Man of the Year in 1975 and Italian American of the Year in San Diego, California, in 1978.

Renato Dulbecco is accorded such a high ranking on *The Italian 100* because his work, like the work of other scholars and researchers who strive toward the elimination of disease, is some of the most important work ever done in the name of science. His name may not be known to most people, but, since cancer strikes one in three, the odds are that Dulbecco's efforts will directly impact most people at some point in their lives.

22

Ugo Cerletti
1877–1963
Lucio Bini
1908–64

> The experience and behaviour that gets labeled schizophrenic
> is a special strategy that a person invents in order to live in an
> unlivable situation.
> — R. D. LAING
> *Politics of Experience*

Ugo Cerletti and Lucio Bini developed the pioneering medical
technique of electroconvulsive therapy (ECT) in 1937. Electroshock therapy is a dramatic and controversial procedure that has
become part of our popular culture and is often perceived as a
nightmarish experience, thanks in part to popular films such as *One
Flew Over the Cuckoo's Nest* (1975), in which a mental patient experiences violent convulsions while undergoing ECT. Because of such
images, prospective candidates for the treatment are often terri-
fied.

Electroconvulsive therapy is a psychiatric procedure used to
treat severe depression (currently the most common psychiatric dis-
order), manic depression, schizophrenia, and schizophrenic catato-
nia. Prior to an ECT treatment, patients are given an anesthetic
and a muscle relaxant drug, rendering them extremely drowsy if

not actually putting them to sleep. A conductant gel is applied to the temples, and a bite guard is inserted into the mouth. Electrodes are affixed to the temples. Then a specified voltage of electric current (always low) is deliberately passed through the patient's brain via the electrodes at the temples.

The electrical current causes immediate unconsciousness and a convulsive seizure of the central nervous system which somehow short-circuits those parts of the brain that are causing the depression or schizophrenia. The seizure usually lasts between five and twenty seconds. The patient remains in a drowsy state (or sleeps) for thirty minutes to an hour, after which he or she becomes more alert and is usually able to converse coherently. Sometimes there is a short-term memory loss and/or intermittent confusion after a treatment and occasionally some patients complain of headaches.

After a short recovery period, the patient is usually in a better state of mind, can think more clearly, and is less depressed. Electroconvulsive therapy is not a onetime treatment, however. A standard course of treatment is two or three times a week for three or four months for a total of eight to twelve "shocks."

Prior to the widespread use of relaxant drugs and anesthetics, ECT would sometimes cause spinal injuries, muscle pulls, or other injuries due to the violent thrashing of the convulsive patient. With the judicious use of extremely effective drugs, now most patients only experience some mild muscular twitching, and there is almost no incidence of injuries during a treatment. Tranquilizers and other sedative-type drugs also work wonders in alleviating the often intense anxiety (sometimes bordering on full-blown panic) on the part of a pre-ECT patient. It is estimated today that serious complications of electroconvulsive therapy occur in less than one-tenth of one percent of all patients who undergo the treatment.

Although isolated from their colleagues around the world by World War I (1914–18) and the twenty-two-year reign of Italian Fascism (1922–44), Ugo Cerletti and Lucio Bini spent their professional careers working in psychiatry and advancing the effective use of electroconvulsive therapy. Bini (with T. Bazzi) published in Milan from 1963 to 1967 a comprehensive three-volume text on psychiatry. Cerletti wrote extensively on electroshock and published widely in journals throughout his life, including in the renowned *American Journal of Psychiatry.*

The use of electroconvulsive therapy still remains controversial, but the argument over its use seems to stem in large part from the public's misconception of the treatment (thanks, in no small way, to Hollywood) and the fact that in the past ECT was abused by unscrupulous mental health workers who often overused it to stun difficult patients into a stupor.

Nevertheless, ECT is recommended by the American Psychiatric Association for depression and schizophrenia patients who do not respond to drug therapy, and its effectiveness is indisputable.

Drs. Ugo Cerletti and Lucio Bini's identification of the "electrical" function of the brain as it pertained to mental disorders led to their development of electroshock therapy, a treatment that rescued countless people from the horrors and torment of mental depression and schizophrenia.

23

Gasparo Tagliocozzi
1546–99

Had Cleopatra's nose been shorter, the whole face of the world
would have changed.
— BLAISE PASCAL
Pensées

In the town of Bologna, Italy, Gasparo Tagliocozzi's place of birth
and the city where he taught and practiced medicine, a statue of
the great surgeon stands in the University of Bologna's anatomy
theater. The statue shows Gasparo holding a nose in his hand—
such was the enduring importance of the procedure he developed.

During the sixteenth century, the period during which Tagliocozzi lived and practiced, crime and punishment were vastly different than they are today, and justice was often meted out with a

sword instead of a gavel. A common sanction during this era was to lop off a convicted criminal's nose. Interestingly, the victim of this procedure was then allowed (if the resources were available) to have reconstructive surgery. Gasparo Tagliocozzi's technique was not quick, pretty, or comfortable, but it worked.

In the Yale University Medical Historical Library, there is an illustration of one of Tagliocozzi's nasal reconstruction patients following surgery. The surgical technique he used involved cutting a thick slab of skin from the left upper arm and surgically grafting it to the patient's face—*without removing it from the arm.* Thus the patient's upper arm was grafted to his face. A series of straps and splinting materials were then wrapped around the arm and upper body of the patient so that the arm could not be moved. This was critically important, because once the arm was sewed to the face, the patient could obviously do severe damage if he moved the limb and tore off the graft. The purpose of this step of the procedure was to allow the skin flap to acquire a blood supply from the veins and arteries in the patient's face.

This step of the process took *twelve (or more) full days* to accomplish. For that entire period, the patient's arm was held immobile by a splint (his left hand was usually positioned on top of his head) while the skin graft "healed." Once the skin had securely adhered itself to the patient's face, his arm was freed by surgery, and Tagliocozzi would then shape the thick new skin into something resembling a nose. The surgeon also used this technique for lips and ears that had been removed.

These repair procedures were the beginning of plastic surgery, and Tagliocozzi is the surgeon who is credited with being its founder. An interesting and important aspect of Tagliocozzi's work with nasal reconstruction, or rhinoplasty, was his discovery about the rejection of transplanted tissue. He learned early on that if he tried to graft skin from another person onto a patient, the skin would die. He thus confirmed the necessity of autografting—the use of the patient's own skin—for a reconstruction. (Doctors today use homografts—organs from other people—all the time when performing kidney, liver, lung, cornea, and even heart transplants, but the recipient must be on drugs for the rest of his or her life to suppress their immune system's natural defense mechanism and prevent rejection.)

Tagliocozzi explained this phenomenon in his treatise on rhinoplasty:

The singular character of the individual entirely dissuades us from attempting this work on another person. For such is the force and power of individuality, that if anyone should believe that he could accelerate and increase the beauty of union . . . we consider him plainly superstitious and badly grounded in the physical sciences.

Gasparo Tagliocozzi was born in 1546 in Bologna and was a professor of anatomy and surgery at the University of Bologna. Not much is known of his personal life except that he spent most of his life in his hometown and died there on November 7, 1599. During his short life (he was only fifty-three when he died) Tagliocozzi made an enormous contribution toward an important medical skill. Reconstructive facial surgery has aided countless accident victims, as well as patients suffering from conditions such as rhinitis and sinusitis. Currently, the most common use of the skills pioneered by Tagliocozzi is the practice of cosmetic surgery. In the United States alone, more than 400,000 cosmetic procedures were performed in 1994. Many involved rhinoplasty, which—fortunately for patients— no longer requires that the upper arm be grafted to the face. Though these surgeries do not involve life-threatening conditions, they have helped to promote the self-esteem and psychological well-being of many individuals.

Ascanio Sobrero

1812–88

If I have ever made any valuable discoveries, it has been owing
more to patient attention, than to any other talent.

—ISAAC NEWTON

Ascanio Sobrero was born in Casale Monferrato, Italy, which is
known today not for being Ascanio's birthplace but instead for
being the cement capital of Italy and for having Italy's largest and
most elaborate synagogue. Casale is a tiny town in the northern
Piemonte region of Italy about fifty miles east of Turin, the gracious
city where Sobrero would spend his life studying and teaching.

Sobrero was born on October 12, in the year 1812; a twelve-
month period that saw an outbreak of belligerence in many parts of

the globe as Napoleon invaded Russia, and England and the United States began the War of 1812. Perhaps there was something symbolic in Sobrero's birth during this particular year, considering that he was responsible for the discovery of one of the most powerful explosives known to man, nitroglycerine, and that his work would directly lead to the invention of dynamite by Alfred Nobel in 1866.

As a young man, Sobrero studied under the chemists Berzelius and Leibig. In 1847, at the age of thirty-five, he became a professor of chemistry at the Institute of Technology at the University of Turin. That same year he conducted his experiments that would lead to nitroglycerine and in the years 1851 through 1857, he wrote and published a three-volume series on chemistry. He died in Turin on Saturday, May 26, 1888, at the age of seventy-five.

Since its introduction, nitroglycerine has achieved worldwide recognition due to two distinct applications. The first is its remarkable volatility: Nitroglycerine will explode if it is shaken or if its container is jostled. This deadly sensitivity has been used as a plot device countless times in movies and books. In addition to its obvious importance in the manufacture of explosives—ammonium nitrate and c-4 are two of the better-known later applications in addition to dynamite—the second factor in nitroglycerine's worldwide importance is its adaptation for use as a cardiac-anginal agent.

Shortly after Sobrero's discovery of nitroglycerine, the wizards of the pharmaceutical world discovered that the chemical, in a refined form and in extremely low doses, when administered sublingually (dissolved under the tongue), reduced or completely eliminated the symptoms of angina pectoris and could, in some cases, prevent an actual heart attack until the patient could seek treatment. Apparently, the "explosive" nature and characteristics of nitro (as it came to be known) also worked on painfully constricted arteries; the chemical acts as a vasodilator, expanding the vessels and lowering the blood pressure, so that blood flow returns to a more normal state.

As is often the case with important scientific discoveries, serendipity played a role in Sobrero's discovery of nitroglycerine and its astonishing explosive properties. In 1846, a German scientist named Christian Friedrich Schönbein was performing chemical experiments in an attempt to create a practical artificial textile fiber. While working with a cellulose paste that he hoped to weave into such a fiber, he accidentally created the chemical nitrocellulose by treating the cellulose paste with the transparent, corrosive liquid known as nitric acid. This new material was of the right physical consistency for use as a fiber, but it was completely unsuitable for the making of textiles because it was extremely flammable.

Shortly after Schönbein's discovery, Sobrero, then thirty-five, learned of the properties of nitrocellulose. He became extremely interested in its combustible properties and, following the German scientist's lead, began experimenting with other materials that he would likewise treat with nitric acid in an attempt to create "ignitable" materials. One of his experiments involved treating (at room temperature) glycerol, a syrupy liquid obtained from fats and oils, with both nitric acid and sulfuric acid. The result of this mixture was the compound trinitroglycerine, now called simply nitroglycerine. This was an exceedingly dangerous product, and even its manufacture was extremely hazardous because of its aforementioned sensitivity to jarring.

It has since been learned that the detonation of nitroglycerine generates gases that occupy more than 1,200 times their original volume, creating temperatures of approximately 9,000 degrees Fahrenheit. This creates a pressure of 20,000 atmospheres with detonation waves moving at 17,000 miles per hour.

With a capacity to generate forces like these, it wasn't long before other adaptations of nitroglycerine were being developed, most notably by Alfred Nobel. In 1866, the Swedish inventor perfected a way of harnessing the power of nitroglycerine by allowing a porous soil-based substance to absorb it, thus stabilizing it and creating the explosive dynamite. (Four years earlier, Alfred's brother Emil Oskar had lost his life as he was working with nitroglycerine. Apparently, the factory he was working in did not have adequate safety measures in place, and he and several other workers were killed instantly by a powerful explosion.) Alfred Nobel later created and endowed the Nobel Prize because he did not want to be remembered as a "merchant of death," as he had been called in a premature obituary that accidentally ran in a newspaper when he was still alive.

Thus, Ascanio Sobrero's legacy is one of both destruction and salvation. His nitroglycerine has been used for over a century in the manufacture of dynamite, an explosive which is used for both good (construction, landscaping, and so forth) and nefarious (bombs, weaponry, and the like) purposes. His discovery has also saved countless lives in its application as a heart medication. As with his fellow countryman Enrico Fermi, Sobrero's genius has been utilized in both tragic and wonderful ways.

25

Francesco Redi

1626–97

Se vi è alcumo, a cui non piaccia
 La vernaccia
 Vendemmiato in Pietrafitta,
 Interdetto,
 maledetto
 Fugga via dal mio cospetto
 E per pena sempre ingozzi
 Vin di Brozzi,
 Di Quaracchi e di Peretola.

If there is anyone who doesn't like
 The white wine that is
 Harvested in Pietrafitta,
 Let him flee away from my presence,
 Interdicted,

Maledicted;
And for punishment
Let him ever guzzle the
Wine of Brozzi,
Of Quaracchi, and of Peretola.
            — FRANCESCO REDI
              from *Bacco in Toscano*

In the fourteenth through seventeenth centuries, the prevailing views on the origins of life, shared by both scientists and nonscientists, were often twofold: The first was that life on earth was due to the direct action of a supernatural being (God) who created it out of nothing; the second, that life came about through spontaneous generation, that is, arising from nonliving matter with no outside catalyst or power. (This second view probably came from the ancient Greeks, in whose mythology the earth goddess, Gaea, was said to be able to create living things out of stones.) One seventeenth-century writer insisted that believing in spontaneous generation was mandated by "reason, sense, and experience," and all the "doubter" had to do was "go to Egypt, and there he will find the fields swarming with mice begot of the mud of the Nile, to the great calamity of the inhabitants." Other "evidence" of spontaneous generation often cited was the appearance of maggots on putrefying meat without any apparent external cause. We now know that maggots are the larvae of insects, but back then, it was assumed they were creatures unto themselves, and no one made the connection between the presence of houseflies and the appearance of maggots.

In 1651, the seventy-three-year-old English physician William Harvey published his book *Exercitationes de generations animalium,* in which he mainly discussed his belief that all living creatures evolve out of an egg. However, he also posited the erroneous theory that all of the lower forms of life were capable of spontaneous generation.

Years later, Harvey's book came into the hands of Francesco Redi, an Italian physician and poet. Redi immediately doubted Harvey's theory of spontaneous generation among the lower lifeforms (though he did completely accept Harvey's theory that lifeforms did arise out of eggs). In 1668, at the age of forty-two, Redi performed a series of biological experiments—some of the first experiments ever done with proper scientific controls—to disprove Harvey's spontaneous generation theory.

Redi placed different varieties of meat in a number of flasks. He sealed some of the flasks and left others open to the air. As Redi expected, all of the meats in the flasks—whether they were open or sealed—putrefied.

He then repeated the experiment, only this time he left some of the flasks open while covering others with a thin piece of gauze. Again, all the meat eventually rotted, but the flasks left open to the air were the only ones in which maggots appeared on the meat. The thin layer of gauze Redi had placed over certain flasks had prevented flies from getting into the flasks and laying their eggs. These results disproved the theory of the spontaneous generation of maggots from meat and conclusively proved that the maggots needed to be hatched from eggs in order to come into being. (Redi knew that he had proved that maggots came from the eggs laid by the flies, but he shortsightedly continued to believe for years that parasitical intestinal worms *could* be spontaneously generated.) Redi had, with one series of experiments, proven that William Harvey was both right and wrong in his thinking about the generation of life, and his findings were published in a book titled *The Generation of Insects.*

Even though Redi had made an important scientific breakthrough with his experiments, many people, including the educated elite, continued to believed in spontaneous generation. Redi's work, however, effectively complemented the work that Dutch scientist Antony van Leeuwenhoek was doing with the microscopes he fashioned (Leeuwenhoek also discounted the theory of spontaneous generation and discovered the microbe during his research) and aided Louis Pasteur's work with germ theory in the nineteenth century.

Francesco Redi was born in Arezzo, Italy, on February 19, 1626. He attended medical school and developed a wide range of interests, including the writing of comic poetry and a fascination with vipers. Redi was the naturalist who determined conclusively that a viper's poison originated in a bladder covering the teeth—not in the tail, as had been previously believed. Redi's poetry was also highly popular. His best-known work was *Bacco in Toscano* (*Bacchus in Tuscany*), published in 1685.

His collected writings were published in a nine-volume edition in 1809–11. This thousand-line dithyramb (a choral song of praise to Bacchus) fantasized that Bacchus himself visited Italy's Tuscan hills (with Ariadne as his companion) and spent his time sampling the various wines of the region until he ended up staggering and incoherent. In the poem, Bacchus ultimately pronounces the wine of the Montepulciano region the finest of them all. (Redi was a genuine elitist when it came to wine: He had Bacchus refuse all other beverages during his earthly sojourn, including beer, water, tea, lemonade, cider, and coffee: "Never shall I make use of chocolate or tea;/Such medicines shall never be for me;/I'd rather drink poison/Than a cup full of bitter and evil coffee.")

Redi spent many years working on the poem, and when it was published (along with his own detailed commentary), it immediately became very popular.

Redi died on March 1, 1697, at the age of seventy-one, in Pisa, Italy. His important contributions to science and medicine came about because of his refusal to accept an archaic, supernatural explanation for the genesis of life, committing himself instead to a search for the truth through experimentation.

26

Girolamo Cardano
1501–76

> Although various abortive medicines, as I have heard, were tried
> in vain, I was born on September 24, 1501. Since Jupiter was in
> the ascendant and Venus ruled the horoscope, I was not
> maimed save in the genitals, so that from my twenty-first to my
> thirty-first year I was unable to lie with women; and many a time
> I lamented my fate, envying all other men their good fortune.
> — GIROLAMO CARDANO
> *Book of My Life*

As the epigraph above reveals, Girolamo Cardano began his
shocking autobiography by revealing that his mother tried to abort
him *in utero* and that he was impotent until he was thirty-one.

Such candor—which prevailed throughout the entire book—
was not unusual for one of the most truly unique men to have ever
lived during the Italian Renaissance.

Girolamo Cardano's name appears often in reference books
and textbooks that chronicle the sixteenth century. His important
contributions to a wide range of scientific disciplines are a documented part of history.

But what is not generally known is the nature of Cardano's
personality, a bizarre blend of elements that historian Mario Gliozzi
noted encompassed "Encyclopedic learning, powerful intellect
combined with childlike credulity, unconquerable fears, and delu-

sions of grandeur."

There is no denying that the brilliant Girolamo Cardano was an authentic eccentric, and some of the events of his life are truly astounding. As a child, he was abused and neglected by his ignorant (and apparently explosive-tempered) mother; and yet he was encouraged to study and excel by his brilliant father, a judge who was a good friend of LEONARDO DA VINCI [10]. As already noted, Cardano relates in one of his autobiographies (he wrote three) that he was completely impotent from the age of twenty-one until his marriage at the age of thirty-one; but that after he wed, the union resulted in three children, two boys and a girl. But his family life was also touched by tragedy: In 1560, despite his efforts to stop it, his favorite son was executed for poisoning his unfaithful wife.

In 1570, Cardano was imprisoned by the Inquisition for casting Jesus Christ's horoscope and controversially concluding that Jesus' life and crucifixion were due to unfavorable influences of the planets and stars.

Throughout his life, Cardano wrote 230 books, of which 138 have been published. (Harshly self-critical, he was known to burn some of his own manuscripts if they did not please him.)

Cardano also suffered from an amazing array of physical problems and ailments, including: stuttering; chronic hoarseness; nasal discharge; heart palpitations; hemorrhoids; indigestion; malaria; gout; chronic itching; hernia; colic; insomnia; dysentery; and a malignant growth on his left nipple. He also had some truly *odd* physical problems. He wrote that "in 1536 I was overtaken with an extraordinary discharge of urine; and although for nearly forty years I have been afflicted with this trouble, giving from sixty to a hundred ounces a day, I live well."

Considering these weighty burdens, then, it is truly impressive to review Girolamo Cardano's contributions to the sciences:

Mathematics: Cardano's *Practica arithmetice* first revealed his skill with calculation and equations. His later work, *Ars magna*, published in 1545, established and defined the rules for algebra and is considered to be the work that began the era of modern mathematics. In that work, Cardano claimed credit for NICCOLÒ TARTAGLIA [32]'s method for solving third-degree equations, after six years of promising Tartaglia that he wouldn't. (Tartaglia was outraged and wrote scathingly of Cardano, thus ruining Cardano's reputation.)

Hydrodynamics: Cardano studied water flow and proved that Aristotle was wrong when he declared that nature "abhorred a vacuum."

Earth Sciences: Cardano studied erosion, the formation of mountains, and was one of the first to posit the (correct) theory that water is in a constant cycle from ocean to sky and back again.

Probability Theory: Cardano's *Liber de ludo alea* was the first book to suggest that there are laws that govern seemingly random occurrences, thus setting forth a theory of probability that he then illustrated with examples from games of chance, including dice and cards.

Mechanics: Cardano unequivocally declared that perpetual motion was impossible. He also described "Cardano's suspension," a device which drew from his studies of the lever and his research with projectiles contributed to the science of ballistics.

Medicine: While still in his thirties, Cardano was the most famous physician in Europe after Andreas Vesalius, and was sought after by rulers and other important men, most of whom Cardano was able to cure.

Cardano was also keenly interested in cryptography, and his writings on codes and ciphers contributed to the advancement of that science as well. And among other pursuits, in 1551 Cardano used torches on towers to spell out letters, thus contributing to the development of long-distance visual signaling.

Almost all of Girolamo Cardano's published works were collected in a massive ten-volume set called *Opera omnia*, which was edited by Charles Sponi and published in 1663, almost one hundred years after Cardano's death.

Yet despite his personal peculiarities, Cardano's writings and research paved the way for the expansion of mathematics and for advancements in many other sciences as well. It is often said that there is a thin line between genius and insanity, and it seems as though Girolamo Cardano straddled that line for almost all seventy-five years of his impressive life.

27

Francesco Bonaventura Cavalieri
1598–1647

[F]ew, if any, since Archimedes, have delved as far and as deep
into the science of geometry.
> —GALILEO GALILEI
> writing about Francesco
> Bonaventura Cavalieri

[I]t is certain that this geometry represents a marvelous economy of labor in the demonstrations and establishes innumer-
able, almost inscrutable, theorems by means of brief, direct,
and affirmative demonstrations, which the doctrines of the
ancients was incapable of. The geometry of indivisibles was
indeed, in the mathematical briar bush, the so-called royal
road, and one that Cavalieri first opened and laid out for the
public as a device of marvelous invention.
> —EVANGELISTA TORRICELLI
> writing about Cavalieri's work

The Italian mathematician Francesco Bonaventura Cavalieri's
development of the geometry of indivisibles predicted and paved
the way for the development of two mathematical inventions: integral calculus and differential calculus, two branches of mathematics
that were critical to the many advances in science that followed
their widespread dissemination and use.

Grossly oversimplified, Cavalieri's method of indivisibles was essentially a way of calculating the size of geometric figures by using logarithms, a similar approach that integral calculus would later use after Newton and Leibniz defined and refined it. (Logarithms are mathematical factors defined as those exponents to which a number must be raised in order to produce a second number. For example, the logarithm of 25 to a base of 5 is 2, because 5 must be raised to the second power to produce the result 25. Or, the logarithm of 27 to a base of 3 is 3, because 3 must be raised to the third power to produce the result 27.)

Cavalieri, therefore, can be seen as one of the forefathers of these two types of calculus, which science historian Gerald Messadié describes as "major inventions in the history of the human brain." Messadié makes the point that "the significance of integral calculus [after its invention] was to spread to all sciences, from physics and astronomy to thermodynamics and mechanics." (Integral calculus deals with the method of adding together the effects of constantly changing variables using, among other tools, logarithms; differential calculus deals similarly with rates of change.)

Francesco Bonaventura Cavalieri was born around 1598 in Milan, Italy. (We do not know his exact birthdate because records are missing; the year 1598 is an estimate by Urbano d'Aviso, a student of Cavalieri's who also served as his biographer.) As a young boy, Cavalieri joined the Apostolic Clerics of St. Jerome, a religious order known as the Jesuati. Around the age of seventeen he received his minor orders and was transferred in 1616 to the order's monastery in Pisa. There he met a Benedictine monk named Benedetto Castelli, a lecturer in mathematics at Pisa, and a former student of the renowned scientist and astronomer Galileo. Brother Castelli gave the young Cavalieri a reading list, directing him to study the works of the Greek mathematicians Euclid and Archimedes and the poets Pappus and Appollonius. Cavalieri was immediately intrigued by the writings of these ancient thinkers, and he soon became knowledgeable enough in the fields of geometry and mathematics to fill in for Castelli as an instructor at the University of Pisa.

Castelli was so impressed with Cavalieri and his enormous potential that he eventually introduced him to Galileo, probably when Cavalieri was still in his late teens. Until his death, Cavalieri considered himself a student of Galileo's and, as the epigraph to this chapter illustrates, Galileo likewise held Cavalieri and his work in high regard. During their association, Cavalieri wrote Galileo over 100 letters, all of which are reproduced in *The Works of Galileo.*

Cavalieri developed his method of indivisibles during the years 1620 through 1623, when he was teaching theology at the San Girolamo monastery in Milan. He postponed publishing his work, however, for six years out of deference to his mentor Galileo, who had hinted that he himself might be publishing something on indivisibles. (Galileo eventually did publish, but his work with indivisibles was different than Cavalieri's.)

In 1632, Cavalieri published *Directorium generale uranometricum* (*A General Directory of Uranometry*) in which he introduced the use of logarithms as part of an intricate calculating process. That year, Cavalieri also published a treatise on conic sections. Finally, in 1635, Cavalieri published his new geometry under the title *Geometria indivisibilibus continuorum nova quadam ratione promota* (*A Certain Method for the Development of a New Geometry of Continuous Indivisibles.*) In 1643, his writings on plane, spherical, linear, and logarithmic trigonometry were published. (His *Trigonometria* [*Trigonometry*] contained superbly constructed logarithm tables.) And in 1647, Cavalieri wrote and published *Exercitationes geometricae sex* (Six Geometric Exercises).

Throughout his life, Cavalieri was accorded great respect and high honors for his work, including the chair in mathematics at the University of Bologna. He wrote and published eleven books while teaching at Bologna.

Also during his relatively short life (he was only in his late forties, apparently, when he died) Cavalieri suffered from crippling gout, an inflammatory type of arthritis that he had had since he was a child, even though gout usually strikes later in life.

In addition to his work in mathematics, Cavalieri also made contributions in the sciences of optics and acoustics. Devoutly religious, Cavalieri was also an astrologer, a pursuit that was not held to conflict with science in his day. He wrote a treatise on astrology titled *Practica astrologica* (*The Practice of Astrology*) but claimed that he did not suggest making predictions based solely on the position of the stars and planets.

Because of his innovative work in the field of geometry, Francesco Bonaventura Cavalieri can be credited with greatly advancing many sciences.

28

Amedeo Avogadro
1776–1856

Stanislao Cannizzaro
1826–1910

Chemistry took so long to come up from the Dark Ages because even after physics and astronomy and anatomy had assumed something vaguely like their modern contours, instruments didn't exist to isolate gases and no one troubled much to weigh or measure anything.
— JUDY JONES AND WILLIAM WILSON
An Incomplete Education

602,252,000,000,000,000,000,000.
— AVOGADRO'S NUMBER

There are certain moments in history that seem to contain an extraordinary concatenation of events and human achievements.

The year 1811 qualifies as one of those landmarks. It witnessed several notable milestones, including the launching of the first steamboat in the Mississippi Valley; the patenting of the two-cylinder steam locomotive; the discovery of iodine; the discovery of nitrogen chloride; the discovery of the functions of the sensory and motor nerves; the (anonymous) publication of Jane Austen's novel *Sense and Sensibility*; the first performance of Beethoven's Emperor Concerto; and the formulation of Avogadro's hypothesis.

The Italian chemist and physicist Amedeo Avogadro discovered that there was a determinable, fixed relation between the density of a gas and the number of molecules that it contains in a specific volume. Science historian Gerald Messadié says of this discovery, "From this time onwards chemical analyses of compounds would rest on precise numerical bases." Avogadro published his hypothesis in a paper in 1811, theorizing that at a given temperature all gases contain the same number of particles. In this paper he also coined the term *molecule*, thereby distinguishing for the first time between the two particles now known as atoms and molecules.

As is sometimes the case with brilliant, pioneering insights, Avogadro's hypothesis was met with both positive and negative reactions. Part of the problem was that Avogadro had come to his ingenious conclusions by the sheer power of his intellect: He did not really do too much to support his theories with a body of experimental verification. Some of his fellow scientists backed him up, most notably the French physicist André-Marie Ampère, who supported Avogadro's theories (and for a time was given credit for Avogadro's findings, an honor he always rejected). Other prominent scientists of the day, such as Britain's John Dalton and Jöns Jacob Berzelius of Sweden either rejected Avogadro's findings or ignored them.

In 1858, two years after Avogadro's death, the Italian chemist Stanislao Cannizzaro gave the first widely publicized presentation of Avogadro's theory, detailing Avogadro's number, which represents the number of particles found in one mole of any gaseous substance. After Cannizzaro spoke out in defense of Avogadro, and other physicists demonstrated the universal application of Avogadro's number, Avogadro's work was honored for being a "brilliant conception ignored for fifty years" (as it was described in the

Biographical Dictionary of Scientists, published in London). As is often the case, Avogadro, who was never given the acclaim his discovery deserved while he was alive, found the fame and respect he was entitled to after his death.

Cannizzaro then used Avogadro's findings to develop and construct a system of chemistry, thus making Amedeo Avogadro one of the true fathers of modern chemistry. Cannizzaro, born in Palermo, Sicily, on July 13, 1826, must subsequently be acknowledged for the determination of true atomic weights, a development that (once it was accepted in 1864) gave rise to a true system of chemistry, complete with proper notation.

Amedeo Avogadro was born in Turin, Italy, on August 9, 1776. His father was the count of Quaregna, and in 1787, when Amedeo was eleven, he inherited his father's title. In 1796, when Avogadro was twenty, he was awarded a doctorate in law (many of his family members were lawyers) and for three years he worked as a practicing lawyer. He tired of the law, however, and around the year 1800 he turned his attention to science, with a particular interest in chemistry and physics.

Avogadro was especially interested in the work of the French chemist Joseph-Louis Gay-Lussac. In 1787, Gay-Lussac had published his findings that all gases expand at the exact same amount for a given rise in temperature when the gases are held at a constant pressure. (Gay-Lussac had actually *rediscovered* a forgotten law that had been originally put forth in 1699 by Guillaume Amonton, but because Amonton's law had been forgotten, Gay-Lussac got the credit for it.) Avogadro thought deeply about Gay-Lussac's contention about the phenomenon of equal expansion and came to the conclusion that, if Gay-Lussac was correct (and Avogadro knew he was), then all gases contain exactly the same number of particles per unit volume. And thus was born the scientific breakthrough now known as Avogadro's hypothesis.

Avogadro continued his study of chemistry and physics throughout his life, with a special interest in gases and their properties. In his later years, he was a professor of physics at the University of Turin. Avogadro died in Turin on July 9, 1855, one month short of his eightieth birthday. His disciple Stanislao Cannizzaro survived him by fifty-five years, dying in Rome on May 10, 1910, at the age of eighty-three. Canizzaro's legacy was the final acceptance of Avogadro's findings, which helped provide the science of chemistry with the structure it needed to advance. Together, Avogadro and Cannizzaro were responsible for defining the modern science of chemistry.

29

St. Fabiola

d. 399

I think it frets the saints in heaven to see
How many desolate creatures on earth
Have learnt the simple dues of fellowship
And social comfort, in a hospital.
—ELIZABETH BARRETT BROWNING
Aurora Leigh

During the years between A.D. 375 and 400, the power of Rome was in decline, a self-serving egotism pervading the upper echelons of its society. The counterforce to this egotism was the growing influence of Christianity, now officially established after more than two centuries of persecution. During this period of self-centeredness, an affluent Roman matron named Fabiola opened the first hospital and hospice in the Western world, committing herself and all her energies to the Christian concept of caring for the sick and the dying in a loving, charitable, and above all, selfless way. Fabiola, a wealthy society woman, personally tended the sick and dying in her hospital. It is said that when Fabiola died in A.D. 399, all of Rome attended her funeral. Though little known, St. Fabiola deserves a place in *The Italian 100* because she is credited with establishing, in A.D. 390, the first centralized, public health care facility in the Western world, the archetype of the modern hospitals and medical centers of today. Fabiola is also responsible for opening the first known Western hospice for indigent and ill travelers, an important forerunner of present-day hospices.

Fabiola was a member of the aristocratic Fabia family. Little is known of her early years, and St. Jerome's account of her life (particularly the seventy-seventh letter of his 120 extant epistles) is the most complete source now available. We do know that before Fabiola entered a life of religious service, she divorced her immoral and irresponsible first husband and then married again, a decision that placed her at odds with the Church. In Butler's *Lives of the Saints,* St. Fabiola is described as "lively, passionate" and having a "headstrong disposition." When her second husband died, she made her peace with the Church and did public penance at the Lateran basilica. Pope St. Siricius personally gave her absolution and allowed her to again receive Holy Communion. After her reconciliation, Fabiola began doing charitable work, and donated huge sums of money to churches and poor Italian towns. At this time she founded her pioneering hospital in Rome. She then scavenged the filthy streets and hidden alleys of the city, gathering the sick, the homeless, the poor, and even lepers, bringing them all back to her hospital.

Prior to the establishment of a centralized place for the sick, the ill were often outcasts from society. Families, if they had them, bore the responsibility for their care and, ultimately, their burial. After Fabiola's hospital opened, though, similar institutions began appearing across Europe, all of which were forerunners of the modern hospital.

It is true that Fabiola did not actually originate the idea of the hospital. There are records of healing centers well before the Christian era. In ancient Rome, for example, there were the *valetudinaria;* but these hospitals were reserved for injured Roman soldiers and were not open to the general populace. Fabiola opened the doors of her hospital to everyone and applied a strict Christian ethic to caring for the sick and dying. This approach to health care is still the paradigm in modern hospitals.

Five years after establishing her hospital, Fabiola traveled from Rome to Bethlehem to visit her mentor and friend, St. Jerome. She considered staying in Bethlehem and living a holy life in the company of St. Jerome's students and companions, but she could not accept their spartan lifestyle. She returned to Rome and in 395 opened a hospice at Porto, Italy, with St. Pammachius, a Roman senator and a friend of St. Jerome's. According to Butler, this hospice "was the first of its kind and within a year of its opening 'became known,' says St. Jerome, 'from Parthia to Britain.' "

It is said that after the establishment of this hospice, Fabiola grew restless and wanted to embark on a journey. She died before she could fulfill this last wish, and she was buried in Rome in 399.

30

Luigi Galvani
1737–98

[F]or it is easy in experimentation to be deceived, and to think one has seen and discovered what we desire to see and discover.
—LUIGI GALVANI

In 1791, the Italian physician and scientist Luigi Galvani published a paper called *De viribus electricitatis in motu musculari commentarius* (*Commentary on the Effect of Electricity on Muscular Motion*) in which he concluded that animal tissue contained a previously unknown force, which he christened "animal electricity." (The paper was part of a series that published the proceedings of the Bologna Academy of Science.)

Galvani stated his belief that this newly identified force was an additional form of electricity, similar to yet different from "natural" electricity as was found in lightning and eels, or "artificial" electricity such as could be generated in a laboratory through friction.

Galvani had reached his conclusions through a series of experiments with amputated frogs' legs. Galvani biographer Bern Dibner calls this discovery "one of the most important in the history of science." It essentially led to the invention of Alessandro Volta's electric battery (see VOLTA [5]) and can be credited as being the genesis of all future developments in the science of electricity generation.

In the first paragraph of Galvani's classic treatise, he describes one serendipitous frog experiment that utilized an "electrostatic machine," a device that could be used to generate static electricity and large sparks:

> I had dissected a frog and had prepared it . . . and had placed it upon a table on which there was an electric machine, while I set about doing certain other things. The frog was entirely separated from the conductor of the machine, and indeed was at no small distance from it. While one of those who were assisting me touched lightly and by chance the point of his scalpel to the internal crural nerves of the frog, suddenly all the muscles of its limbs were seen to be so contracted that they seemed to have fallen into tonic convulsions. Another of my assistants, who was making ready to take up certain experiments in electricity with me, seemed to notice that this happened only at the moment when a spark came from the conductor of the machine. He was struck with the novelty of the phenomenon, and immediately spoke to me about it, for I was at the moment occupied with other things and mentally preoccupied. I was at once tempted to repeat the experiment, so as to make clear whatever might be obscure in it. For this purpose I took up the scalpel and moved its point close to one or the other of the crural nerves of the frog, while at the same time one of my assistants elicited sparks from the electric machine. The phenomenon happened exactly as before. Strong contractions took place in every muscle of the limb, and at the very moment when the sparks appeared, the animal were seized as it were with tetanus.

Twelve copies of *De viribus electricitatis* were printed; one was sent (inscribed "From the Author") to Alessandro Volta, who referred to the work to replicate Galvani's experiments. Volta had a problem with some of Galvani's conclusions, though. He did not believe that the animal generated electricity itself but rather that Galvani had made two different metals come into contact with each other, thus generating what he termed "metallic electricity."

The debate raged gently between these two great minds for years (each continuing to hold the other in the highest regard). We now know that they were both right, and they were both wrong: Galvani was incorrect in deducing that animal tissue was a source of the current, and Volta was wrong in believing that every electrical current was due to metallic conduction. But as is often the case with notable discoveries and sudden advances, the attempt to prove something right or wrong led to Volta's invention of the battery and all the innovations that followed from it.

Luigi Galvani was born in Bologna, Italy, on September 9, 1737. As a child he was urged to study medicine by his father, Domenico, and in 1759, at the age of twenty-one, he graduated from the University of Bologna with degrees in philosophy and medicine. (His doctoral thesis, *De ossibus*, was on bone formation and the human skeleton.) In 1762, when he was twenty-five, he was named a lecturer in anatomy at the university, and nine years later, in 1773, he was named professor of anatomy and surgery.

Also in 1762, Galvani married Lucia Galeazzi, his teacher's daughter, and moved in with his in-laws. For ten years he and Lucia lived in the Galeazzi home, and it was during this period that he performed his most famous frog electricity experiments. The next two decades were marked by his most well-known and important publications and also his friendly rivalry with Volta.

In 1790, Lucia Galvani died at the age of forty-seven, a tragedy that emotionally devastated Luigi. For the next eight years, until his death, he lived in his childhood home, having been dropped from the faculty of the University of Bologna for his refusal to swear allegiance to the new republic proclaimed by Napoleon Bonaparte, whose armies then controlled northern Italy.

Galvani died on December 4, 1798, at the age of sixty-one, shortly before the truly major developments in electricity occurred, milestones that he had played a part in bringing about. He left his papers and equipment to his nephew (Lucia had died childless) Dr. Camillo Galvani who, ironically, published a work on galvanism after his uncle's death and dedicated it to Napoleon.

As Bern Dibner has written in *Galvani-Volta*:

In an age opened by the observation, ingenuity, and perseverance of Luigi Galvani and Alessandro Volta, the phenomenon which they discovered, be it called Galvanism or Voltaic electricity, bears enough honor for both—for him who first observed and described the phenomenon, and for him who first correctly understood it. The very light which their genius has made available to the succeeding generations in such abundance does most to honor their contributions to all mankind.

Francesco Maria Grimaldi

1618–63

Light is the first of painters. There is no object so foul that
intense light will not make it beautiful.
> —Ralph Waldo Emerson

Optics is that branch of physics that deals with the study of light
and vision, particularly shadows, mirror images, lenses, cameras,
telescopes, and microscopes. The diffraction of light occurs when
light rays bend or are deflected as they pass some obstacle.
Diffraction is, thus, a modification that light waves undergo when
they encounter a surface. The discovery and understanding of diffraction as a specific, quantifiable result of light being deprived of
an unobstructed flow was a seminally important development in

the sciences of astronomy, physics, and medicine, and it served to advance improvements in telescopes, microscopes, and other optical devices that use lenses and light. The discovery and defining of diffraction in 1665 also contributed to the advancement of Isaac Newton's later scientific theories.

Francesco Maria Grimaldi is the Italian who discovered the diffraction of light and who greatly influenced physics and all its related disciplines for centuries to come. In 1665, two years after his death, Grimaldi's major work was published: a lengthy and comprehensive treatise on light, detailing his discoveries and defining what he described on the title page as "the unknown diffusion of light; the manner and causes of reflection, refraction, and diffraction; vision and the intentional species of visibles and audibles; the substantial effluvium of the magnet, which pervades all bodies; and in a special argument the atomists are attacked." The complete title of Grimaldi's foundational work on light was (translated from the original Latin):

> *A physicomathematical thesis on light, colors, the rainbow and other related topics in two books, the first of which adduces new experiments and reasons deduced from them in favor of the substantiality of light. In the second, however, the arguments adduced in the first book are refuted and the peripatetic teaching of the accidentality of light is upheld as probable.*

Prior to Grimaldi's work, what was known as the "corpuscular" theory of light held sway over scientific minds. Light was thought to be made up only of tiny particles in rapid movement. (This theory extended as far back as the ancient Greeks.) In both of his books, Grimaldi opposed the corpuscular theory of light, instead coming to the conclusion that light is fluid, and noted the break that could occur in the uniformity of the flow of light, known as diffraction.

As is often the case with important works that proceed from an intuitive leap however, Grimaldi was both right and wrong: He was right in describing light as a "fluid," which we now call a "wave." But—although science would not be able to confirm this until centuries later, when Albert Einstein explained the photoelectric effect of light—Grimaldi was wrong in his complete rejection of the corpuscular theory of light; we now know that there *are* instances when light can also behave as a particle.

Francesco Maria Grimaldi was born on April 2, c. 1618, in Bologna, Italy. His parents were Paride Grimaldi, a wealthy nobleman who was also a silk merchant, and Paride's second wife, Anna

Cattani. (Paride's first wife had died childless.)

After his father's death, Francesco entered the Society of Jesus (the Jesuit order) in March 1632, at the age of fourteen. Three years later, in 1635, he traveled to Parma, where he studied philosophy for a year. Then, in 1636, he moved to Ferrara for his second year of philosophical study. After completing his three-year program in Bologna in 1636, he taught rhetoric and the humanities at Bologna's College of Santa Lucia from 1638 to 1642.

Over the next five years, Grimaldi studied theology and received a doctorate in philosophy. In 1648, however, at the age of thirty, he contracted tuberculosis and he abandoned his studies to teach the less-demanding discipline of mathematics. On May 1, 1651, he was ordained as a priest. For the next ten years he worked in the fields of astronomy and physics. He died in 1663, three days after Christmas, after an eight-day fever, at the age of forty-five.

Prior to his work on light and diffraction, Grimaldi also made some important observations of the moon that included recording the heights of lunar mountains. Grimaldi is credited with the centuries-old scientific tradition of naming lunar regions after physicists and astronomers. It is thought that he was one of the first to use a telescope with crosshairs and a micrometer, another important innovation in astronomy.

In the 1650s, Grimaldi worked on his theories pertaining to the diffraction of light. Grimaldi's scientific writings, his work in astronomy, his experiments with light, and of course, his identification of diffraction make him one of the more important contributors to several sciences. Although he is less well known than some of his predecessors and successors, Francesco Maria Grimaldi nonetheless left a legacy that changed science and helped define a number of its fundamental principles.

32

Niccolò Tartaglia
1499–1557

Political power grows out of the barrel of a gun.
—MAO TSE-TUNG

Outside of Milan, in the homely industrial town of Brescia, Italy, on top of the Cydnean Hill, there stands the Castello, a place the *Rough Guide* describes as a "confusion of towers, ramparts, halls and courtyards."

The Castello is about a half mile from Via Tartaglia, the avenue named for Brescia's most famous son, Niccolò Tartaglia. When we consider Tartaglia's contribution to modern warfare, it is understandable that the Castello houses Italy's largest museum of weaponry and arms.

Niccolò Tartaglia, born in 1499, a mathematician and teacher of mathematics by trade, is considered today to be the father of the science of ballistics, although certain segments of his seminal work on ballistics were in error. As historian Gerald Messadié wrote,

"Paradoxically, it can be said that Tartaglia invented the concept of ballistics without any understanding of it."

Ballistics, which developed from the science and study of mechanics, is the study of everything and anything having to do with projectiles and weaponry, including the dynamics, motion, impact, and flight characteristics of projectiles; the functioning of firearms; and the firing, flight, and effect of ammunition.

In 1537, Tartaglia, then thirty-seven years old, published his treatise *Nova scientia* (A New Science), which discussed the motion of heavenly bodies as well as the size and shape of projectiles, essentially inventing and defining the science then called gunnery. Even though *A New Science* was a pivotal work, Tartaglia perpetuated an error in maximum projectile range, stating a maximal range for a projectile at 45 degrees, a conclusion he arrived at by averaging maximal vertical shooting range and maximal horizontal shooting range. This was later corrected by the Swiss scientists Jean Bernoulli and Leonhard Euler, with contributions by the English physicist Benjamin Robins. Nonetheless, Tartaglia is credited with being the first to quantify and describe a previously unnamed science.

Niccolò Tartaglia's last name comes from the word *tartagliare* (to stutter or stammer). It is not the name he was born with. In 1512, when Niccolò was thirteen years old, French forces under the command of Gaston de Foix fiercely raided and pillaged Brescia, and the young man, then probably known by the surname Fontana, was seriously injured.

During the terrible attack on the city, a French soldier lashed out at Niccolò with a sword and slashed open the boy's lower face, cleaving his palate (the roof of the mouth) and also splitting open his upper and lower jaw. Medical care being rudimentary at the time, the adolescent was treated as best as was possible with existing techniques and palliatives, but his mouth was allowed to heal without any surgical correction or repairs. This grievous injury severely impaired his speech, and he soon became known as "the stutterer," or "tartaglia." Thus, his true surname was eventually forgotten.

For the next twenty years, Tartaglia pursued his studies and ultimately earned a degree in mathematics. He moved to Venice and taught mathematics there. During this period he wrote and published the aforementioned *Nova scientia*, applying his mathematical knowledge to this "new science."

In addition to his work on ballistics, Tartaglia was also working on advanced mathematical techniques and procedures. In 1535, for instance, he worked out a method for solving cubic equations (a polynomial equation in which the highest sum of exponents of variables in any term is three). For some reason (perhaps his preoccupation with ballistics and *Nova scientia*) Tartaglia did not publish his findings on how to solve these equations. But then, as often happens with great discoveries and the vagaries of human nature, he was presented with what he probably perceived as a golden opportunity.

The Italian physician and lecturer GIROLAMO CARDANO [26], then working and studying in Milan, had heard of Tartaglia's new solutions to cubic equations and came to him with a request to publish his new mathematical findings. Tartaglia, again for some unknown reason, refused, but then his self-interest was aroused, and he began to see the possibilities of advancement if his scholarship were made public. He specifically had his eye on a position as the artillery adviser to the Spanish army, so he succumbed to Cardano's entreaties and made a mistake in judgment: He put his trust in Girolamo Cardano and revealed his new discoveries to him. In 1545, Cardano published his own treatise, *Ars magna* (*Great Art*) completely appropriating Tartaglia's work and his technique for solving cubic equations. *Ars magna* is today considered to be the beginning of the science of modern mathematics and contains pioneering information on algebra and geometry, but there are important findings in the work that can be directly attributed to Niccolò Tartaglia, not Girolamo Cardano.

Tartaglia continued to pursue his interests in mathematics, and in the years 1556 through 1560, he published an important three-volume encyclopedia on mathematics called *Trattato di numeri et misure* (*Treatise on Numbers and Measures*). He also did additional work on ballistics. In 1546, for instance, he published a lengthy volume on artillery and fortification that he dedicated to England's King Henry VIII. Tartaglia was a literary scholar as well: His translation of the works of Euclid, the first ever in Italian, was published in 1543.

Niccolò Tartaglia died in Venice on December 13, 1557, at the age of fifty-eight. He is remembered today for his seminal work on defining the science of ballistics, as well as for his important work in Euclidean geometry and algebra, achievements that he unfortunately did not receive credit for until after his death, thanks to the questionable use of his work by Cardano. Nonetheless, Niccolò Tartaglia's contributions to mathematics and science were significant and enduring, and thus his ranking in *The Italian 100*.

33

Andrea Cesalpino
(Andreas Caesalpinus)
1519–1603

> If I were to name the three most precious resources of life, I
> should say books, friends, and nature; and the greatest of
> these, at least the most constant and always at hand, is nature.
> — JOHN BURROUGHS
> "The Art of Seeing Things," in *Leaf and Tendril*

Botany is defined as the scientific study of plants. But such a broad definition oversimplifies a complex and meticulously structured and specialized science, which today includes the following subdivisions:

- **Taxonomy:** The identification and classification of plants.

- **Plant Anatomy:** The study of the internal formation of plants.

- **Plant Morphology:** The study of the external formation of plants.

- **Plant Histology:** The microscopic examination and study of plants.

- **Plant Physiology:** The functioning of plants and the study of their life history.

- **Plant Ecology:** The study of the distribution of plants over Earth's surface in relation to their geographic surroundings.

- **Paleobotany:** The study of fossil plants.

- **Economic Botany:** The study of the functional utility of plants.

Specific branches of botany include *horticulture* (the science of cultivating plants, fruits, vegetables, and flowers); *agriculture* (the science of cultivating soil and producing crops); and *forestry* (the science of developing, maintaining, and managing forests).

Modern botany and all its intricacies owes an enormous debt to a sixteenth-century Italian named Andrea Cesalpino. Cesalpino profoundly influenced later botanists and he also laid the groundwork for understanding the circulation of the blood. Cesalpino anticipated (and paved the way) for the scientists Carolus Linnaeus, William Harvey, and Marcello Malpighi (see MALPIGHI [14]).

Andrea Cesalpino was a physician, botanist, and a philosopher. He was the first scientist to propose a comprehensive system of plant classification that was not based on the alphabetical order of the plants' names or on the plants' curative properties. Cesalpino began with a wide-ranging theoretical evaluation of all plants and their respective places within a larger hierarchy and then essentially reevaluated over 1,500 plants, defining them within a coherent system of his own design.

Andrea Cesalpino was born in Arezzo, in the Tuscany region of Italy, on June 6, 1519. After acquiring degrees in medicine and botany, Cesalpino took over his teacher Luca Ghini's position as director of the Botanical Gardens and professor of medicine at the University of Pisa. He spent a good portion of his life teaching and studying at the university, staying there until he was in his seventies. In 1592, when Cesalpino was seventy-three, he became Pope Clement VIII's personal physician in Rome and also taught at Rome's Sapienza University.

In 1583, while still at the University of Pisa, Cesalpino published the work for which he is remembered today: the sixteen-volume series titled *De plantis libri XVI* (*The 16 Books of Plants*, or *The Book of Plants, Volumes 1–16*). This massive work is believed to be the first full-length textbook on the science of botany.

Cesalpino used the works of the Greek philosophers Aristotle and Theophrastus as his paradigm and then proceeded to classify over 1,500 plants in his sixteen-volume botanical encyclopedia. He had read and studied Theophrastus's text, *The History of Plants and Theoretical Botany*, written in 350 B.C. This work discussed plant diseases and provided other (often incorrect) botanical information. Cesalpino had also carefully read the writings of Aristotle, which had appeared prior to Theophrastus between the years 344 and 335 B.C. The rabidly curious Aristotle had spent two years on the Aegean island of Lesbos studying natural history and marine biology. Around 335 B.C., Aristotle opened a lyceum in Athens which contained an extensive museum of natural history as well as an impressive display of zoological gardens.

Cesalpino's work went far beyond the efforts of the ancient writers. He classified plants according to their roots and their fruit organs. He avoided the temptation to assign medicinal values to plants whose external shapes resembled human organs, as did the botanist Giambattista della Porta. In 1588, della Porta tried to establish a relationship between the shape of a plant and its effect on the human organ that looked like it. He believed, for instance, that a plant resembling a vagina would be useful in healing gynecological disorders.

Though he corrected many of della Porta's errors, Cesalpino did err in one area. In his books, he retained the incorrect classifications of woody and herbaceous plants, and he perpetuated the erroneous belief that plants were not sexual.

In addition to his botanical work, Cesalpino also studied the physiology and circulatory characteristics of human blood, influencing the work of William Harvey thirty years later.

When the great Swedish botanist Carolus Linnaeus devised his system of scientific classification during the eighteenth century, he disagreed with Cesalpino on some points, but he was nonetheless greatly influenced by the Italian botanist's work. Linnaeus published his *Systema naturae* in 1735, classifying flora according to the number of their stamens and pistils. He also developed the binomial nomenclature used to classify plant genera and species that is still in use today. And in 1681, just over a hundred years after Cesalpino's *De plantis*, the Italian physician Marcello Malpighi (see chapter 14) founded the science of plant anatomy, a field for which the groundwork had been laid by Cesalpino.

Andrea Cesalpino died in Rome on February 23, 1603, at the age of eighty-three. He is best remembered today as a pioneer in the field of botany and also for his innovative work in human anatomy.

The Medicis
1434–1737

We read that we ought to forgive our enemies; but we do not read that we ought to forgive our friends.

—COSIMO DE' MEDICI

Quant è bella giovinezza
Che si fugge tuttavia!
Chi vuol esser lieto, sia:
Di doman nonc'è certezza.

How beautiful is youth,
    That is always slipping away!
    Whoever wants to be happy, let him be so:
    About tomorrow there's no knowing.
        — LORENZO DE' MEDICI
            Trionfo di Bacco ed Arianna
            (The Triumph of Bacco and Arianna)

Three centuries.

That is the length of time that the wealthy and noble Medici family ruled the city of Florence, Italy.

During those 303 years—to be exact—the thirteen generations of the Medici family gave Italy and the world three popes; many patrons of sculptors and artists; discerning collectors of art (whose diligence is appreciated today); legendary soldiers; renowned intellectuals and poets; and incredibly powerful political leaders.

The Medici family consisted of three consecutive lines of leaders: the fourteenth-century Minor Branch (headed by Chiarissimo II), which failed to acquire enough power to rule Florence; the Principate of Cosimo the Elder in the fifteenth century; and the Grand Duchy founded by Grand Duke Cosimo I in the sixteenth century. The Principate is the most well known of the three branches, having produced Cosimo the Elder, Lorenzo the Magnificent, Pope Leo X, Pope Clement VII, and Catherine, queen of France.

In the introduction to his 1910 biography, *The Medici*, Colonel G. F. Young, expounded on the sweeping history of the family:

> The history of the Medici is a deeply interesting story; while, besides its intrinsic interest, it helps us to acquire much knowledge about the re-birth of Learning and Art, about the history of Europe in perhaps its most important period, about the birth of Science, and about the great collections of Art possessed by Florence. For without referring largely to all these subjects no true picture of the Medici can be given.

Volumes have been written about the many characters in the Medici family and the countless historical events they were involved in, and the reader is referred to the volumes listed in the bibliography for a more comprehensive look at the dynasty.

Here, however, in the limited space available, is an overview of three of the most influential and important Medicis:

- *Cosimo de' Medici (1389–1464):* Cosimo the Elder, known as *Pater Patriae* (father of his country); founder of the Principate line of the Medici family; expanded the Medici bank and became phenomenally wealthy; managed the finances of the papacy of Pope Pius II; sponsored the artists Ghiberti, Donatello, and others; created the Medici Library; was imprisoned for "having sought to elevate himself higher than others"; dominated the Florentine government from 1434 until his death.

- *Lorenzo the Magnificent (1449–92):* The grandson of Cosimo the Elder and son of Cosimo's incompetent son and successor Piero (Piero the Gouty); modeled himself after his grandfather; appears as a soldier with a sword in Botticelli's *Adoration of the Magi*; an intellectual giant who distinguished himself as a scholar and poet; established a balance of power among the Italian city-states; patron of artists such as Michelangelo, Botticelli, and Ghirlandaio; father of Pope Leo X; died young at the age of forty-three.

- *Catherine de' Medici (1519–89):* The daughter of Lorenzo II, duke of Urbino; married Henry II of France when they were both fourteen and ultimately became queen of France; introduced broccoli, artichokes, and cabbage to France; mother of King Francis II, King Charles IX, and King Henry III; signed the Peace of Amboise, which ended the hostilities between Catholics and Huguenots.

In addition, other influential Medicis included the popes Leo X; Clement VII; Leo XI; and Queen Marie of France.

The last of the Medici rulers was Gian Gastone, who acceded to the throne in 1723 following the death of his father, Cosimo III.

At first Gian Gastone attempted to live up to the past greatness of his august family. He lowered taxes and the price of corn; he stopped public beheadings; he provided a shelter for the homeless; he rescinded the Church's control of the government; he eliminated sanctions on scientists and scholars; and he reversed the anti-Semitic laws that had been passed before his reign.

But Grand Duke Gian Gastone was not all philanthropist and benevolent ruler. Later in his reign he began to spend most of his time in bed, eating and drinking to excess and indulging his sexual appetites. When he did venture out in his carriage, he was usually drunk. Such was the depth to which the great Medici clan had fallen. When Gian Gastone died on July 9, 1733, without a male heir, the reign of the Medicis in Tuscany came to an end.

Historians agree that the Medicis were the incarnation of the spirit and spark of the Renaissance. They controlled the world of art, the papacy, and the political policies of the European continent with their wealth, often bribing enemies and buying whatever they might need or want, from frescoes to favors. Paintings of their many villas and estates survive, and the splendor, size, and opulence of these establishments leave one awestruck even today. Excess was the norm for the Medicis: Cosimo III's June 1661 wedding in the Boboli Gardens featured a gargantuan figure of Atlas that moved through the stadium and then transformed itself into an enormous mountain, complete with vestal maidens perched at its summit. In fact, wedding festivities celebrating Cosimo's marriage to Marguerite-Louise (the niece of France's Louis XIII), went on for days. On June 24, the festival of St. John the Baptist took place, an annual event marked by the most elaborate and opulent processions and pageants the Florentine nobility could muster. The streets were carpeted for the ceremonies. In one notable procession, the most renowned members of the Florentine clergy carried sacred relics through the streets, including St. Andrew the Apostle's elbow; St. John the Baptist's thumb; a nail from Jesus's cross; and a thorn from Jesus's Crown of Thorns.

The Medicis were influential simply because they essentially "owned the world" during their "reign," and the deeds and actions of the *family*—financial, artistic, military, judicial, religious, marital—had more impact on Italy and her surrounds than the regimes of any individual political or religious leader of the Renaissance.

Guido of Arezzo
(Guido Aretinus)
c. 990–1050

Sure there is music even in the beauty, and the silent note
which Cupid strikes, far sweeter than the sound of an instrument. For there is a music wherever there is a harmony, order
or proportion; and thus far we may maintain the music of the
spheres; for those well ordered motions, and regular paces,
though they give no sound unto the ear, yet to the understanding they strike a note most full of harmony.

—SIR THOMAS BROWNE
Religio Medici

The small Italian town of Arezzo lies southeast of Florence in Tuscany. Arezzo is the birthplace of five monumental Italian historical, cultural, and scientific figures: the writers Petrarch and Giorgio Vasari, the physician Francesco Redi, the botanist Andrea Cesalpino, and the music theorist Guido of Arezzo.

Guido of Arezzo is a significant figure in the history of music, not for a piece of music he composed or for his performance skills, but for what he invented: Guido is responsible for conceptualizing and then charting the musical staff, one of the most important developments in musicology. Guido's staff and system of music notation allowed music to be systematically written, read, played, and, above all, preserved.

Today, one need not know how to read or write music in order to be a successful composer. If a person can play an instrument and hum or sing a melody, an inexpensive tape recorder can save any and all melodic musings, some of which may result in a popular song or instrumental composition. Former Beatle Paul McCartney, for example, can neither read nor write music, yet he has achieved great success as a songwriter.

But prior to the eleventh century, this was not the case. There was no standardized system of musical notation, and ecclesiastical singers would have to tediously memorize melodies before they were prepared to sing in the cathedrals and at religious ceremonies. Guido of Arezzo changed all that with his revolutionary musical staff and system of "solmization," reducing training time for singers from a decade down to a year or less, such was the ease with which notes seen *visually* could be remembered.

Solmization, which is the practice of assigning syllables to notes, greatly simplified the sight-reading of music. Children today, even from an early age, learn Guido's system—an impossible-to-forget mnemonic device that renders the scale as *do, re, mi, fa, sol, la, ti, do.* (The "Do, a deer" song from the extremely popular 1965 movie *The Sound of Music* also added to the awareness of Guido's system in the twentieth century.)

Prior to the year 1000, the only musical notation in use utilized "neumes," which were irregularly shaped symbols placed on one or two lines (very common in Gregorian chant) in order to orient a singer as to pitch and tone. In addition to his note-naming technique of solmization, Guido devised a four-line musical stave of different colors to chart melodies. (The *five*-line staff appeared around the year 1200 with the development of polyphonic music.)

In *Aliae regulae*, Guido's prologue to his now lost antiphoner (a collection of devotional compositions), the music theorist made his case for his system of notation:

> So that you may better detect these levels [of pitch], lines are drawn close together, and certain levels of notes become these same lines, while certain others fall between the lines, in the intermediate distance or space between the lines. . . . [W]hichever lines or spaces you wish are preceded by certain letters of the monochord and also colors are marked over them.

(The monochord was a rudimental musical instrument that consisted of a single string stretched over a sounding board, with a movable bridge set on a graduated scale. The monochord measured and demonstrated the mathematical relationship between musical tones. A twelfth-century illustration shows Guido of Arezzo with his sponsor, Bishop Theodaldus, standing over a monochord.)

Guido of Arezzo was born sometime around 990. He was educated at a Benedictine monastery in Pomposa, north of Commacchio (on the Adriatic Sea), where he began to develop his musical theories (with the help of a fellow monk named Michael). Using his nascent system of musical notation, he quickly achieved a reputation for being able to teach singers hymns and chants quickly and accurately. Guido decided to leave the abbey around 1025 because his fellow monks refused to accept his novel approaches to music notation, and many were also jealous of the fame and acclaim he was achieving in the outside world for his work.

After leaving Pomposa, Guido took a position as a teacher and was then commissioned by the Bishop of Arezzo to write a treatise on music. When completed, this work became his most famous literary composition, the *Micrologus de disciplina artis musicae*. The *Micrologus*, which was dedicated to Theodaldus, the bishop who sanctioned it, became enormously popular and was used throughout the twelfth and thirteenth centuries in monasteries and universities. The musical treatise of Boethius (see chapter 54) was the only music instruction book that was copied and distributed more often during these centuries.

Arezzo's musical son, the Benedictine monk Guido, left his mark on Western culture and made an enormous contribution to the widespread dissemination and availability of music in all its forms. An international choral competition, the Concorso Polifonico Guido d'Arezzo, was founded in his honor, and still takes place annually in Arezzo.

The Pomposa Abbey where Guido did much of his early work still stands about fifteen miles north of Commacchio. At the center of the complex is a basilica that houses frescoes by artists of the Bolognese school. It seems that a few hundred years after Guido studied at the abbey, the surrounding delta became malarial, and the monks ultimately decided to abandon it in the seventeenth century.

Guido died in 1050, probably in the Avellana monastery in Arezzo. Several of his manuscripts are still extant and have been translated into many languages, such has been the impact of his work on the development of music in the Western world.

Aldo Manuzio, The Elder
1449–1515

Aldo Manuzio, The Younger
1547–97

Oh that my words were now written! Oh that they
were printed in a book!
—THE BOOK OF JOB; 19:23

Aldo Manuzio the Elder and his grandson Aldo the Younger are responsible for three huge leaps forward in printing, publishing, and orthography: the creation and distribution of the first inexpensive, pocket-size books; the design and implementation of the first italic typeface; and the definitive cataloging of what is now considered to be modern punctuation, including the comma, semicolon, colon, and period.

History recognizes that printing had its beginnings in China. As far back as A.D. 350, the Chinese were producing printed texts using wooden blocks on which raised, reversed symbols were cut, smeared with ink, and then pressed onto paper made from wood or rags. In 1041, movable type made from clay blocks was first used by the Chinese printer Pi Sheng, and by 1450, the Chinese were printing complete pages using movable type. Six years later, in 1456, the German printer Johannes Gutenberg, using a printing press he designed and built himself based on the Chinese techniques, published the Mazarin Bible at Mainz, Germany, creating the first European book printed from movable type. It took Gutenberg five full years to design and set the book. It was published in two volumes, folio (folded in the middle), with two columns, forty-two lines each on each page.

Though the art of printing was born in China and Germany, less than ten years after the Gutenberg Bible was published, Aldo Manuzio realized the gargantuan potential and possibilities of the printing press, and the trailblazing Aldine Press was born.

Aldo the Elder (also known by his Latin name Aldus Manutius) was born in 1449 in the Papal State of Bassinia. At the age of twenty-one, Aldo, with the assistance of a group of Greek scholars, started a rudimentary publishing company in Venice. He published his first book in March 1495—*Erotemata* by Constantine Lascaris. This was the beginning of what would become known as the Aldine Press. In the following years, Aldo subsequently published books by Aristotle, Theocritus, Aristophanes, Virgil, Juvenal, Petrarch, Catullus, Sophocles, Dante, Herodotus, Euripides, Homer, Aesop, Horace, and Plato. His five-volume edition of Aristotle, published in 1498, achieved especially wide recognition.

In 1500, Aldo's type cutter, Francesco Griffo, designed an elegant italic typeface that the Aldine Press first used in 1501 in an edition of Virgil. This was the first of the Aldine Press's compact and inexpensive editions, comparable to the modern paperback.

Aldo was a shrewd man: As his company grew and his editions

became more popular, he pursued a practice now widespread in the publishing industry. He realized that after the initial set-up costs were accounted for, it was less expensive to print larger quantities of a book. So instead of ordering print runs of 250 copies, he ordered 1,000 copies of his editions. This not only kept his costs down, it increased fourfold the availability of each book, thus contributing to the widespread acceptance of inexpensive books, making them available to everyone. The Aldine Press also employed scholars as editors and proofreaders, to make sure that their editions were accurate.

Aldo Manuzio the Elder died on February 6, 1515, in Venice, and after his death, his brothers-in-law, and eventually one of his sons, Paulus, took over the press. In 1561, Paulus's son and Aldo's grandson, Aldo the Younger, continued his grandfather and father's work by taking over the management of the press.

Aldo the Younger was born in Venice on February 13, 1547. He took over the Aldine Press when he was only fourteen and continued publishing books in the tradition of his father and grandfather. Aldo the Younger also had other interests, such as the art and science of orthography; the practice of writing words using the correct spelling, punctuation, placement, and so on. In 1566, at the age of nineteen, Aldo the Younger published an important text called *Orthographiae ratio* (*A System of Orthography*). This was the first book to define what is now the modern system of punctuation.

Aldo (basing his work on the ancient Greeks) specifically classified such punctuation marks as the comma [(,) which separates clauses and phrases], the semicolon [(;), which separates different statements), the colon [(:), which indicates a transition to an item of information or a list], and what he called the "full point," but which we now know as the period [(.)]. He also covered such devices as the question mark (?), the exclamation point (!), the apostrophe ('), and the quotation marks (" ").

In addition to his work with typographic symbols, Aldo the Younger also expounded on the purposes of punctuation: clarification of syntax, or the way in which words are put together in sentences in order to express meaning. (Writings before the advent of punctuation did not even have space between the words!) In 1575, Aldo published *Epitome orthographiae*, another work on orthography, and the following year, his lengthy commentary on Horace's *Ars poetica.*

Aldo the Younger died in Rome on October 28, 1597, at the age of fifty. He was the last member of the Manuzio family to work in the Aldine Press. As is often the case in dynastic, entrepreneurial families, none of his children took over the family business.

Aldo and his grandfather made enormous contributions to literacy. They not only made books available to almost everyone, but their innovative work with typefaces also made them easier to read and therefore to understand.

This contribution to the education of the masses grants the two Manuzios a respected place in *The Italian 100*.

37

St. Thomas Aquinas
c. 1225–74

I am receiving thee, Price of my soul's redemption: all my studies, my vigils and my labors have been for love of thee. I have taught much and written much of the most sacred body of Jesus Christ; I have taught and written in the faith of Jesus Christ and of the holy Roman Church, to whose judgment I offer and submit everything.

—THOMAS AQUINAS'S DYING DECLARATION

St. Thomas Aquinas was an intellectual giant who sought to incorporate the principles of Aristotelianism (which stated that the ultimate human goal should be the most logical and effective use of the intellect) into Roman Catholic doctrine.

Thomas was a bold figure, both physically and intellectually, and in 1273, with the publication of his *Summa theologica* and his "Five Proofs for the Existence of God," he attempted to prove the existence of God through logic and reason rather than faith or revelation. In the minds of many people, he succeeded.

Thomas Aquinas was born sometime around the year 1225. (There is disagreement on exactly when, although most authorities and reference works today accept 1225 as his birth year.) He died in 1274, was canonized a Roman Catholic saint by Pope John XXII in 1323, and was declared a doctor of the Church by Pope Pius V in 1567. Between 1323 and 1879, St. Thomas's philosophies and theological thinking were intensively studied by Catholic scholars. In his 1879 encyclical *Aeterni patris*, Pope Leo XIII declared St. Thomas's system the official doctrine of the Roman Catholic Church.

St. Thomas's monumental and enduring influence on centuries of religious and philosophical thinking continues to this day. The Roman Catholic Church, with over 900 million followers, is the largest Christian religious group in the world, and its believers base their spiritual lives, in part, on the teachings of Thomas Aquinas.

Thomas Aquinas was born in his family's castle of Roccasecca in the small town of Aquino, Italy, situated about fifty miles northwest from Naples in Italy's fertile Campania region. He was the son of Count Landulf, a knight, and when he was five, his father placed him in the nearby Monte Cassino abbey, where he received his schooling until he was thirteen.

In 1239 he entered the University of Naples for further studies. In Naples, Thomas became very interested in a religious order known as the Order of Preachers, and it was there that he began moving toward a spiritual life dominated by prayer and meditation. At the age of nineteen, Thomas joined the Dominican friars and embraced the "beggar" lifestyle of the order. Thomas's mother, Theodora, who had wanted her son to join the more prestigious Benedictine order, had Thomas kidnapped by his soldier brothers. He was then held prisoner by his own family in a castle near Roccasecca for two years. In 1245 his family surrendered to Thomas's implacable determination to remain a Dominican and set him free. Over the next thirty years or so, Thomas taught at universities, wrote and lectured on the Scriptures, and became a trusted adviser to France's king Louis IX (later St. Louis) and others. Thomas had many religious visions throughout his life and often claimed that his writings and views on religious and spiritual matters were imparted to him through visions of Jesus Christ.

Thomas Aquinas died on March 7, 1274, in the Cistercian abbey of Fosso Nuova. (He had been taken there when he got terribly ill on a journey to Lyons at the bidding of Pope Gregory X.)

Thomas's novel approach to spiritual questions and issues involved applying the principles of mathematics to religion. His famous "Five Proofs" uses the principles of geometry to prove a theological "theorem," namely, How can the existence of God be proven?

Stated briefly (and paraphrased), Thomas formulated the following "five ways":

- **1. The "Unmoved Mover":** We know there is motion in the world. We know that whatever is in motion was moved by another thing. This other thing also had to be moved by something. To therefore avoid an impossible infinite regression, there must be a "First Mover," and that is God.

- **2. The "First Cause":** Everything in reality comes into existence due to a cause: A house is built by a builder who came into being because of his parents, who came into being because of their parents, and so on. To again avoid an infinite regression, there must have been a "First Cause," which is God.

- **3. The "Something from Nothing" Argument:** All physical things are finite (they have a beginning and an end). Since time is infinite, there had to have been a time, therefore, when nothing existed. So then how could there be anything now if at one point in time there was nothing? Nothing cannot bring into being something. There had to have always been something outside of nothingness, and that something is God.

- **4. The "Goodness" Argument:** Since everything in the world has varying degrees of goodness, and since a thing's "goodness" is a relative term definable only by comparison with something else, there has to be a "maximum goodness," and that is God.

- **5. The "Design" Argument:** Things in the world function with a purpose: they have a "design." In order for this to be there must exist an ultimate "designer," and that designer is God.

Thomas's other surviving writings include *Summa contra Gentiles, Summa theologica, Quaestiones disputatae, Quaestiones quodlibetales, De unitate intellectus contra Averroistas,* as well as writings and commentaries on Boethius, Dionysius, and of course, Aristotle.

St. Thomas's works have remained strong during the twentieth century, inspiring philosophical movements such as Neo-Scholasticism. The leaders of this movement, the Catholic theologicians Etienne Gilson and Jacques Maritain, sought to apply the principles of Thomism (as Aquinas's system is now known) to contemporary social and political issues.

Thomas Aquinas was neither a scientist nor an inventor, and he did not build something that would change the material existence of the world's peoples. He is ranked highly in the *The Italian 100* because his brilliant reasoning and essential work on matters of the spirit profoundly influenced the religious lives of a quarter of the world's population. His contributions to the defining principles of one of the world's largest churches were enormously significant, and his prodigious writings continue to be important to religious thinkers the world over.

38

Dante Alighieri

1265–1321

PER ME SI VA NELLA CITTÀ DOLENTE,
PER ME SI VA NELL'ETERNO DOLORE,
PER ME SI VA TRA LA PERDUTA GENTE . . . .
LASCIATE OGNI SPERANZA VOI CH'ENTRATE!

This way for the sorrowful city.
This way for eternal suffering.
This way to join the lost people. . . .
Abandon all hope, you who enter!
　　　—DANTE
　　　　The Divine Comedy, from *Inferno*
　　　　(the inscription at the entrance to Hell)

125

Michelangelo's nightmarish masterpiece *The Last Judgment* (painted in the Sistine Chapel) was inspired by Dante's vision of God's wrath as related in the *Inferno* section of *The Divine Comedy*. He was only one of many great artists to be inspired by Dante's vision.

The twentieth-century poet and critic T. S. Eliot said, "The poetry of Dante is the one universal school of style for the writing of poetry in any language." Eliot also said that Dante and Shakespeare share a literary throne for two: "There is no third." Historian Daniel Boorstin has said that Dante's work has an "awesome immortality," and quotes the oft-repeated description of Dante's writings as "Saint Thomas Aquinas set to music." And the poet William Butler Yeats described Dante as the "chief imagination of Christendom."

It is true that artists as a group have not had the overwhelming impact on world history and culture that scientists, inventors, and explorers have had, yet in the case of the thirteenth-century Italian poet Dante Alighieri, one must defer to a different standard. Dante must be acknowledged as one of the creators of modern literature and, as such, be included in this ranking in a position higher than that of other artists. (Although, in Dante's case, the term *artist* is far too limiting for someone who was so brilliantly gifted in the fields of philosophy, political theory, prose writing, and literary theory.)

Dante Alighieri was born in Florence, Italy, in the year 1265, sometime between May 21 and June 20. (His birth was recorded only as being under the astrological sign of Gemini.) His father was a moneylender of noble ancestry, and Dante grew up involved in the political strife and struggles of his native Florence. In 1300, at the age of thirty-one, Dante was elected to the highest office in Florence, a development that led ultimately to his banishment (on phony corruption charges) and the assurance that if he ever returned to the city of his birth, he would be burned at the stake. "All my woes and all my misfortunes had their origin in my unlucky election," Dante wrote.

In 1274, when Dante was nine, he first set eyes on the greatest love of his life, Beatrice Portinari, also nine. It seems, however, that Dante's awe-inspiring love for Beatrice was utterly unrequited. He kept his feelings secret. When Beatrice died in 1290, Dante finally felt free to write of his undying love for her. He did so in *La vita nuova* (*The New Life*), published in 1293, in which he chronicled his many years of frustration and repressed passion, beginning with his first glimpse of Beatrice and continuing until the death of the woman he called *la gloriosa donna della mia mente* (the glorious lady of my mind). Despite his grief and devotion to Beatrice's memory, Dante married Gemma Donati, and the couple had three children.

But it is Dante's magnum opus, his masterpiece of world literature, *The Divine Comedy*, that secured, indeed, *necessitated*, his high ranking in *The Italian 100*.

This 100-canto epic poem may be the greatest poem ever written, and its brilliance was immediately recognized by medieval scholars and lay people alike, since it was written in the vernacular of Italian, rather than in the scholarly language of Latin. As Italian historian Valerio Lintner put it, Dante's use of Italian, his "*dolce stil novo* ('sweet new style') as exemplified in the *Divina Commedia*, was the basis [and beginning] of modern Italian." If he had done nothing more than instigate the change in literature from Latin to the vernacular, Dante would have to be reckoned as a major influence on world culture. But he did much more than just that.

Dante began writing his monumental epic when he was forty-three. *The Divine Comedy* is in three sections of thirty-three cantos each (with one introductory canto): *Inferno*, *Purgatorio*, and *Paradiso* (Hell, Purgatory, and Heaven) and tells the story of Dante's journey through the afterlife, guided by the Roman poet Virgil and his last love, Beatrice.

It begins:

> In the middle of the journey of our life I came to myself within a dark wood where the straight way was lost.

Dante did not include the word *divine* in his original version. As Michelangelo's admirers would later honor the great sculptor "divine" upon seeing his magnificent works, it seems as though Dante's enthusiasts did likewise with him, and in 1555, a printed edition of the epic in Venice first christened the work *The Divine Comedy*. Dante, in a letter to his patron Can Grande della Scala of Verona (to whom Dante dedicated the *Paradise* section of the poem), wrote:

> The title of the book is "Here beginneth the Comedy of Dante Alighieri, a Florentine by birth, but not by character."

The Divine Comedy has retained its power, importance, and popularity for almost seven centuries. It is taught in schools throughout the world and stands today as the ultimate manifestation of poetic imagination wielded on behalf of an unapologetically spiritual sub-text. The Encyclopedia Brittanica makes the revealing point that "Later readers have been eager to show the poem to be a polyphonic masterpiece, as integrated as a mighty work of architecture, whose different sections reflect and, in a way, respond to one another." Dante's world view, as expressed in *The Divine Comedy* and his other writings, was thoroughly Christian: The only true salvation for man comes through adherence to the will of God and atonement for sin. Dante was definitely a political animal, though, acknowledging the divine mandate of the emperor in worldly matters. Dante wrote *De Monarchia* (*The Monarchy*) to prove to his readers that the only way for mankind to achieve its highest goals was to join under the authority of one ruler. Dante scholar Thomas G. Bergin sees a theological defense to this view:

> [I]t is the duty of man, God's creature, to imitate his Maker as closely as possible, and unity is of course supremely realized in God. Finally, it may be argued that since mankind is the child of the heavens (man is begotten by man and the sun, said Aristotle), it should rightly imitate the rule of the heavens, all of which follow the *primum mobile* [ninth heaven].

Dante saw freedom of choice as God's greatest gift to mankind, believing that this would bring happiness on earth as well as in heaven. His argument was simple: If one ruler (God) was enough for all of creation, and humans had the duty to imitate God as best they could, then one ruler should be more than enough for the perfect functioning of mankind.

Bergin adds:

> Clinching his point, Dante asserts that, as the human race depends—just as a town or nation does—on concord for its "best disposition," and this calls for one dominating will, then clearly *one prince* is essential. [emphasis added]

Dante's political views were synthesized within a Christian gestalt in *The Divine Comedy*, focusing on the poet's journey through the land of the dead. This parallels the Christian belief that life is a pilgrimage and that we each determine how we make our way through the world by using our God-given freedom of choice. Dante's body of work still stands today as one of the most explicit and unambiguous illustrations of Aristotelian commitment to the perfection of the intellect within a devotedly Christian design.

Dante Alighieri died in Ravenna, Italy, on September 13 (or 14), 1321. His legacy is strong today: His sublime love for Beatrice remains moving, and his masterful writings have inspired poets and other writers for centuries. His influence continues to dominate Western literature. And as this passage from the *Inferno* section of *The Divine Comedy* illustrates, the great Dante teaches us still:

> *Considerate la vostra semenza:*
> *Fatti non foste a viver come bruti,*
> *Ma per seguir virtute e canoscenza.*

> Consider your origins:
> you were not made that you might live as brutes,
> but so as to follow virtue and knowledge.

39

Niccolò Machiavelli

1469–1527

As a prince must be able to act just like a beast, he should learn
from the fox and the lion; because the lion does not defend
himself against traps, and the fox does not defend himself
against wolves. So one has to be a fox in order to recognize
traps, and a lion to frighten off wolves.

> —NICCOLÒ MACHIAVELLI
> *The Prince,* chapter 18

We are much beholden to Machiavel and others, that write
what men do, and not what they ought to do.

> —FRANCIS BACON
> *Advancement of Learning*

I affirm that the doctrine of Machiavelli is more alive today
than it was four centuries ago.

—BENITO MUSSOLINI, 1924

History tells us that there are many sides to the personality of
the Italian statesman, writer, historian, and social philosopher
Niccolò Machiavelli. The most pervasive perception of him is as a
cynical and dissolute opportunist whose belief system revolved
around the notion that man is essentially evil and that the end justi-
fies the means. So ingrained into Western consciousness is this
interpretation of Machiavelli, his name has transmuted into an
adjective. The *American Heritage Dictionary* defines "Machiavellian"
as "suggestive of or characterized by the principles of expediency,
deceit and cunning attributed to Niccolò Machiavelli." Historian
Will Durant, in *The Renaissance*, called Machiavelli "the most cynical
thinker of his time, and yet a patriot fired with a noble ideal"; he
added that the Florentine thinker "left upon history a deeper mark
than almost any other figure of this age."

Machiavelli is most remembered for his seminal work, *The
Prince*, which has been called by literary scholars Frederic Raphael
and Kenneth McLeish "a handbook for enlightening despots." To
be fair, there is much in *The Prince* that warrants such a reading,
and yet the book contains many views that can be easily applied to
politics and social consciousness now, almost five hundred years
later:

- "The first method for estimating the intelligence of a ruler is to
  look at the men he has round him."

- "It is more secure to be feared than to be loved."

- "Only those means of security are good, are certain, are lasting,
  that depend on yourself and your own vigor."

- "Hate is gained through good deeds as well as bad ones."

- "One who deceives will always find those who allow themselves to
  be deceived."

The painfully pragmatic philosophical principle running
throughout *The Prince* is that the good of the state takes precedence
over *everything*, and morality must play absolutely *no role* in governing. Machiavelli states this baldly when he writes, "Hence it is necessary for a prince who wishes to hold his own *to know how to do wrong,*

and to make use of it or not according to necessity" [emphasis added]. According to Machiavelli, the prince's concern for the public good invests him with the power and obligation to do whatever is necessary to maintain the integrity of the state. Religious dogma and precepts (including such fundamental guiding principles as the Ten Commandments) are irrelevant to the proper functioning of a healthy government.

Machiavelli believed that liberty was incompatible with a smoothly functioning bureaucracy; and yet he acknowledged that in order to prevent revolt, the citizenry must possess the *illusion* of liberty and be confident that they are, in essence, free, regardless of the actual truth. And ironically, underlying all of this deviousness and amorality, is Machiavelli's passionate patriotism and his dedication to the flourishing of the state, at any and all costs.

Niccolò Machiavelli was born on May 3, 1469, in Florence, Italy, and died there on June 21, 1527, at the age of fifty-eight. He was married to Marietta Corsini, with whom he had six children. (Machiavelli apparently spent a great deal of time in brothels. Some of his letters describe his sexual encounters with prostitutes in such graphic terms that none of his biographers have seen fit to publish them.)

Niccolò was born into a poor family and had a very frugal childhood; he once wrote that he had "learnt to do without before he learnt to enjoy." Because of his family's poverty, Niccolò did not receive the type of education a young man with his intellect deserved. Instead, he read widely and taught himself, a course of learning that did not corrupt his thinking by exposing him to the humanistic philosophies prevalent at the time.

One area that immediately engaged the young Machiavelli was politics. Of Machiavelli's embrace of the art of government, Will Durant wrote, "His one absorbing interest was politics, the technique of influence, the chess of power." In 1498, Machiavelli began his political career, although he never actually held an elected office; instead, he served in various appointed government posts throughout the following fifteen years.

Machiavelli's first assignment was as secretary to the Council of Ten for War. He was twenty-nine at the time, and this position allowed him a glimpse into the inner workings of government. He then undertook a number of diplomatic missions, one of which introduced him to the man who would be the biggest influence on his intellectual development, Caesar Borgia. Machiavelli was impressed and humbled by the younger man's political and military accomplishments, and Borgia became his role model and seminal inspiration. Seeking to emulate his hero, Machiavelli returned to Florence and convinced the government that the city needed its own militia and should no longer depend on paid mercenaries for its defense. The government finally acquiesced to his impassioned arguments and created the militia in 1507.

In 1512, however, Machiavelli's militia crumbled under the onslaught of Pope Julius II's Holy League. Florence fell, and the Medici were returned to power. This effectively ended Machievelli's political career. He was ultimately arrested and tortured, on suspicion of being in league with the invading army. He was eventually released and moved his family away from Florence and for the next fifteen years, wrote his most important and acclaimed works.

In the years between 1512 and the end of his life in 1527, Machiavelli wrote prolifically, publishing, among other works, *The Prince* (1513), *Discourses Upon the First Ten Books of Titus Livius, A History of Florence,* and the play *The Mandrake.*

Machiavelli's influence on modern political thought has been profound and complex. On the one hand, *The Prince*'s teachings were embraced by, among others, Napoleon, Mussolini, Hitler, and Stalin. The book's secular—and essentially heartless—advocacy of authoritarian regimes appealed to these despots, and history is clear on their own legacies.

But Machiavelli must be credited with unemotionally and dispassionately acknowledging the need for strength on the part of governments, a principle that has also been embraced by liberal political figures. "Strength through power" is an important political tenet; modern history has shown that its potential ruthlessness needs to be tempered by an agreed-upon public morality that does not sacrifice human rights and welfare for the benefits of a strong bureaucracy.

The Prince initiated the discussion of these crucial issues, and thus the book has endured as Niccolò Machiavelli's contribution to political thought.

That Machiavelli was an Italian writing about Italian government gives an interesting historical slant to his work. In the end, Machiavelli did not believe that his philosophies would be accepted by Italians. He knew that Italians tended to be antagonistic toward authority in principle and would not be able to fight together effectively. He concluded *The Prince* with the following observation:

Look at the duels and the combats between a few, how

the Italians are superior in strength, in skill, in inventiveness; but when it is a matter of armies, they do not compare. All this because of the weakness of the leaders. Those who are capable are not obeyed. Everyone imagines he is competent.

The Italian sensibility, in the end, doomed widespread acceptance of Machiavelli's political philosophy in Italy. Instead, Machiavelli's emotionally charged views contributed to forging foreigners' perception of Italians in a way that survives to this day.

40

St. Francis of Assisi

c. 1181–1226

He who knows how to be poor knows everything.

—JULES MICHELET

St. Francis of Assisi was born into wealth; was never ordained into the clergy; spent his youth reveling in a decadent lifestyle; went willingly and with glee into war; spent time in prison; and was often so disheveled and obsessive that he was sometimes dismissed as a madman.

Yet this one Italian, in his short forty-five years on earth, is remembered and venerated as the founder of the worldwide Franciscan religious order and also as the man who established the custom of the Christmas nativity scene. His short life created a legacy that lives to this day. As religious historian John Delaney expressed it, "Francis' impact on religious life since his times has been enormous. Probably no saint has affected so many in so many different ways as the gentle saint of Assisi who, born to wealth, devoted his life to poverty, concern for the poor and the sick, and so delighted in God's works as revealed in nature."

Francis was born in either 1181 or 1182 in Assisi in the Umbria region of Italy. His father, Pietro de Bernardone, was a wealthy merchant who sold silks and cloths. His mother was known only as Giovanna, although history records that she was also called Pica, which some take to mean *La Pica,* or "from Picardy." The author of *The Anonymous Life of Saint Francis* (now in the Royal Library at Brussels) related the story of Francis's birth, a narrative that has the stuff of legend about it:

> Giovanna was a woman devout above the ordinary; she had visited the holy sepulchre, the place of the Blessed Archangel Michael, the house of the Apostles, and daily made efforts to visit other shrines. And she begged the Lord most earnestly in her prayers to give her a son, but always asked that things might be accomplished as was well-pleasing to God. So then she conceived a child. And when she realized that she was near her time, she happened to be alone. And she began to grow faint because of her labour-pains. And she could not give birth to her child on her own. And suddenly there flooded into her mind a recollection of the childbearing of the glorious Virgin, and the humble place in which the Lord had been born. So she followed that pattern, going down into their own stable, where the cows and the donkeys were led in, and there, by his Benevolent Will, she gave birth to her son in the middle of them, with very little pain.

This story illustrates the powerful belief in Francis's Christlike persona and emphasizes the gravity with which his teachings have been honored for nearly eight hundred years.

Francis was christened Giovanni (John) by his mother during one of his father's frequent buying trips, but when Peter returned, he insisted that the baby be renamed Francesco (Francis), meaning "the Frenchman," a sign of Pietro's admiration for France, which he often visisted. In his early years, Francis seems to have made good use of his family's wealth. He indulged himself in all manner of earthly delights and had no interest in either an education or in following his father into business. He spent a great deal of money and lived lavishly.

When Francis was twenty, he was captured during a battle between Assisi and Perugia and imprisoned for an entire year. But even this hardship did not seem to faze him, and he supposedly bore his jail time "with cheerfulness and good temper." Following his release from prison, he continued to live the high life on his father's money until his twenty-fifth year, when he became gravely ill. Francis's biographer Thomas of Celano had a pointed interpretation of this illness: "God suddenly decided to deal with him . . . For some time, he was laid low by sickness, the just deserts of human perversity." When Francis finally recovered, Celano reports that he had a very cynical view of the world: "The beauty of the meadows, the delight of the vineyards, and all the lovely things there are to see gave him no pleasure."

At this point, Francis began to experience what can only be described as mystical, supernatural events. Crucifixes spoke to him; he witnessed miraculous cures; and he had prophetic dreams that came true. Written off by his father as insane, Francis retreated to a cave, where he prayed night and day for an answer to what seemed to be his growing madness. Upon leaving the cave, he was much more sober of spirit and seemed to be quite distracted. His family and friends joked that he must be in love, to which he replied, "I am going to take a wife more beautiful and worthy than any you know."

He then spent several years repairing churches (a painted icon of Christ in a church had spoken to him, telling him, "Francis, repair my house"). After this he retired to a chapel, where he devoted himself to preaching and committed himself to a life of total poverty.

On April 16, 1209, he officially founded the Franciscan religious order, (which he humbly called the Friars Minor) and in 1210 the order was sanctioned by Pope Innocent III. For the next decade, Francis sent missionaries out throughout the world, all of whom preached the Franciscan creed of humility, simplicity, and poverty.

In the year 1224, on September 14, gravely ill and in intractable pain, Francis received the stigmata, those inexplicable bleeding wounds that correspond to Christ's wounds of crucifixion.

This was the first instance in which anyone was said to receive the stigmata, and it remains the only such occurrence that is celebrated in the liturgy of the Catholic church. Francis died at Assisi on October 3, 1226, and was canonized only two years later by Pope Gregory IX, his close friend. His selfless devotion to the poor and the sick continues to inspire religious thought today, almost eight centuries after his death. The order he founded is now the second largest in the Church (only the Jesuits have more members), and no order has seen more of its members canonized than have the Franciscans.

41

Giuseppi Mazzini
1805–72

Giuseppe Mazzini . . . believed the unification of Italy to be not only possible but necessary. He insisted upon it with single-minded obstinacy, and dedicated his whole life to realizing this ideal, from his early, ardent youth to his grief-stricken old age.
—GAETANO SALVEMINI
Mazzini

A nation must be to humanity what the family is, or should be, to the fatherland. If it acts harmfully, if it oppresses, if it becomes the vehicle of injustice and sponsors and supports temporary interests, it loses the right to existence and digs its grave.
—GIUSEPPE MAZZINI, IN A LETTER TO A GERMAN PATRIOT

Astory is told of Giuseppe Mazzini as a child: One day, when he was out walking with his mother, Maria, they came upon a wretched old man begging on the streets of Genoa. Rather than shun the filthy pauper, the young Mazzini embraced him and attempted to comfort him. The beggar looked up at Mazzini's mother and told her, "Love him well, lady; he is one who will love the people."

Giuseppe Mazzini, the indispensable contributor toward Italian unification and the creation of contemporary Italy, was born in Genoa on June 22, 1805. His childhood home was just a few blocks away from the home of violinist Nicolò Paganini, then twenty-two and already a star (see chapter 82).

In his 1862 treatise *The Duties of Man*, Mazzini articulated the principles that would serve as a driving force in the Risorgimento (Resurgence), the movement to create an independent and united Italy, a goal finally achieved in 1870:

> Your first duties—first as regards importance—are, as I have already told you, towards Humanity. You are *men* before you are either citizens or fathers. If you do not embrace the whole human family in your affection, if you do not bear witness to your belief in the Unity of that family, consequent upon the Unity of God . . . if, wheresoever a fellow-creature suffers, or the dignity of human nature is violated by falsehood or tyranny—you are not ready, if able, to aid the unhappy, and do not feel called upon to combat, if able, for the redemption of the betrayed or oppressed—you violate your law of life, you comprehend not that Religion which will be the guide and blessing of the future.

Second only to Giuseppe Garibaldi in the eyes of the Italian people in terms of admiration and respect, Mazzini is commonly called the "father of the Italian nation" and the "prophet of Italian unity," and his ideology and efforts to create a unified Italian republic (*not* the monarchy it became during his lifetime) are viewed as the kindling of the fire of Italian independence (see GARIBALDI [76]).

Early in his life, Mazzini, the son of the physician Giacomo Mazzini, exhibited great intellectual potential and literary talent. He entered the University of Genoa when he was only fourteen, and at age sixteen he witnessed political refugees from the crushed Piedmontese uprising being hustled through Genoa, on their way to exile. (At this time the fragmented Italian states were dominated by repressive regimes controlled by noble families or foreign powers such as Austria.) This event changed his life, and an electrifying idea immediately blossomed in his mind. Mazzini recounted this moment of enlightenment in his *Life and Writings*:

> That day was the first in which a confused idea presented itself to my mind—I will not say of country or of liberty—but an idea that we Italians *could* and therefore *ought* to struggle for the liberty of our country.

In 1827, at the age of twenty-two, Mazzini graduated with a degree in law and began working as a lawyer while writing essays and considering a literary career. His dreams of becoming a historical novelist were put on hold, however, when he joined the Carbonari, a secret society that had as its goal the overthrow of tyranny in all its forms. The Carbonari was a ritualistic fraternal organization that had its roots in the Freemason movement that had begun in Europe during the eighteenth century.

Three years later, in November of 1830, at the age of twenty-five, Mazzini was betrayed by Raimondo Doria, the Grand Master of the Spanish Lodge of the Carbonari, and imprisoned for ten weeks in a fortress at Savona. This imprisonment marked the end of Mazzini's subservience to the Grand Masters and Supreme Lodges of the Carbonari, and while in prison he began to work out in his mind the specifics of a new type of revolutionary movement, one that would not be tainted by the corruption plaguing the Carbonari.

When he was released from prison in early 1831, Mazzini fled to Marseilles, France, where he lived for two years. In France he formed the Young Italy organization (Giovine Italia), the group he had conceived while in prison. He intended this group to encompass people of all social classes because he believed that a revolution could succeed only if the common people were behind it. While noble in intent and clever in conception, the feasibility of a grassroots movement focused on insurrection was, in the end, impractical, because of one critical factor: Mazzini was a literate, intelligent spokesperson who was trying to use propaganda to rally an illiterate, uneducated populace. Most of the rural peasants didn't read, nor did they have the exposure to culture necessary to understand Mazzini's dogmas. Working in Mazzini's favor was the *spirit* of his new organization. Even the uneducated poor could understand passion and crave freedom and thus, within two years,

Young Italy boasted 60,000 members. Sheer numbers did not, however, guarantee the success of Young Italy, and after several failed insurrections, the group disbanded.

Revolutions in France, Germany, Austria, and Hungary in 1848 greatly influenced the people of Italy and further aroused their growing passion for freedom. Mazzini (and the more theologically minded revolutionary Vincenzo Gioberti) was able to use the European uprisings as a catalyst for similar revolts in the monarchies of Naples, Tuscany, and Piedmont, culminating in enormous uprisings against Austria in Milan and Venice. A new republic, headed by Mazzini, was formed in February 1849.

In 1851, Mazzini formed another revolutionary society, the Friends of Italy. He then supported Milanese workers in their 1853 uprising against Austria, and in 1857 he was involved (with Carlo Pisacane) in the failed insurrection at Calabria. Mazzini started another political journal, *Pensiero ed Azione* (*Thought and Action*), in 1858.

The united Kingdom of Italy was established in 1861. This development devastated the democratically-minded Mazzini, whose whole life had been devoted to a free and independent Italy, not a monarchy. Bitterly disappointed, he called Italy "a corpse" and continued his revolutionary activity. He died of pleurisy in Pisa on March 10, 1872, at the age of sixty-seven. His legacy, however, is one of unwavering commitment to an Italian nation not bound by the shackles of foreign rule.

It is true that Giuseppe Garibaldi is more beloved by Italians and that his work as a military leader is legendary. Yet, as Italian scholar Dr. Michael Vena has astutely described the two men, Mazzini (who supported Garibaldi's endeavors) was the *mind* of the new Italy; while Garibaldi was the *heart*. And since the mind must inevitably control the heart, Mazzini is thus ranked higher in *The Italian 100* than Garibaldi.

The epitaph on Mazzini's tombstone in Staglieno fulfills the prophecy of that Genoese beggar from Mazzini's childhood:

L'uomo
Che tutto Sacrificò
Che amò tanto
E molto compatì e non odiò mai

"He was that man who sacrificed everything, who loved greatly and suffered much and never hated."

42

Benito Mussolini
1893–1945

It is well known that Hitler's favourable opinion of [Mussolini],
of Italian military preparations, and the people's devotion to
the régime and to the Axis, made him commit several miscalculations, one of which probably cost him the war. He believed, in
the end, that he lost the Russian campaign because he had
started four weeks too late; he was four weeks late because he
wasted time to rescue the Italians bogged down in Albania, in
their ill-prepared attack on Greece. If this were true, Mussolini
could be considered the greatest negative military genius the
world has ever seen, who defeated two great nations single-
handed, his own and Germany.

— LUIGI BARZINI
The Italians

Here lies one of the most intelligent animals who ever
appeared on the face of the earth.

—MUSSOLINI'S EPITAPH, WRITTEN BY HIMSELF

Influence on world history and culture is not always positive. During his twenty-year reign as dictator of Italy, Benito Mussolini had a major impact on not only his own country but, as the quotation from Barzini illustrates, also on the outcome of World War II.

Benito "Il Duce" ("the Leader") Mussolini was born on July 29, 1893, in Predappio, Italy. He was an unruly child and student and was expelled from a religious boarding school for stabbing a classmate in the buttocks with a pocketknife. In his teens and twenties he wrote for and edited Socialist newspapers, including *The Class Struggle* and *Avanti!* Gradually he developed the ideology of fascism, which exalts the nation above all else and suppresses individual freedoms in the name of a national unity that is often based on concepts of racial superiority.

During World War I, Mussolini edited the paper *Il Popolo D'Italia* (*The People of Italy*). Even though the paper initially proclaimed itself socialist in ideology, Mussolini soon began calling for Italy to enter the war on the side of the Allies (Britain and France), shrewdly utilizing the country's growing nationalistic fervor through inflammatory exhortations to working-class Italians. Mussolini himself ultimately served in the army until he was wounded in 1917, a year before the war's end. Historian Dennis Mack Smith states that "for anyone prepared to read or listen, Mussolini made it obvious that he was becoming a nationalist with great ambitions for his country," and he also notes that Mussolini's ultimate goal was to "raise the flag of imperialism throughout the Mediterranean and make Rome once again the center of European civilization."

After the war, Mussolini began to organize his followers into the black-shirted *Fasci di combate*, who took violent action against opponents such as Socialists and Communists. The Fascists marched on Rome on October 28, 1922, and this bold move was the catalyst for Mussolini's ascent to power.

Mussolini's reign as dictator of Italy began three days later, on October 31, 1922, when, at the age of thirty-nine, he was installed as the youngest prime minister in Italy's history. Italy's King Victor Emmanuel III, bowing to Mussolini's threats to take over the government by violence if necessary, surrendered authority to the young Fascist, and within a year, Mussolini had complete dominion over Italy and the Italian people. In 1928, Mussolini said, "The eighteenth and nineteenth centuries experimented with democracy. The twentieth century will be the century of Fascism." He also proclaimed that "Democracy is beautiful in theory; in practice it is a fallacy."

Much to Mussolini's delight, he was embraced by the Italian people as a savior. He was a consummate showman who, by using a highly theatrical blend of inflammatory oratory and rhetoric, was able to get things done. Roads were paved, labor strikes stopped, bridges and public buildings were built and, most memorably, the trains ran on time. Mussolini is reported to have told a stationmaster, "We must leave exactly on time ... From now on everything must function to perfection." In 1929, Infanta Eulalia of Spain, writing in *Courts and Countries after the War*, noted, "The first benefit of Benito Mussolini's direction in Italy begins to be felt when one crosses the Italian Frontier and hears 'il treno arriva all'orario' ['the train is arriving on time']." Historian Valerio Lintner correctly notes, however, that "Fascism may have 'made the trains run on time,'. . . but it also turned Italy into a vulgar, corrupt, cynical and conformist society, in which fear and intellectual poverty dominated."

Mussolini's administrative brilliance was, in essence, a sham. Luigi Barzini, who knew the fiery dictator and once described him as "the master of make-believe" noted that "behind the scenery of modernization and industrial investments, millions of Italians still lived a life of prehistoric squalor, and most of the fundamental problems of the country had been left practically untouched."

In October 1935, Mussolini made a huge miscalculation, one that stemmed from his megalomaniacal delusions of an Italian empire and his eagerness to believe the exaggeratedly flattering things the Italians and others in the world were saying about him and his purported accomplishments. With the advice and encouragement of his one European supporter, Adolf Hitler, Mussolini invaded the African country of Abyssinia (now known as Ethiopia) and seven months later, on May, 9, 1936, announced to a throng of 400,000 supporters that Italy had successfully begun the building of its empire.

The world was outraged by this blatant expansionism. The League of Nations imposed economic sanctions on Mussolini, but since the league did not restrict Abyssinian oil exports, the Italian occupation held fast. That same year, Mussolini and Hitler formed an alliance known as the Axis, with Italy playing a secondary role to Germany and its massive, well-organized military machine. (Japan joined the Axis in 1940.) In 1938, Mussolini embraced Nazi Germany's reprehensible racial policies and began the persecution of Italian Jews.

In April 1939, Mussolini misguidedly invaded Albania, forcing Germany to devote resources to the extrication of Italian forces, and on June 10, 1940, Italy officially entered World War II. Following the successful Allied landings in Sicily in 1943, Mussolini was forced from power by his followers on July 25 and placed under arrest in Rome. In September, German forces rescued Mussolini, and Hitler installed him as head of a puppet regime, the Italian Social Republic, in northern Italy. Two years later, after the Germans had essentially abandoned him to anti-Fascist factions, Mussolini was captured trying to flee to Switzerland in a German uniform. On Saturday, April 28, 1945, Il Duce and his mistress were shot; their bodies were hung upside down from the roof of a Milan gas station with the bodies of other captured Fascists. Ironically, Mussolini had once told a friend, "Everybody dies the death that corresponds to his character."

43

Amerigo Vespucci
1454–1512

All men are liable to error; and most men are, in many points, by passion or interest, under temptation to it.
— JOHN LOCKE
An Essay Concerning
Human Understanding

Christopher Columbus may have received credit for the European discovery of the Americas, but it was Amerigo Vespucci who corrected Columbus's mistaken belief that his discoveries were part of Asia, and it was Vespucci who stated unequivocally that the Americas were a "New World."

Amerigo Vespucci was born in Florence, Italy, in 1454, the son of a notary. Amerigo's uncle Giorgio tutored him in his youth, schooling him in the Renaissance school of thought called humanism. Humanists looked beyond the accepted spiritual and religious sources of knowledge and focused on secular learning and studies. Amerigo traveled to France in 1479, and when he returned, he joined the Medici Bank in Florence, where he trained and worked until 1491. He then worked with a ship's outfitter in Seville, Spain, and in all likelihood was in the city when Christopher Columbus returned from his first voyage.

In the years after Columbus's momentous 1492 voyage, Vespucci made several voyages to South America in the employ of Spain and Portugal, most notably discovering the Río de la Plata estuary between Uruguay and Argentina, and then continuing on to the southern coast of Argentinea (Patagonia) before turning his caravels back. When Vespucci returned from his voyages, he wrote many letters to friends in which he described what he had found. These letters were ultimately collected, bound, and published in several languages. These letters became enormously popular; Vespucci's accounts of his 1502 voyage expressly challenged Columbus's assertion that the Americas were actually part of the Asian land mass. In one of these letters, Vespucci used the term *Mundus Novus* (New World) to describe what we now know as the South American continent, correctly asserting that the lands he had been exploring had never before been written about or charted.

Vespucci's letters aroused and intrigued the Europeans. His descriptions of the New World and the natives living there seemed to describe an earthly paradise:

> They wear no clothes or linen or cotton because they have no need of them. There is no private property; everything is held in common. With neither king nor magistrate each man is his own master. They have as many sexual partners as they want. . . . They have no temples, no religion, worship no idols. What more can I say? They live according to nature.

But Vespucci's letters also appealed to the baser, more sensationalistic tastes of his European readers as well. John Hale, in his *Civilization of Europe in the Renaissance* (pp. 48–9), explains:

> The Vespucci account catered for a readership avid for myths and marvels and prepared to believe that while these had evaded the investigations of travelers in the old continents they would be encountered in the new. Much was made of the theme that was associated with personifi-

cations of America: cannibalism. According to his editors, Vespucci had spoken to a man who had helped to eat three hundred others, had seen salted human hams dangling for future consumption in native huts, and who remarked that it was not just enemies who were eaten but, on occasion, wives and children. The same flair for titillation marked Vespucci's discussion of sexual customs; not only were the women so lubricious that they would offer themselves freely to any male, but they envenomed the penises of their regular partners to make them swell into ever more satisfying proportions.

Aside from his historical travels, Amerigo Vespucci can also be credited with being the first European to record the use of coca in the New World. In 1499, while in Venezuela, South America, Vespucci asked the natives for some drinking water for himself and his crew. Instead of bringing water, the natives reportedly offered him coca leaves, indicating by signs that he should put the leaves in his mouth. Vespucci came to the conclusion that the natives "kept this herb in their mouths to stave off thirst." This was the first mention by a European of the leaves of the coca plant (from which cocaine is derived).

In 1507, a German geographer and cartographer named Martin Waldseemüller published a map that used the name *America* for the first time. The map was part of a collection of charts and maps called *Quattuor Americi navigationes*, or, the "Four Voyages of Amerigo." Accompanying the map was a recommendation by Waldseemüller that the New World be named after Amerigo Vespucci: "*ab Americo Inventore . . . quasi Americi terram sive Americam,*" which translated means "from Amerigo the discoverer . . . as if it were the land of Americus or America."

Waldseemüller's suggestion was not widely accepted until 1541, when the Flemish geographer Gerhardus Mercator (whose actual name was Gerhard Kremer) published a map of the New World in which he placed the letters AME on the northern land mass, and RICA across the southern one. Mercator was the cartographer who conceived of making longitude and latitude lines equidistant on maps, thereby greatly simplifying navigation and the charting of courses. Mercator's marking of latitude and longitude followed the system devised by Vespucci, who also made an estimate of the equatorial circumference of the earth that was later found to be off by only fifty miles.

Vespucci returned to Spain in 1502 and gained high honors, including the prestigious nautical rank of pilot major. However, he had contracted malaria during his American explorations, and recurrent bouts of the disease brought about his death, which occurred in Seville in 1512.

44

Marco Polo

c. 1 2 5 4 – 1 3 2 4

In Xanadu did Kubla Khan
A stately pleasure-dome decree:
Where Alph, the sacred river, ran
Through caverns measureless to man
Down to a sunless sea.
—SAMUEL TAYLOR COLERIDGE
Kubla Khan

Though a merchant by profession, Marco Polo lived an adventurer's life, spending years in exotic places, witnessing strange customs, and eating unfamiliar foods. He spent the seventeen years from 1275 through 1292 traveling on behalf of the Chinese monarch Kublai Khan, the founder of the Mongol dynasty, and when he returned to Europe in 1295, he brought back with him

151

milk ices (an early form of ice cream), spices, cashmere, new and different culinary ideas, and enthralling tales of cannibalism and hedonistic sexual customs.

Marco Polo wrote about his travels in a book that was originally titled *Il Milione* (*The Million*), but ultimately came to be called *The Travels of Marco Polo* (it was also known simply as *Travels*). Polo's book about his exploits and adventures in China and the Far East was enormously popular in Europe. Two hundred years after his travels, long after Kublai Khan was buried and contact with the Orient had ended due to the Black Death and the rise of the Ottoman Turks, Polo's book was still being copied, translated, and read.

In his book *Travel and Discovery in the Renaissance 1420–1620* the historian Boise Penrose wrote of Polo's influence:

> [T]he memory of the medieval journeys lived on, and the number of surviving manuscripts and incunabula editions [books printed before 1501] shows how popular this literature was in pre-Columbian as well as Columbian times. Judged on this basis, the *Travels of Marco Polo* was by all odds the most popular and most influential book of the type, being represented by at least 138 manuscripts still in existence. Of the early printed editions, that by Leeu of Gouda, 1483–1485 (Hain 13244) was owned by Columbus, and is preserved in Colombina in Seville. . . . [I]t is obvious that the medieval tradition of Asiatic land travel lived on, and . . . we know that Polo's geographical information went where it counted most.

It would be an oversimplification to claim that Polo was responsible for the European exploration of the New World. But it is undeniable that Polo's fascinating accounts of his journeys to China and other Asian places motivated Columbus (and many others) almost two hundred years later to try and find a westward sea route to those enchanting lands and in so doing encounter two vast continents previously unknown to Europe.

Marco was born in Venice around the year 1254 (although it is possible that he was actually born on the island of Curzola in the Adriatic Sea, then part of Venetian Dalmatia and now Korcula, Croatia). Because Marco's father, Niccolò, and his uncle Maffeo were traders for whom travel was a way of life, Marco did not really get to know his father until he was in his mid-teens. In 1271, the seventeen-year-old youth accompanied his father and uncle on a lengthy expedition that took them to what is now Turkey, Iran, Afghanistan, Pakistan, and finally China, which remained Polo's principal home until he returned to Venice in 1292.

In 1280, Polo visited the Chinese city of Hangzhou, (known to him as Kinsai), and immediately saw it as an eastern Venice. The city had a population of 900,000, and Marco was so overwhelmed by its wonders that he effusively wrote that Hangzhou was "beyond dispute the greatest city which may be found in the world, where so many pleasures may be found that one fancies himself in Paradise."

During his two-decade stay in China, Polo served under Kublai Khan as a military advisor and diplomat. At one point he constructed out of lumber an artillery engine capable of hurling 300-pound stones, a useful device for an emperor who fought many battles. Polo was held in high esteem by Kublai Khan, for he was well spoken, clever, and possessed an almost photographic memory that he would use to regale the emperor with stories of his many travels. While in China, Polo also observed and recorded many of the rituals and customs of the times. These included elaborate hunts, some of which involved upward of 20,000 men and hounds. Another was the solemn selection process of the emperor's concubines, each of whom had to prove not only that she was a virgin but also that she emitted no unpleasant odors.

Marco Polo arrived back in Venice in 1295. Valerio Lintner describes the impact he had on his fellow Venetians:

> On his return [from China], Marco was reportedly indistinguishable from a Tartar, with enormous drooping mustachios and oriental attire. At a banquet he is said to have ripped open his clothing, showering fabulous jewels over the table and the unsuspecting guests, which earned him the somewhat ironic nickname of Ser Marco il Milione (Sir Marco, the Millionaire).... Marco Polo in many ways typifies the Venetian character of the time: adventurous and daring in pursuit of profit, whilst financially extremely conservative and prudent—he was noted for his ruthless pursuit of interest on loans he had made both inside and outside his family circle.

Polo fought in Venice's war against Genoa and was taken prisoner at the Battle of Curzola. During his two years of captivity in a Genoese prison, he met a fellow political prisoner from Pisa named Rustichello. While regaling Rustichello with the tales of his travels, Polo conceived the idea to compile a book. Rustichello volunteered to act as transcriptionist, and Polo began dictating his story. The result was *Il Milione* (originally given the ambitious title *Description of the World*), a book that would inspire and thrill readers for centuries to come. However, the book contained so many fantastical tales that many Europeans believed that Polo had made up much of what he related.

Many different versions of Polo's book exist today, the result of what was often an exceptionally haphazard and undependable translation process. Nonetheless, the book was so widely read and disseminated that its fairly accurate geographical information became a valuable resource to later explorers. Until the late 19th century, it was the only source of information available to Europeans who wished to learn about central Asia.

Marco Polo died in Venice on January 8, 1324, at the age of seventy. Supposedly, when asked on his deathbed to admit that he had made up the fantastic stories in his book, the great adventurer replied that he didn't reveal *half* of what he had actually seen.

In March of 1996, British librarian Frances Wood published a book titled *Did Marco Polo Go to China?* in which she claimed that Polo's trip to China and his subsequent account of it were nothing but fantasy. "It is a terrific story; the only trouble is that there is no evidence to support it," she told Associated Press. "Like so many other great historical legends, the story is a myth." Wood bases her claim on the fact that Polo did not refer to Chinese tea-drinking ceremonies, the Great Wall, or the practice of binding girls' feet to keep them small. She did concede, however, that the Wall was incomplete at the time of Polo's journey and thus may not have impressed him enough to write about it; and that young girls with bound feet were probably confined to their homes and Polo may not have come into contact with them. Earlier attempts to discredit Polo's account of his travels have failed, and it remains to be seen whether or not Wood's theory is widely accepted by historians. For our purposes, it is moot: Whether Polo wrote his book from actual experience or made it up, it nevertheless inspired other explorers and set into motion a monumental chain of important historical events.

45

John Cabot
(Giovanni Caboto)
(c.1450–c.1498)

To discover the planet, mankind would have to be liberated from ancient hopes and fears, and open the gateways of experience. The largest dimensions of space, the continents and the oceans, were only slowly revealed. The West proved a vantage point, and for most of history the West would be the discoverer, the East the discovered. The first reaches from the West to another half of the planet came from laborious and lonely overland travelers. But the full extent of the planet could be glimpsed only by organized communities of adventure on the sea, which became a highway to grand surprises.

— DANIEL J. BOORSTIN
The Discoverers

There is a strong likelihood that somewhere off the coast of North America, between the shores of Newfoundland and the shoals of Cape Hatteras, the wreckage of a sailing ship on the bottom of the ocean floor serves as the watery tomb of an intrepid adventurer and explorer, the Italian John Cabot.

On his first sea voyage westward from England in 1497, Cabot encountered the coast of North America. His second voyage, in 1498, consisted of five ships (one of which was damaged and turned back shortly after embarking) and two hundred men. Cabot's four ships were bid farewell by the crew of the retreating ship and were never seen again. Some historical records suggest that Cabot's ships reached Chesapeake Bay before sinking, but the issue is still open to debate and speculation, like Cabot's life itself.

In the United States, Christopher Columbus has long been credited with the "discovery" of America because of his 1492 landing in the Bahamas. But the Italian Giovanni Caboto (now known by his English name, John Cabot) was the first modern European to actually reach the North American continent. Indeed, Cabot had a more direct influence on the history of the United States than did Columbus. Cabot was sailing under the flag of King Henry VII of England, and his successful 1497 voyage enabled Britain to claim the entire North American continent and eventually on May 14, 1607, to establish the colonies that became Canada and the United States.

Giovanni Caboto was born in Genoa, Italy, around the year 1450. In 1461, the Cabotos moved to Venice, and sixteen years later, at the age of twenty-six, Giovanni became a Venetian citizen. When he was in his twenties, Cabot worked for a Venetian merchant and also traveled to Arabia on business. He became an expert navigator and sailor and began to think (around the same time Columbus was conceiving the same idea) of a western sea route to the Orient.

Cabot moved his family to London in 1484, and there is little or no surviving information on his activities during the next ten years. Some scholars theorize that he spent some time traveling through England, Spain, and Portugal trying to secure funding for an Asian voyage, but there is no actual extant historical documentation to prove this.

In 1496, Cabot persuaded England's King Henry VII to sanction an exploratory journey to find new worlds in the name of England and share in whatever trade might be established as a result of his discoveries. Henry VII was notoriously cheap, however, and the monarch did not put up a single shilling to finance Cabot's journey. He did, however, issue a patent (or royal charter), which essentially permitted Cabot to sail under the British flag.

With his son Sebastian at his side, Cabot set sail from Bristol, England, on May 2, 1497, on the ship *Matthew*, with a crew of eighteen men. He proceeded westward, and approximately eight weeks later, sighted land. Again, history is uncertain as to the exact spot where Cabot made landfall. A 1929 historical atlas shows Cabot traveling *south* from Ireland (other sources say he went north around Ireland before moving west) and finally sailing through the Strait of Belle Isle before landing in southeastern Labrador.

Cabot believed he had found the eastern coast of Asia. He made the return voyage to Bristol, landing on August 6, 1497. He reported that the sea off the coast of "Asia" teemed with so many fish that it was sometimes difficult for his ship to get through them, and that if you dropped a weighted basket into the ocean, you would pull it back up filled to overflowing with fish. King Henry was thrilled with this news, and on February 3, 1498, Cabot received a royal charter for a second voyage, from which he never returned. (Sebastian Cabot survived his father by more than half a century, making a number of voyages on behalf of Spain. During the 1520s he explored the coast of South America for three years and also drew a superb map of the world in 1544.)

History must acknowledge that John Cabot opened the North American continent to European expansion. In later years, the Cabot Strait between southwestern Newfoundland and the northern tip of Cape Breton Island was named after this intrepid explorer. John Cabot was the first to make a complete transatlantic voyage to the North American continent, traveling over 3,000 miles in about eight weeks, an admirable pace of close to fifty nautical miles a day.

46

Giovanni da Verrazano
1485–1528

> The natives were very much like those we had recently met. . . .
> They came cheerfully toward us with loud cries of admiration,
> showing us where we could conveniently ground the boat. We
> went up river for half a league into the interior and saw that it
> formed a fine basin about three leagues in circumference.
> — GIOVANNI DA VERRAZANO, describing his meeting with
> natives in what would ultimately become New York harbor

Born in Florence, Italy, around 1480, the navigator Giovanni da Verrazano is best known for his explorations of the North American coast, including the island of Manhattan and New York harbor. His contributions are today acknowledged by a statue at the Battery in New York harbor, as well as the Verrazano-Narrows Bridge, named in his honor, linking Brooklyn and Staten Island.

In 1523, at the age of thirty-nine, Verrazano set sail from Dieppe in northern France under a charter from King Francis I. He had his sights set—both literally and figuratively—on finding a sea passage through the North American continent that would lead him to Marco Polo's famed Cathay (present-day China) and all its enormous wealth; his own writings show that he was familiar with Polo's book of travels.

The belief that Cathay was reachable by sailing west was strong, and the "route" to reach the mysterious land was even shown on maps. There exists a 1506 map of the world, drawn by Italian cartographer Giovanni Matteo Contarini, that has the first appearance on a printed map of America, although it was not yet called by that name. The three distinct parts of America included South America and Columbus's West Indies. The northern third of America was shown as being joined to Cathay.

Verrazano reached the North American land mass a few weeks after his departure from Dieppe and made landfall on the shores of North Carolina. He did not try to establish a camp on dry land, but he did go ashore now and then for brief reconnaissance trips. Verrazano was afraid of both the animals in this untamed land and the Indians. In his journal he wrote that the animals in this place were "much wilder than in our Europe."

For the next few months Verrazano traveled up the eastern seaboard of America, recording the coastal features of what would become Georgia, North and South Carolina, Virginia, Maryland, Delaware, and New Jersey; at length he found himself in what we now know as New York harbor. Upon first seeing the expansive harbor, he wrote that he had "discovered a very pleasant spot situated between two hills where a very large river flows into the sea." After a brief exploration of the harbor by small boat, Verrazano continued his exploration northward, eventually reaching as far as the coast of Maine, before turning east and heading back to Dieppe. He arrived back in France in July, 1524.

Giovanni da Verrazano made a major contribution to the accurate charting of America, the "New World," but the Italian navigator was genuinely misguided and actually succeeded in advancing man's knowledge of the New World in spite of himself. Verrazano was absolutely convinced that there was, indeed, a sea route through America that would allow sailors to reach China and the Pacific Ocean by traveling west. In *The Age of Exploration,* John Hale explains:

Verrazano refused to face facts. Although he had recon-
ciled himself to the reality of continental America, he
remained convinced that there must be a gap in the bar-
barous Atlantic coast which would lead to Asia. When he
looked across the Hatteras sandpit off North Carolina
and saw the wide waters of Pamlico Sound that lay
beyond, he thought he saw not only a strait but the western ocean itself. He promptly concluded that the Pacific
invaded the American continent right up to the Carolina
cape which juts far out into the Atlantic to constitute one
of the worst shipping hazards of that coast. On the map
based on his voyage, and on most of the maps of North
America for more than half a century thereafter, the
Pacific—under the name "Verrazano's Sea" [*Mare de
Verrazano*]—is so depicted.

This misconception persisted for years, with what seems to be
one exception: In the year following Verrazano's journey up the
American coast from south to north, the Spanish explorer Estevan
Gómez made the same journey, only he started in the north in
Nova Scotia and traveled south to the Caribbean Sea. His journey
convinced the Spaniards (at least) that there was no truth to
Verrazano's contention that the Pacific was actually visible from the
eastern seaboard of America.

Verrazano did not return to America after his important 1524
voyage. Instead, he explored other lands, including the eastern
coast of South America. His explorations came to an abrupt end in
1528, when he was killed by natives during an expedition in Brazil.
It seems as though Verrazano's (perhaps overly cautious) fear of
strange peoples, in his case, was warranted.

Verrazano deserves a place in *The Italian 100* for his meticulous charting of the eastern coast of North America.

47

Bartolommeo Cristofori

1655–1731

Like the cithara in antiquity and the lute during the
Renaissance, the piano is today our most important musical
instrument. We could not imagine our musical life without it.
— ERNEST CLOSON
History of the Piano

In an 1838 letter to the Paris magazine *Gazette Musical*, the brilliant
and revolutionary Hungarian pianist and composer Franz Liszt elo-
quently explains why pianists are so passionate about their chosen
instrument:

Perhaps I am deluded by this mysterious feeling which
binds me to the piano, but I regard its importance as
enormous. To my mind, the piano occupies the highest
place in the hierarchy of instruments: it is the one most
widely cultivated, the most popular of all, and it owes this
importance and popularity partly to the harmonious

resources which it alone possesses, and, because of this, to its ability to epitomize and concentrate the whole musical art within itself. Within the compass of seven octaves it covers the spectrum of the orchestra, and the ten fingers of one man are enough to reproduce the sounds created by a hundred musicians in concert. It is thanks to the piano that we have an opportunity to become familiar with works that would otherwise be little known or completely unknown because of the difficulty of assembling an orchestra to perform them. It has the same relationship to orchestral music as engraving does to painting: it multiplies it and makes it available to all; and if it does not reproduce its colors at least it reproduces its light and shade.

Bartolommeo di Francesco Cristofori was born in Padua, in the Republic of Venice, Italy, on May 4, 1655. Almost nothing is known of Cristofori's early years or private life but there are historical records that reveal his work with stringed keyboard instruments and his employment by Ferdinando De' Medici from 1690 until Ferdinando's death in 1713. Cristofori's most important contribution to the invention of the modern piano was his replacing the plucking mechanism of the harpsichord with individual hammers that *struck* the strings percussively instead.

In 1709, Cristofori built the first modern piano, the instrument that is the direct prototype of what we have today. It had a hinged hammer mechanism, an escapement (to allow the hammer to fall back away from the string when the key is released), and a damper for each string. In 1720, after over a decade of work and experimentation, he built his "new and improved" version, which also boasted knobs at each end of the keyboard, allowing the keyboard to be shifted to the left so that the hammer struck one or two strings instead of three—this gave the pianist even more dynamic control. Cristofori called this instrument a *gravicembalo col piano e forte*, a "harpsichord with soft and loud." This was soon abbreviated to *pianoforte*, and ultimately the *forte* was also dropped and the instrument became known simply as the piano.

This innovative instrument was not without its faults and drawbacks, however. First, it had only twenty-nine keys, a limitation that had to be extremely frustrating for composers and accomplished pianists. Second, the mechanism was noisy. The French historian Gerald Messadié wrote that "Listening to a perfectly restored pianoforte can be irritating for the 20th-century listener because of the clicking of the falling keys. Consequently many inventors endeavored to improve Cristofori's invention."

But even with its imperfections, Cristofori's invention revolutionized music and was responsible for one of those truly defining moments in the development of certain branches of the arts and sciences. Just as the printing press changed how the written word would be employed for the rest of history, so did Bartolommeo Cristofori's pianoforte change how music would be played and listened to for centuries to come.

After his patron Ferdinando de' Medici's death in 1713, Cristofori stayed in Florence and served the Grand Duke Cosimo III. In 1716 he was made custodian of the Medici collection of musical instruments, which included eighty-four pieces. In this collection there were seven harpsichords or spinet pianos of Cristofori's own construction. Cristofori continued to refine his instruments and seek improvements, and there are still keyboards of his design surviving today.

In New York's Metropolitan Museum of Art (in the Crosby Brown Collection of Musical Instruments), there is a Cristofori grand pianoforte that is believed to be the oldest surviving piano in existence. It has ivory knobs on each end of the keyboard that allow the keys to slide to the left to achieve an *una corda* (one-string) effect (a quieter tone). The concept of the damping foot pedal had not been conceived when this instrument was built in 1720.

Bartolommeo Cristofori died in Florence on January 27, 1731, at the age of seventy-five. Piano players the world over owe him a huge debt. Thanks to this Paduan's inspired genius, we possess the most versatile instrument in the whole realm of music.

48

Alessandro Manzoni
1785–1873

By their actions, my good fellow—men are known by their actions.

— ALESSANDRO MANZONIA
The Betrothed (chapter 7)

Along with Petrarch, Boccaccio, and (in modern times) Calvino, Alessandro Manzoni must be included as one of those handful of Italian writers who produced work of such excellence and importance that they defined a unique style and enormously influenced those who followed them (see chapters 55, 50, and 87).

Alessandro's Manzoni's "territory" was that of the modern novel: He claimed it decisively with his 1827 masterpiece, *Il Promesso Sposi (The Betrothed)* and in so doing, he also defined the modern Italian language as we know it today, as well as helping to form a unified Italy. Manzoni's stature was such that upon the first anniversary of his death, the great composer Giuseppe Verdi wrote his brilliant *Requiem* in Manzoni's honor.

Francis Haskell, in *The Italians*, discusses Manzoni and his achievement:

> Alessandro Manzoni—largely on the strength of one novel—has become celebrated in Italy as the greatest writer since the Renaissance. . . . In its final form his novel *The Betrothed* . . . constituted among other things a deliberate self-conscious attempt to write a masterpiece in a living Italian language that did not yet exist. . . . Manzoni had to go to Tuscany in order to master an idiom and a style which would be as expressive and intelligible in Milan as in Naples, in Venice as in Rome. His triumphant success in doing so earned him a natural place among the founders of united Italy. . . . No great novel relies more on the most basic of all fictional plots: two poor, virtuous young people—Renzo and Lucia—are in love and want to get married. After meeting every conceivable obstacle they eventually manage to do so. Against their love are set the intrigues and struggles for power of a ruthless and incompetent society which quite fails to live up to the noble and high-sounding forms and rituals that it uses to disguise its greed and ambitions. The contrast between ideals and reality provides Manzoni with an opportunity to display his sometimes sardonic humor to telling effect.

Haskell also notes that "*The Betrothed* is surpassed only by *War and Peace* in the wholly unpedantic and wholly unforced image of the past that it brings to life."

In one powerful scene from *The Betrothed*, which is set in the seventeenth century, Renzi searches Milan frantically for his beloved Lucia, who he fears has died in the devastating plague that has struck the city. During his search, he comes across a small camp in which abandoned infants are being cared for by nurses, as well as by some unlikely nursemaids:

> He arrived at length before a cracked and disjointed wooden partition, from within which this extraordinary sound proceeded; and peeping through a large aperture between two boards, he beheld an enclosure scattered

throughout with little huts, and in there, as well as in the spaces of the small camp between the cabins, not the usual occupants of an infirmary, but infants, lying upon little beds, pillows, sheets or cloths spread upon the ground, and nurses and other women busily attending them; and which above everything else attracted and engrossed his attentions, she-goats mingled with these, and acting as their coadjutrices: a hospital of innocents, such as the place and times could afford them. It was, I say, a novel sight, to behold some of these animals standing quietly over this or that infant, giving it suck, and another hastening at the cry of a child, as if endued with maternal feeling, and stopping by the side of the little claimant, and contriving to dispose itself over the infant, and bleating, and fidgeting, almost as if demanding someone to come to the assistance of both.

Alessandro Manzoni was born to noble parents on March 7, 1785, in Milan and was educated in Lugano, Milan, and Pavia. After he received his university degree in 1805, he joined his mother in Paris, where she was involved with a circle of rationalists and was living with her lover, Count Carlo Imbonati. Alessandro was greatly influenced by his mother's skeptical views on religion, and he soon left the Catholic church.

In 1808, at the age of twenty-three, Manzoni married Henriette Blondel. Two years later, he had a rebirth of his Catholic faith, and both he and his wife rejoined the church. His religious beliefs were paramount to him from this point on, and they greatly influenced his writings.

In 1827, at the age of forty-two, Manzoni published five *Sacred Hymns* (*Inni Sacri*). By this time, he had also written two historical plays, *Il Conte de Carmagnola* and *Adelchi*, and two poems, including *The Fifth of May* (*Cinque Maggio*), which was an ode to Napoleon.

In 1827, he also published his first version of *The Betrothed*, which he had begun in 1821. The book was very well received, but Manzoni was not pleased with the language of the novel. He spent the next decade completely rewriting it, using a pure Tuscan dialect. This revised version was published in 1840 and is the rendition read today.

A historical novel, a love story, and an adventure tale rolled into one, *The Betrothed* enthralled readers with its meticulous detail and its insights into Italian life. It also solidly endorsed Roman

Catholic doctrine and thus won the approval of the Church. By the 1870s, more than 100 editions of the work had appeared. After Italy was unified in 1870, Manzoni was made a senator.

Manzoni died on May 22, 1873, at the age of eighty-eight. This poet laureate of Italian reunification, the man Verdi looked to as his idol, this dauntless advocate of Catholicism left behind an extraordinary legacy—the book he wrote and the great work of music his memory inspired.

49

Giuseppe Verdi

1813–1901

I do not hesitate at all to declare that this most recent Verdi work [is] the best, as regards novelty, knowledge and musical beauty. I say this to you honestly: I have no words to express the wonder that such a noble work aroused in me. . . . I am immensely pleased especially that people admire true beauty. From my heart, I congratulate the man who wrote it, who is justifiably renowned.

— ITALIAN CONDUCTOR ANGELO
MARIANI, in his August 15, 1852,
review of Verdi's *Rigoletto*
in the *Gazzetta Musicale di Milano*

Two days after Giuseppe Verdi died, the famed opera house of La Scala in Milan presented a musical program in the great composer's honor. The music performed in the legendary concert hall that day included overtures, choruses, preludes, duets, and quartets from Verdi's brilliant body of work, and the money raised went toward erecting a monument to Verdi to be raised in front of his estate, Casa di Riposo.

Such laudatory tributes are not unusual when a great man dies. The La Scala tribute on January 29, 1901, however, was especially glittering: The 200-member orchestra and chorus were conducted by famed Italian conductor Arturo Toscanini, and the role of the duke in Verdi's *Rigoletto* quartet was sung by the renowned tenor Enrico Caruso.

When Verdi had a stroke and became gravely ill in Milan in early 1901 at the age of eighty-seven, his deteriorating condition became a subject of national attention. The king and queen of Italy were sent hourly telegrams detailing his condition; and the hotel in which he was residing posted bulletins on a board next to its front door (some of which even specified his respiratory and heart rates). Verdi biographer Mary Jane Phillips-Matz summed up the reasons for this extraordinary public concern:

> Few heads of state have been tendered higher honours than Verdi, universally hailed as an artist, a model citizen, and a philanthropist. To the world, as to the nation he helped to found, he left an enduring legacy of music, charity, patriotism, honour, grace, and reason. He was and remains a mighty force for continuing good.

Giuseppe Fortunino Francesco Verdi was born in Roncole in northern Italy on October 10, 1813. (Even though Verdi repeatedly insisted that he was actually born on October 9, existing birth records confirm October 10 as his actual date of birth. As Phillips-Matz explains, regarding this discrepancy, "Verdi held to his own ways. He and history remained at odds on this point.")

Verdi's father was a grocer and tavern keeper and was too poor to give his son a proper education. But a local teacher and organist named Pietro Baistrocchi took a liking to young Peppino (as he was called by his family and friends) and agreed to teach him Latin, Italian, arithmetic, and music.

Phillips-Matz quotes recollections of the young Verdi by his Roncole neighbors:

> [Peppino was] quiet, all closed within himself, sober of face and gesture, a boy who kept apart from happy, loud gangs of companions, preferring rather to stay near his mother or alone in the house. There lingered about him an air of authority; and even when he was a boy, the other children pointed him out as someone different from the rest of them; and they admired him in a certain way.

The young Verdi seemed to have been an especially serious lad, and his musical abilities manifested at an early age, around six or seven, when the sound of any instrument mesmerized him. When Verdi was eighteen, he was sent to Milan in the hope that he might study at the Milan Conservatory of Music, but his application was rejected because he was too old. He spent three years in the city, however, studying under the composer Vincenzo Lavigna, whose own works had been produced at La Scala.

In 1836, at the age of twenty-three, Verdi returned home, married Margherita Barezzi, and became municipal music master of Bussetto, a large town near Roncole. The couple had two children, but between 1838 and 1840, Verdi's daughter, son, and wife all died. Neither historical records nor Verdi's own writings (letters, his autobiographical narrative, or the like) reveal what caused the death of his children. We do know, however, that his wife died from acute encephalitis shortly after the death of their children.

Verdi had begun to compose when he was around thirteen years old. He began with piano pieces and works for solo instruments. Here, from a 1913 collection of his letters, is Verdi's account of his early efforts:

> From my thirteenth to my eighteenth year ... I wrote a wide variety of music, marches by the hundred for the band, perhaps hundreds of little works to be played in church, in the theatre, and in private concerts; five or six concerti and variations for the piano, which I played myself in private concerts; many serenades, cantatas (arias, duets, many trios) and several religious compositions, of which I remember only a Stabat Mater.

One of Verdi's most notable early compositions was a new overture for Rossini's opera *The Barber of Seville.* As Verdi biographer George Martin explains, "To substitute an overture to an opera in 1828 was not the presumptuous thing it would be today. Then there was hardly a concept of a standard repertory with masterworks that could not be tampered with." Other early (pre-*Oberto*) Verdi works included a cantata in eight movements called *I deliri di Saul* (*The Madness of Saul*); and a piece for orchestra, tenor, and solo flute, based on the text of Psalm 70. On Sunday, November 17, 1839, Verdi's first opera, *Oberto*, premiered at Teatro alla Scala (La Scala) in Milan.

The opera had come into existence thanks to the support (both financial and artistic) of Verdi's father-in-law Papa Barezzi, and the efforts of Verdi's friend Pietro Massini, who gave him the *Oberto* libretto, written by Antonio Piazza. Even though *Oberto* was a popular and critical success, Verdi found himself mired in financial difficulties. His next work, the comic opera *Un Giorno di Regno* (written when Verdi was distraught over the death of his wife and children), was met with boos at La Scala. Only after the success of his next opera, the popular *Nabucco*, could Verdi become confident that his future works would be sought after and produced.

Over the next fifty years Verdi's career can be divided into three distinct parts:

- **The Early Works:** This period includes *Oberto* (1839); *Nabucco* (1842); *I Lombardi* (1843); *Ernani* (1844); *I due Foscari* (1844); *Giovanni d'Arco* (1845); *Alzira* (1845); *Attila* (1846); *Macbeth* (1847); *I masnadieri* (1847); *Jérusalem* (1847); *Il corsaro* (1848); *La battaglia di Legnano* (1849); *Luisa Miller* (1849); and *Stiffelio* (1850).

- **The Middle Years:** *Rigoletto* (1851); *Il trovatore* (1853); *La traviata* (1853); *I vespri siciliani* (1855); *Simon Boccanegra* (1857); *Aroldo* (1857); *Un ballo in maschera* (1859); *Inno delle nazioni* (1862); *La forza del destino* (1862); *Macbeth* (1865); *Don Carlo* (1867); *Aida* (1871); *Quartetto perarchi* (1873); and *Messa de Requiem* (1874).

- **The Final Works:** *Otello* (1887); *Falstaff* (1893); and *Quattro pezzi sacri* (1898).

Verdi was mercurial, intense, compelling, energetic, generous, lusty, and complex. He stimulated a nationalistic fervor with his music and after his death, opera never again had the epochal scope of his works. Verdi's letters show a man with a fiery and diverse mind who devoted his entire being to his music.

It is a daunting task to explain the enduring popularity of Verdi's work. One can look to the lyricism and the passion of Verdi's melodies; his focus on strong vocal lines and the moving expression of human emotions; the stirring and memorable orchestrations; but these do not succeed completely in illuminating his ongoing appeal. Verdi was unquestionably the greatest operatic composer who ever lived: Opera reached its zenith with his works. Perhaps the failure of subsequent composers to surpass his achievements is the simplest way of explaining his influence.

In 1897, following the death of his second wife, Giuseppina Strepponi, Verdi funded the construction of Casa di Riposo in Milan, a rest home for aged composers, singers, and musicians. His will directed that all royalties from the performances of his operas go to support the Casa. The home is still in operation today, housing one hundred musicians and supported almost entirely by the music of Verdi.

The following sonnet was written in 1846 by Andrea Maffei in honor of Verdi who, at the age of thirty-three, had become a national Italian idol, because of the patriotic feelings expressed in some of his work.

To Giuseppe Verdi, The Glory of Italy
New is the sweet, angelic magic [of your music];
New is the tender, pure melody . . .
You bring joys and delights to the soul . . .
Already you are the heart of Italian music.
You live and reign in every heart;
And when you interpret fiery emotions,
Because of you, new leafy fronds are woven . . .
What do you fear? You are at the Apex of Glory,
The words Verdi and Victory ring out together.

50

Boccaccio
(Giovanni Boccaccio)
1313–75

Neither relatives nor friends nor priests nor friars accompanied
the corpses to the grave, nor was the office of the dead
recited. . . . And no bells rang, and nobody wept no matter
what his loss because everyone expected death. . . . And people
said and believed, "This is the end of the world."
— AGNIOLO DI TURA OF SIENA
writing about the Black Death

173

If not for the persuasive powers of the great Italian writer Petrarch (see PETRARCH [55]), Giovanni Boccaccio would probably have destroyed the (handwritten) manuscript of his magnificent collection of stories, *The Decameron.* Petrarch understood that the previously worldly Boccaccio had undergone a major spiritual crisis during which he had decided to abandon secular concerns and devote his life to religion. His bawdy *Decameron* tales represented to Boccaccio a life he did not wish to be reminded of and, thus, he conceived the plan to sell his books and burn his writings. "What a strange procedure," Petrarch wrote to Boccaccio in a reproving letter, "to burn what you want to correct, so that nothing will be left to correct!" Petrarch also provided Boccaccio with a new focus: the study of ancient Greek and Latin classics. Boccaccio embraced Petrarch's suggestion with a passion and devoted himself to the preservation and dissemination of ancient Greek texts in the West.

Giovanni Boccaccio is generally considered to be the father of the psychological novel, the novella, and the short story, and his work was (and continues to be) a major influence on literature all over the world. His masterpiece, *The Decameron,* remains a classic over six hundred years after it was written.

The Decameron arose from one of the most horrible events in the history of Europe, the Black Death, an outbreak of bubonic plague that killed so many people so quickly that ravenous dogs were able to dig up the hastily buried bodies and feast on them. At the height of the plague in 1348, surrealistic scenes unfolded in Florence as families piled their dead on their doorsteps and mongrels roamed the streets carrying arms and legs in their mouths.

In the midst of this nightmare, Boccaccio conceived his *Decameron.* His premise for the work was an imagined colloquy involving ten healthy young men and women who retire to a villa two miles outside of Florence, hoping to avoid the plague. To occupy their time, they agree that each of them will tell one story a day during the ten days they plan to stay in the country. (An avid admirer of Dante, Boccaccio mirrored the hundred cantos of *The Divine Comedy.*)

The themes of the stories told during the "ten days" included courage; generosity; tragic love; escaping danger; the attainment of desires through ingenuity; and people who achieve happiness after misfortunes; and many have a blatant (and pioneering) feminist tone and slant.

The Decameron consists of one hundred *novelle* (stories), told by each of the ten people at the rate of one a day for ten days.

The collection begins with Boccaccio's Author's Preface:

> Human it is to have compassion for the unhappy, and a great deal is required of those who are happy, especially if they required comfort in the past, and managed to find it in others. Now, if any man ever had need of compassion or found it dear to him, or received comfort from it, I am that man; for, from my earliest youth until the present time, I have been inflamed beyond all measure with a most exalted and noble love, perhaps too exalted and noble for my lowly station.

The structure of *The Decameron* (as detailed by Boccaccio authorities Mark Musa and Peter E. Bondanella in their 1977 translation) is as follows:

- **Author's Preface and Introduction:** The narrator addresses his reader directly, explains the origins of his novelle, introduces his ten storytellers (Pampinea, Filomena, Neifile, Filostrato, Fiammetta, Elisa, Dioneo, Lauretta, Emilia, and Panfilo), and describes the Black Plague of 1348 in Florence. Each of the storytellers will tell a story on each of ten days of storytelling, and each storyteller (except Dioneo) must tell a story which follows a topic determined by the king or queen of the previous day.

- **Day I:** Subjects freely chosen (the reign of Pampinea).

- **Day II:** Stories about those who attain a state of unexpected happiness after a period of misfortune (the reign of Filomena).

- **Day III:** Stories about people who have attained difficult goals or who have recovered something previously lost (the reign of Neifile).

- **Day IV, Prologue:** The narrator defends himself from the criticism that greeted the stories of the first three days of storytelling.

- **Day IV:** Love stories with unhappy endings (the reign of Filostrata).

- **Day V:** Love stories which end happily after a period of misfortune (the reign of Fiammetta).

- **Day VI:** Stories about how intelligence helps to avoid danger, ridicule, or discomfort (the reign of Elisa).

- **Day VII:** Stories about tricks played by wives on their husbands (the reign of Dioneo).

- **Day VIII:** Stories about tricks played by both men and women on each other (the reign of Lauretta).

- **Day IX:** Subjects freely chosen (the reign of Emilia).

- **Day X:** Stories about those who have performed generous deeds and who have acquired fame in so doing (the reign of Panfilo).

- **Author's Conclusion:** The narrator defends the tone of his work against those critics who view it as obscene or others who claim the stories are sometimes too long, as well as against those who accuse him of slandering churchmen or betraying his scholarly inclinations by composing such a frivolous work as *The Decameron*.

Boccaccio was born in Paris, France, in 1313. He was born out of wedlock yet was welcomed warmly into his father's home. (His stepmother was related to Beatrice, Dante Alighieri's eternal love, and it is likely that Boccaccio later used her as his source when he wrote his biography of Dante.) Boccaccio reluctantly studied banking and law in Naples from about the age of fifteen until his father's banking firm went bankrupt in 1340. Freed of his business responsibilities, he returned to Florence and passionately pursued his literary career.

Prior to the publication of his *Decameron*, Boccaccio produced a number of impressive literary works. Notable achievements included the short poem "La caccia di Diana" ("Diana's Hunt"); the five-volume prose work *Il ficolo* (*The Love Afflicted*); and the poem "Il filostrato" ("The Love Struck"), which was told in eight-line rhymed stanzas (octava rima) and which recounted the love story of Troilus and Criseida. Another important pre-*Decameron* work was "Il ninfale d'Ameto" ("Ameto's Story of the Nymphs"), which was rendered in a combination of prose and three-line stanzas (terza rima).

After he completed *The Decameron*, Boccaccio wrote primarily in Latin. His important works in Latin include the comprehensive *De genealogia deorum gentilium* (*On the Genealogy of the Gods of the Gentiles*, 1350); *De Claribus Mulieribus* (*Concerning Famous Women*, 1360–74); *De Casibus virorum illustrium* ("On the Fates of Famous Men," 1355–74); and *Vita di Dante Alighieri* or *Trattatello in laude di Dante* ("Little Tractate in Praise of Dante," 1354–55).

Historian Will Durant stated that "*The Decameron* remains one of the masterpieces of world literature. . . . It is perfectly constructed—superior in this respect to *The Canterbury Tales.* Its prose set a standard that Italian literature has never surpassed. . . . every European language translated it . . . Chaucer and Shakespeare took leaves from it admiringly."

Giovanni Boccaccio died four days before Christmas in 1375 in Certaldo, Tuscany (Italy), leaving behind, among all of his brilliant writings, one classic work that would influence literature and writers for centuries to come.

51

Filippo Brunelleschi
1377–1446

How charming a thing is this perspective! Ah, if I could only
get you to understand its delights!
— RENAISSANCE PAINTER PAOLO UCCELLO, to his wife

Architecture in general is frozen music.
— FRIEDRICH VON SCHELLING
Philosophie der Kunst

One of the most distinctive aspects of ancient Egyptian art is its
relentless two-dimensionality: Figures are usually all the same size,
regardless of their position in the composition. The Egyptians did
not employ perspective, the technique of rendering three-dimensional objects in proper proportion relative to their distance from
the foreground. Contemporary viewers often find this unsettling,

because they are accustomed to paintings and drawings that make them feel that they are viewing a scene in the real, three-dimensional world. Plato actually defended the stilted Egyptian style of art for *not* using perspective. Even those who love Egyptian art would be unlikely to endorse Plato's condemnation of perspective as too "innovative" or echo his view that "no painter or artist is allowed to . . . leave the traditional forms and invent new ones."

Even though a rudimentary form of perspective was used by the ancient Greeks on vases as far back as the fifth century B.C., the use of this technique was abandoned during the Middle Ages. Its reintroduction was due to the insight and genius of the subject of this chapter, Florentine architect and engineer Filippo Brunelleschi. Through experimentation and study, Brunelleschi identified the phenomenon of the "vanishing point," the point at which parallel lines appear to meet at the horizon. He put this theory to work in 1420, creating two panels that depicted views of Florence, with the streets and buildings receding from the foreground exactly as the eye would perceive them. This was the basis for further studies in perspective made by the architect Alberti and the artists Donatello, Masaccio, Ucello, and Piero della Francesca.

Brunelleschi was born in Florence in 1377, the son of a respected notary. He spent his early years learning goldsmithing and sculpting, and in 1401, he competed with several other sculptors to create bronze panels for the doors of the Florence Baptistery. Brunelleschi lost the competition to Lorenzo Ghiberti; even though his sample panel, *The Sacrifice of Isaac,* was a brilliant accomplishment, he was so shaken by losing that he essentially abandoned sculpture from that point on and concentrated instead on architecture. (According to art historian Giorgio Vasari, Ghiberti was chosen over Brunelleschi because Ghiberti's piece was "well designed and the composition excellent, the figures being slender and graceful, the pose admirable and so beautifully finished that it did not look as if it had been cast and polished, but rather as if it had been created by a breath.")

With his friend and fellow sculptor Donatello, Brunelleschi traveled to Rome, where the two artists intently studied the ancient buildings, often drawing them to scale on notepads. Of this trip, Brunelleschi's biographer Antonio Manetti wrote that "Neither was bothered by family cares and worries because neither had a wife or children there or elsewhere. . . . Neither was much concerned with how he ate, drank, lived or dressed himself; provided he could satisfy himself with these things to see and measure." Brunelleschi's diligence and eagerness to absorb all he could from the buildings of the Eternal City served him well, as Daniel Boorstin has confirmed in his book *The Creators*:

> From Rome Brunelleschi brought back to Florence the vocabulary and the grandeur of the Roman style with some of the secrets of Roman building technology, and gave them new life. Just as Dante had translated Christian mythology from Latin into the Italian vernacular, and as Giotto had translated painting from the Byzantine ("Greek") into the Latin ("Roman"), Brunelleschi revived a Tuscan order in architecture. He aimed to prove that "the years between" were not a gulf but only an interruption, as he adapted the grandiose Roman forms to Florentine buildings on a smaller scale with a new grace and light elegance.

Brunelleschi's first major architectural achievement was designing and building Florence's Church of San Lorenzo, completed in 1428 after seven years of construction. In this building, Brunelleschi carefully employed the principles of perspective in proportioning the structural elements and interior spaces.

But his greatest accomplishment, and the feat for which he is best known, was designing the huge, double-shell dome for the uncompleted Florence cathedral of Santa Maria del Fiore, something no one thought was possible due to the building's enormous size. Brunelleschi's task was daunting: His dome would have to be 138 1/2 feet wide, 133 feet high, extend 300 feet from the ground to its peak, and reach a total height of 351 feet.

In 1420, construction of the dome began. The usual technique for building a dome was to use a wooden framework that would support the stones as they were put into place. However, in this case there were no trees tall enough to serve as the centering supports. Brunelleschi solved the problem by building two separate domed shells, each of which reduced the weight of the other. According to Boorstin, "Separate brickwork was laid for the inner and the outer domes as the work proceeded, reducing the thickness of each as the dome went up. The result was a cellular system, with an increasing space between the layers till the space between the layers became six feet at the crown." This was unexplored architectural territory, and the old rules—and old tools—simply would not do. Brunelleschi actually invented and built innovative cranes and derricks for the construction of his revolutionary new dome.

Brunelleschi's dome was completed in 1436, when the great architect was fifty-nine. It still lacked the lantern that was designed to hang from the open eye at the top, but Brunelleschi did not live to see that final element put in place. He died in Florence on April 15, 1446, at the age of sixty-nine. Appropriately, he was buried in the Florence Cathedral.

Leon Battista Alberti
1 4 0 4 – 7 2

Men can do all things if they will.
—LEONE BATTISTA ALBERTI

"Nothing pleases me so much as mathematical investiga-
tions and demonstrations, especially when I can turn
them to some useful practice."
—A CHARACTER FROM ONE OF ALBERTI'S DIALOGUES

The archetypal Renaissance man, Leone Battista Alberti, possessed an enormous range of talents, skills, and personal graces, as
Will Durant notes in *The Renaissance*:

> He was both handsome and strong; excelled in all bodily
> exercises; could, with feet tied, leap over a standing man;

could, in the great cathedral, throw a coin far up to ring against the vault; amused himself by taming wild horses and climbing mountains. He was a good singer, an eminent organist, a charming conversationalist, an eloquent orator, a man of alert but sober intelligence, a gentleman of refinement and courtesy.... Like Leonardo half a century later, Alberti was a master, or at least a skilled practitioner, in a dozen fields—mathematics, mechanics, architecture, sculpture, painting, music, poetry, drama, philosophy, civil and canon law.

As a writer, Alberti tackled a breathtaking range of topics, including the following:

- **Family life:** *Della famiglia* (*On the Family*); begun in Rome in 1432 when he was twenty-eight, this was the first of a series of moral tracts written in the form of dialogues in which Alberti attempted to bring the wisdom of the ancient philosophers to his contemporaries.

- **Painting:** *Della pittura* (*On Painting*); written in 1436, this three-volume work explained for the first time how to use the vanishing point and other techniques of the science of perspective (developed by Brunelleschi) to draw three-dimensional objects on two-dimensional surfaces. *On Painting* revolutionized Renaissance painting and influenced everyone who read it, including Leonardo da Vinci.

- **Architecture:** *De re aedificatoria* (*Ten Books of Architecture*), published in 1485; this massive and seminal work became known as the bible of Renaissance architecture and is regarded as the first printed book on architecture.

- **Lorenzo de' Medici:** *De iciarchia* (*On the Man of Excellence and the Ruler of His Family*); published in 1468, this admiring portrait of the great patron of the arts, written in the form of a dialogue, also elucidates of Alberti's own philosophy.

In *Art History*, Marilyn Stokstad notes that Alberti and his work defined an era:

Alberti's various writings present the first coherent exposition of early Italian Renaissance aesthetic theory, including the Italian mathematical perspective system credited to Brunelleschi and ideal proportions of the human body derived from classical art. With Alberti began the gradual change in the status of the architect from a hands-on builder—and thus manual laborer—to an intellectual expected to know philosophy, history, and the classics as well as mathematics and engineering.

In addition to his influence on painters, architects, sculptors, and writers of the fifteenth century, Alberti was also an important adviser to Cosimo de' Medici (see THE MEDICIS [34]) and significantly for the history of the New World, to Paolo Toscanelli. Toscanelli is the cartographer who supplied Christopher Columbus with the maps he needed for his first voyage in search of the sea route to Asia. It is believed that Alberti assisted Toscanelli with the preparations of these maps and that he also worked with Toscanelli on his astronomical studies.

Leone Battista Alberti was born on February 14, 1404, in Genoa, Italy, to a wealthy family that gave him the best that money could buy. His family had moved to Genoa from their native Florence because of political differences with Florence's ruling Albizzi family, who had arranged for the explusion of these opponents. When Leone Battista was ten, his family sent him to a boarding school in Padua, where he excelled at his studies in a wide range of subjects. When he was twenty, Alberti wrote a comedy in Latin that he pretended was the long-lost work of a great ancient Roman poet. This misconception endured (throughout Alberti's life and beyond) and in 1588, the Aldine Press of Aldo Manuzio (see chapter 36) was still publishing the play as a genuine work of antiquity.

In his later years, Alberti also invented the cipher wheel, a device for encrypting text into an undecipherable code, thereby establishing himself as a pioneer in the science of cryptography.

From the years 1445 through 1470, Alberti focused his architectural genius on the designing of magnificent buildings that still stand today. His most important works include the Palazzo Rucellai in Florence, begun in 1452, a building that art historian Horst Janson declares "[applies] a classical system of articulation to the exterior of a non-classical structure"; the church of San Francesco in Rimini, begun in 1451; part of the facade of Santa Maria Novella in Florence, begun in 1458; and the church of San Andrea in Mantua, completed in 1470.

Alberti lived a life wholly dedicated to ideas and art. Though he moved in the circles of the elite and his intimates included the Medicis, luminaries such as Pope Nicholas V, Donatello,

Brunelleschi, and Toscanelli, Alberti took holy orders and apparently lived a totally celibate life. He died in Rome on April 25, 1472, at the age of sixty-eight. Vasari tells us "he passed away to a better life, content and tranquil, leaving behind him a most honorable reputation."

53

Maria Montessori
1870–1952

Humanity shows itself in all its intellectual splendour during
this tender age as the sun shows itself at dawn, and the flower
in the first unfolding of the petals; and we must respect reli-
giously, reverently, these first indications of individuality. If any
educational act is to be efficacious, it will be only that which
tends to help toward the complete unfolding of this life. To be
thus helpful it is necessary rigorously to avoid the arrest of
spontaneous movements and the imposition of arbitrary tasks.
It is, of course, understood that here we do not speak of useless
or dangerous acts, for these must be suppressed, destroyed.
— MARIA MONTESSORI
The Montessori Method

The human being proves to have a fundamental need for order from the very first years of his life. He is eager to live in orderly surroundings, and he disciplines himself when he can act freely and follow the dictates of his nature. It is not the adult who teaches him this, for the adult has no notion of this sort of discipline, because his development has been constrained. We should remember what the Bible says, "Great things are found among men, kings and riches, but something never seen is inner discipline." This is the cause of the fall of many civilizations.

> — MARIA MONTESSORI, at a lecture given at the International School of Philosophy on Tuesday, December 28, 1937

In the afterword to her authorized 1976 biography of Italian educator Maria Montessori, Rita Kramer makes the case that "[Montessori] passes the test for the real innovator—many of her ideas have become part of our common language of discourse about the subject of educating the young." Kramer then presents "a random list of ideas, techniques, and objects familiar to everyone in the field of childhood education today, all of which go back to Montessori's work at the start of the century, all of which she either invented or used in a new way."

This list includes:

- The idea that children learn through play. The acceptance of this concept is evident today in the wide variety of "educational" toys available.

- The idea that education should begin well before kindergarten or first grade. Hence the popularity of preschools and nursery schools today for children as young as two or three.

- The idea that rigidly disciplining young children and restricting their activity while in school does more harm than good, and the belief that if young children are given interesting and stimulating things to do, they will unknowingly impose discipline upon themselves, thereby rendering a self-defined order to the classroom.

- The idea of age-appropriate learning programs, such as "reading readiness."

- The idea that parents should be intimately involved in their children's education and acknowledge that the school is not a disconnected institution but rather a vital part of the community, like the fire department, the police department, and the seats of municipal government.

Maria Montessori was born in Chiaraville, Italy, in the province of Ancona, on August 31, 1870. Her family moved to Rome when she was five because her father was transferred there to work as an accountant. In Rome, Maria attended the traditional Italian grade school until she was thirteen, when she then broke tradition by entering a technical school, the Regia Scuolo Tecnico Michelangelo Buonarotti. She graduated from the Michelangelo school when she was sixteen and entered the Regio Instituto Tecnico Leonard da Vinci, which she attended until 1890.

While studying at the da Vinci school, she announced her intention to become an engineer, even though at the time the only acceptable role for a woman was to become a teacher. As Kramer notes, "There is a splendid irony in the adolescent Maria's adamant refusal even to consider teaching as her future career." Her father was stunned by her decision, but his independent-minded daughter had even more surprises in store. As Maria neared graduation, she informed her parents that she had changed her mind about becoming an engineer. She now wanted to go to medical school and study to become a doctor. No woman in Italy had ever before attended medical school. Maria Montessori was the first.

Montessori completed two years of premed studies at the University of Rome and in 1892 enrolled in the School of Medicine. She completed the program in 1896 (her final thesis was "A Clinical Contribution to the Study of Delusions of Persecution") and graduated with honors as a doctor of medicine and surgery and began to work as a child psychiatrist.

In 1907, after several years of treating and studying both healthy and retarded children, Montessori opened a school called Casa dei Bambini—The Children's House—the first structured institution established to implement the specific educational ideas Montessori had been developing. According to Kramer, "In 1907 [her ideas and techniques] were revolutionary, and the four- and five-year-olds who learned to write in less than two months and to read in a matter of days after that astonished the world."

Montessori's system of education involved teaching the child's senses as well as the mind; using carefully designed teaching materials that included toys, tools, and household utensils; equipping the classroom with child-sized furniture; and having children care for animals to teach responsibility and discover the wonders of nature. Montessori collected her ideas and thoughts into a book published in Italy as *Il Metodo*. Montessori's ideas soon became the rage in Europe and were officially adopted by schools in Italy and Switzerland.

In 1912, Montessori traveled to the United States, where her book appeared in an English translation as *The Montessori Method*. The first Montessori school in the United States was opened in Tarrytown, New York, shortly thereafter. Montessori's ideas eventually created opposition, as many educators and parents were disturbed by her insistence on free-form classes instead of the traditional discipline imposed by the teacher. After suffering a decline during the 1930s and 1940s, the Montessori method had a rebirth in the United States during the 1950s. After the American Montessori Society was formed in 1960, the movement continued to grow, and Montessori schools proliferated.

Montessori never married, although she did have a son, Mario, out of wedlock when she was eighteen. (She publicly acknowledged Mario only in her will.) She died of a cerebral hemorrhage on May 6, 1952, in Noordwijk aan Zee, Holland. She was buried there because she had always said she wanted to be interred wherever she died.

Maria Montessori's educational practices are still widely used today throughout the United States and the rest of the world. For her pioneering efforts and feminist attitudes, as well as for the groundbreaking educational system she conceived and established, Maria Montessori ranks as one of the most influential Italians of all time.

54

Boethius

c. 480–524

Nam in omni adversitate fortunae infelicissimum genus est infortunii, fuisse felicem.

For in every ill-turn of fortune the most unhappy sort of misfortune is to have been happy.
— BOETHIUS
The Consolation of Philosophy

Boethius is included in *The Italian 100* because of his development of the first liberal arts curriculum; the massive impact of his writings (especially *The Consolation of Philosophy*) on the Middle

Ages; and the contributions he made to the arts and sciences of mathematics, music, and logic.

Anicius Manlius Severinus Boethius was born in Rome around the year 480 into a prominent aristocratic family. His father, a Roman consul, died when he was seven, and he was sent to live with a friend of his father's, Symmachus, who taught the youngster Greek philosophy and the liberal arts. Boethius, who later wed Symmachus's daughter, was an exceptional student and grew to be an erudite man.

Boethius's earliest writings (which were dedicated to his friend and guardian Symmachus) established the foundation for a traditional liberal arts education. He coined the term *Quadrivium* to describe a program of learning that focused on arithmetic, music, geometry, and astronomy (four disciplines that all have "mathematical" rudiments). Boethius's *Quadrivium* offered a detailed, four-part explication of the suggested disciplines. He wrote introductions to each section and then provided a translation of a classic text on the subject:

- **Arithmetic:** *De arithmetica*, by Nicomachus

- **Geometry:** *Elements*, by Euclid

- **Astronomy:** *Almagest*, by Ptolemy

- **Music:** *De musica*, by Nicomachus and *Harmonics*, by Ptolemy

During the Renaissance, the *Quadrivium* was joined to the *Trivium*—the arts of grammar, rhetoric, and logic—to form the seven liberal arts, the course of study that was said to constitute a proper education. Only two of Boethius's works from the *Quadrivium* survived: his *De institutione arithmetica* and *De institutione musica*.

In 510, Boethius became *magister officium* to Theodoric the Great, ruler of Italy. However, Boethius fell from favor in 522 when he passionately defended a fellow official named Albinus, who had been charged with treason. As a result, Boethius was himself charged with treason and imprisoned in a tower in Pavia, near Milan. Boethius used this period of captivity to write his classic *The Consolation of Philosophy*.

Daniel Boorstin has described the influences that contributed to Boethius's new "vision," and explains how they defined the vision that underlay *The Consolation of Philosophy*:

It was Boethius's fatal fall from royal favor, in the very

model of an Aristotelian tragic hero, that made him creator of the solacing classic of later centuries. Personal disaster, the isolation of prison, and separation from his books would stir a new vision all his own. And he managed to transform the subtleties of Plato and Aristotle into a popular philosophy. Boethius's personal tragedy was a symptom of the uncertainties of the age, the rivalries between the Eastern and the Western empires. . . . The imprisonment that provided his unwelcome sabbatical from official duties forced Boethius to concentrate on questions of fate and destiny. And his enduring work, *The Consolation of Philosophy*, was the creation of these last two miserable years of Boethius's life.

One of the most appealing elements of *The Consolation of Philosophy* was Boethius's completely reasonable answer to a problem that had perplexed the faithful for centuries: If God is all-powerful and knows everything, then he must know everyone's future; but if this is so, then how can humans have free will? Boethius's clever and inspiring solution to this conundrum lay in his belief that man and God perceive time differently. Using the goddess Philosophy as his narrator, Boethius assured his readers that the eternal God—a "judge who sees all things"—is able to "[embrace] the whole of everlasting life in one simultaneous present." Boethius explained:

> Whatever lives in time exists in the present and progresses from the past to the future, and there is nothing set in time which can embrace simultaneously the whole extent of its life: it is in the position of not yet possessing tomorrow when it has already lost yesterday. In this life of today you do not live more fully than in that fleeting and transitory moment.

Boethius's thesis was essentially a reaffirmation of the Platonian view that the ultimate reality consisted of absolutes, eternal and unchanging Ideas or Forms, and that all earthly objects are merely lesser parts of the *truly real* Forms. In his *Consolation*, Boethius also emphasized that reason and logic play major roles in the way man must deal with fate, thus once more deferring to the ancients—in this case, Aristotle and his empiricism—and wholeheartedly embracing logic in a quest to understand universal absolutes.

In 524, Boethius was sentenced to death without benefit of trial and was brutally executed by his captors. His writings lived on long after his violent death and were instrumental in transmitting Greek philosophy to the thinkers of the Middle Ages. Along with the Vulgate Bible, Boethius's writings were the most popular texts among medieval scholars; his treatise on ancient music, *De musica*, influenced scholars and musicologists for centuries. One can only wonder about the additional influence this brilliant thinker could have exerted on Western culture if he had not been wrongfully executed at the relatively early age of forty-four.

55

Petrarch
(Francesco Petrarca)
1304–74

Five great enemies to peace inhabit with us: viz., avarice, ambition, envy, anger and pride. If those enemies were to be banished, we should infallibly enjoy perpetual peace.

—PETRARCH

Be reasonable. I know of many who have attained the highest saintliness without literary culture; I don't know of any who were excluded from sanctity by culture. . . . All good men have the same goal, but there are numberless ways thither, and much variety for the pilgrim . . . the way of knowledge is certainly more glorious, illumined and lofty. Give me an example of a saint who arose from the mass of the unlettered, and I will match him with a greater saint of the other sort.

—PETRARCH, advice to Boccaccio after Boccaccio
decided to burn his masterpiece *The Decameron* and
sell his library after a frightening religious experience

Francesco Petrarca (now known in the English-speaking world simply as Petrarch) was a Renaissance writer, scholar, and poet who gave powerful impetus to the philosophical school known as Humanism, a secularly focused doctrine that has thrived for over six hundred years. Petrarch's colleague Dante Alighieri's *Divine Comedy* may have been "Thomas Aquinas set to music," but Petrarch was clearly, as described by historian Daniel Boorstin, "the lodestar of Renaissance humanism" and the defining voice of the fourteenth century.

Petrarch was born in Arezzo, Italy, on July 20, 1304. The Petrarch family home, Casa Petrarca, still stands just south of Arezzo's famous hilltop Duomo in the great poet's hometown. In 1312, when Francesco was eight years old, he and his family moved to Avignon, France. Four years later, he began studying the law in Montpelier, France; at sixteen, he returned to Italy with his brother Gherardo and attended the University of Bologna. Petrarch hated the law and admitted to possessing "an unquenchable thirst for literature." He once wrote, "There is no lighter burden, nor more agreeable, than a pen. . . . As there is none among earthly delights more noble than literature, so there is none more lasting, none gentler or more faithful; none that accompanies its possessor through the vicissitudes of life at so small a cost of effort or anxiety."

After the death of his domineering father in 1326, Petrarch finally abandoned his legal studies and returned to Avignon, where he lived with Cardinal Colonna and his family. On Good Friday, April 6, 1327, Petrarch first saw Laura in church. He fell passionately in love with this young woman and wrote a magnificent series of poems in her honor called the *Canzoniere* (*Songbook*), a work that would place him high atop the roster of authentic Italian literary geniuses. Among his greatest achievements in the *Canzoniere* were his perfection of the sonnet form and his portrayal of Laura as a flesh-and-blood woman rather than one of the idealized female figures common in medieval romances. Petrarch's stature as a poet was recognized officially in 1341, when he was named Poet Laureate at Rome.

To this day, no scholar has been able to identify precisely who Petrarch's Laura actually was. All that is known of her life is contained in the words written by Petrarch in his edition of Virgil, now housed in the Ambrosian Library in Milan:

Laura, who was distinguished by her virtues, and widely

celebrated by my songs, first appeared to my eyes . . . in the year of Our Lord 1327, on the sixth day of April, at the first hour, in the church of Santa Clara at Avignon. In the same city, in the same month, on the same sixth day, at the same first hour, in the year 1348, that light was taken from our day.

Laura was a victim of the Black Death, as was Petrarch's patron, Cardinal Colonna. On May 19, 1348, writing from Parma, the doubly bereaved Petrarch wrote a chilling and elegiac letter to his brother Gherardo, the only survivor in a convent where thirty-five religious had lived.

> My brother! My brother! alas what shall I say? Whither shall I turn? On all sides is sorrow, everywhere is fear. I would that I had never been born, or, at least had died before these times. How will posterity believe that there has been a time, without lightnings of heaven or fires of earth, without wars or other visible slaughter, not this or that part of the earth, but well nigh the whole globe has remained without inhabitants? When before has it been seen that houses are left vacant, cities deserted, fields are too small for the dead, and a fearful and universal solitude over the whole earth?

In addition to the *Canzoniere,* Petrarch's major works include *Africa* (about the Second Punic War); a collection of biographical profiles called *Illustrious Men;* a series of imaginary dialogues with St. Augustine called *My Secret;* a poem about the migration of the soul to Heaven called *Triumphs;* and a collection of letters. He also devoted himself to classical learning and ancient manuscripts: In 1345, he unearthed a priceless cache of letters written by the great Roman orator Cicero.

In 1353, Petrarch returned to Italy. During the last years of his life, he lived quietly in Padua; despite his great fame, it is said that his cat was his principal companion.

The great poet and philosopher died in Arqua, Italy, on July 19, 1374. His beloved feline was immediately put to death and mummified. Petrarch's admirers then buried the cat's remains in a small crypt that was decorated with a handsome marble cat. The tomb bore the inscription "second only to Laura." According to legend, this inscription was written by Petrarch himself.

56

LEVRIDICE
COMPOSTA IN
MVSICA
In Stile Rappreſentatiuo da
GIVLIO CACCINI
detto Romano.

Giulio Caccini
c. 1545–c. 1618

Le nuove musiche was followed by a large number of similar collections of monodic songs by other composers, and to this day
no historical anthology of music is without at least one piece by
[Giulio] Caccini.

—Grove's Dictionary of Music and Musicians

Though far from a household name even among music lovers,
Giulio Caccini merits inclusion in *The Italian 100*. He is credited
with the creation of a completely new vocal singing style, a style that
employs the use of the *basso continuo*, a bass part that consists of a
succession of bass notes with figures that indicate the required

chords to accompany the solo melody. This arrangement is also known as figured bass and has endured to this day in the songs of composers ranging from Schumann and Schubert to Elton John and Marvin Hamlisch.

Caccini was the first composer and teacher to move away from the Flemish emphasis on intricate counterpoint and vocal elaboration, and his innovative compositions were an enormous step forward in the development of the opera, oratorio, and cantata, as well as allowing the consummate realization of the musical style known as Baroque. He introduced his new singing style in a book of songs published in 1602 called, appropriately, *Le Nuove Musiche* (*The New Music*). The musicologist John Wehenham, in *Classical Music and Its Origins*, explains Caccini's contribution:

> [Giovanni de'] Bardi and [Vincenzo] Galilei [father of Galileo] both tried their hands at writing solo songs intended to recreate, in modern terms, the power of Ancient Greek music; but it was Caccini, the experienced virtuoso singer, who made the decisive breakthrough by adopting for his solo songs the technique of *basso continuo*. By restricting the accompaniment of his songs to a simple chordal framework, instead of the elaborate counterpoint typical of songs arranged from polyphonic madrigals, Caccini allowed the singer the rhythmic freedom to declaim the text in a rhetorical manner and to use all the artifices of the virtuoso singer—*rubato*, different methods of vocal attack, *crescendo* and *diminuendo*—to dramatize the emotions suggested by the text. The melodic outlines of his songs, though lyrical in nature, were shaped to support just such a rhetorical manner of delivery.
>
> Caccini also sought to curb what he saw as excesses in the style and quantity of ornamentation customarily added to their songs by professional singers. To this end he wrote out the ornamentation that he considered appropriate to his songs, limiting its use to accented syllables in the text, so that the sense of the text would not be obscured.

Giulio Caccini was born in either Rome or Tivoli, sometime around the year 1545. In addition to the early acclaim he received for his singing, he also played the lute, the viol, and the harp. As an adolescent he studied in Rome under Giovanni Animuccia. When he was in his teens he was taken under the sponsorship of Cosimi de' Medici and brought to Florence to study with Scipione delle Palle. Caccini first sang for the Medici court in 1579, when he was thirty-four years old. He sang at the wedding of Francesco de' Medici, performing a song by Piero Strozzi. His voice at this point in his career was described as sweet and smooth, and court records indicate that he was already famous for his vocal talents throughout Florence.

During the decade from 1575 through 1585, Caccini studied with a group of musicians and scholars known as the Camerata. During this period he perfected his views on singing and worked on the theories that would ultimately become the benchmark for vocalists and composers of songs. In addition to his own writing and composing, Caccini also worked with some of the great composers of the period.

In 1600, at the age of fifty-five, Caccini wrote the music for what is now believed to be the first true opera still extant, Jacopo Peri's *Euridice,* a work that paved the way for the development of the modern opera by CLAUDIO MONTEVERDI [57]. *Euridice* premiered in Florence and aroused great controversy because of the intellectual and cultural rivalries that existed among the courts of northern Italy. Whenman notes that "Caccini rushed his own setting of the opera into print late in 1600, prefacing it with the claim that he had been the first to compose in the new style." Though his rivals may have disputed this claim, Giulio Caccini did in fact change the way songs were written and the way songs were sung, and he ushered in an era replete with marvelous musical forms still being performed today.

It should also be noted that other members of Caccini's family were involved in music performance and composition. Francesca Caccini, Giulio's eldest daughter, and Settima Caccini, his youngest daughter, are both remembered for their compositions. Francesca collaborated with the great Michelangelo Buonarroti during the early 1600s, writing music to accompany the artist's poems. Settima, in addition to composing, performed in works by Monteverdi and others.

Caccini died in Florence sometime in early December of 1618. (Historical records are vague as to the cause of his demise.) He was buried in that city on December 10.

Giulio Caccini was one of the most innovative minds in the development and fulfillment of the tenets of modern Western music.

57

Claudio Monteverdi
1567–1643

No opera plot can be sensible, for in sensible situations people do not sing. An opera plot must be, in both senses of the word, a melodrama.

—W. H. Auden

Claudio Monteverdi is universally considered to be the father of the modern opera. His large-scale dramatic works became the models for the operas that followed and also proved that he was opera's first true musical genius.

Monteverdi was born in Cremona, Italy, sometime in May

1567. (We don't know the exact date of his birth, but there are records showing that he was baptized on May 15. Less then a hundred years later, Cremona would also serve as the birthplace of another Italian musical luminary, the great violin maker ANTONIO STRADIVARI [72].

As a child, Monteverdi studied with Marcantonio Ingegneri, the director of music at the nearby Cremona Cathedral. Ingegneri was a prominent local musician who had published sacred music and madrigals that were popular but not particularly new or innovative. Monteverdi learned much from Ingegneri, however. While still in his teens he published several books of his own compositions, mainly religious madrigals and canzonettas (part-songs resembling the madrigal but less elaborate). This music was disseminated by a respected publisher in Venice and brought early acclaim and respect to the youthful composer. Among the best-known early Monteverdi madrigals was his setting of the poem "Behold the Murmuring Sea," by Torquato Tasso.

Though Monteverdi gave birth to modern opera, credit for the first true opera (a staged work that tells a story in one fluid dramatic musical presentation) belongs to another Italian composer, Jacopo Peri, whose *Dafne* was performed in Florence in 1597. The libretto of this work (written by the poet Ottavio Rinuccini) survives, but only the prologue and one aria of the music are still extant. In 1600, Peri composed a second opera, *Euridice*, which was performed to celebrate the wedding of King Henry IV to Marie de' Medici. The musical score for *Euridice* does survive; along with *Orfeo*, it prepared the way for Monteverdi's advancement of the operatic form.

Monteverdi's musical compositions were quite advanced for his time. He used dissonance and unusual melodic constructions in ways that were quite unfamiliar to the sixteenth-century ear. For this reason, a Bolognese critic named Giovanni Artusi published several scathing attacks, accusing Monteverdi of sundry offenses against the "rules" of musical composition. But Artusi's tirades served only to enhance the public's interest in the composer and his work. At this point, Monteverdi most likely obtained a copy of Peri's score to *Euridice* and that—combined with an often furious rivalry between the courts of northern Italy—appears to have acted as an artistic catalyst. Soon after, Monteverdi was able to synthesize all the elements of his varied influences and create *Orfeo*, now considered the first modern opera, that is, the first large-scale musical work to encompass a genuine theatrical melodrama and to use the orchestra as an expression of the emotions experienced by the dramatic characters.

Orfeo was first performed at Mantua on February 24, 1607. There are no surviving written reviews or accounts of this performance. We do know that the work was published two years later and that it was staged several more times before history lost track of it. It would seem that the courtiers for whom it was performed were pleased with it, or else the later publication of the libretto and score would not have even been considered.

Orfeo brought Monteverdi professional success, but his personal life was marred by tragedy. Seven months after the premiere of *Orfeo*, in September 1607, Monteverdi's beloved wife died: A former singer, she had borne the composer three children, one of whom had died in infancy. Following his wife's death, Monteverdi became deeply depressed and moved back to his father's house in Cremona. He was immediately summoned back to Mantua, however, and ordered to continue working. Between October 1607 and May 1608, Monteverdi composed a second opera, *L'Arianna*. The work was staged in May 1608 and was a huge success.

In 1613, Monteverdi took up the post of choirmaster at St. Mark's Cathedral in Venice and eventually took holy orders. In all, Monteverdi wrote and published an enormous amount of music during his life, including masses, vespers, madrigals, motets, magnificats, secular vocal music, and, of course, operas. He continued to write operas throughout his life, composing several works for the new Venice opera house, which opened in 1637: The most famous of these is *L'incoronazione di Poppea* (1642).

After a brief visit to Cremona and Mantua when he was in his late seventies, Monteverdi returned to Venice and died there on November 29, 1643. He was buried in the church of Santa Maria Glorioso dei Frara, where a memorial to the great composer exists to this day.

Monteverdi paved the way for the great operatic composers of the seventeenth and eighteenth centuries, including Rossini, Puccini, and Verdi. Opera lovers the world over owe him a debt of gratitude.

58

Gioacchino Rossini

1792–1868

[Rossini possessed] an equal genius for shattering melodrama
in tragedy and for devastating humor in comedy.
—NICOLAS SLONIMSKY

In *The Romantic Era,* the musicologist Benedict Sarnaker wrote:

Gioacchino Rossini was the most important composer of
Italian opera during the first half of the nineteenth century. He was recognized by his contemporaries as the
greatest of his time, and he enjoyed the widest popular
acclaim, wealth, prestige and artistic influence, creating
new standards by which other composers were to be

judged. It was not until the appearance of Giuseppe
Verdi that Rossini ceased to hold the central place in
Italian operatic life, and it was only the mature Verdi who
achieved a standing more illustrious than Rossini's.

Rossini was enormously popular during his active composing
years, forming, along with Gaetano Donizetti and Vincenzo Bellini,
a triumvirate of Italy's most cherished composers. And in addition
to Rossini's enormous contributions to the development of the
opera buffa (comic opera about everyday life, regular people, and
romantic liaisons), he is also responsible for the humane elimination of the use of *castrati* (castrated males who retained a high, feminine voice) in opera.

Gioacchino Antonio Rossini was born in Pésaro, Italy, on
February 29, 1792. His father, Giuseppe, was a trumpeter of some
local fame and his mother, Anna, was a singer. Gioacchino's talents
surfaced at a young age. By the time he was in his early teens he was
proficient on several instruments, including the piano, viola, and
French horn, and possessed a fine soprano voice. Before long he
began to compose his own music, including arias and horn duets
that he performed with his father.

In his late teens, Rossini attended the Liceo Comunale in
Bologna. There he acquired extensive knowledge of counterpoint
while studying under Padre Mattei; perfected his singing with
Gibelli; studied cello under Cavedagna; and learned piano with
Zanotti. He left the Liceo when he was eighteen and shortly thereafter was commissioned to write his first opera, *La cambiale di matri-
monio* (*The Marriage Contract*). This work was very well received, and
Rossini was encouraged to create his first serious full-length opera,
Tancredi, which was based on Voltaire's tragedy *Tancrède*. *Tancredi*
was an enormous hit in Venice, so much so that one of its arias, "Di
tanti palpiti," was sung by people in the streets throughout the city
on the day after the opera's premiere.

Rossini followed *Tancredi* with a string of hugely popular
works, including *L'Italiana in Algeri* (*An Italian in Algiers*, 1813);
Elisabetta, Regina d'Inghilterra (*Elizabeth, Queen of England*, 1815); and
what is now considered to be his masterpiece, *Il barbiere di Siviglia*
(*The Barber of Seville* (1816). In rapid succession, he went on to produce *Otello* (also in 1816), *La cenerentola* (*Cinderella*, 1817); *La gazza
ladra* (*The Thieving Magpie*, 1817); *Mosè* (*Moses*, 1818); *La donna del
lago* (*The Lady of the Lake*, 1819); and *Maometto II* (*Muhammad II*,
1820). Rossini's final opera during his Venetian period was

Semiramide, which premiered in 1823.

In 1824, Rossini became director of the Théâtre-Italien in Paris. Five years later he produced the opera that contains what is probably his most recognizable melody. *Guillaume Tell* (*William Tell*) was first staged in Paris on August 9, 1829. The opera was a great success, and its overture eventually became the best-known operatic music of all time when it was used as the theme music for the popular radio and TV series *The Lone Ranger*.

After the success of *William Tell*, the wealthy Rossini retired from writing operas. He was only thirty-seven, and it is not clear why he stopped composing. There is speculation that he originally intended to take a long vacation and simply remained on vacation for forty years. He did compose a variety of songs and piano pieces during this time, in addition to the *Stabat Mater* (*Sorrowful Mother*, 1842) and one last manifestation of brilliance, the 1863 *Petit Messe Solennelle* (*Short Solemn Mass*, although it is never referred to by its English translated title).

Throughout his life, the superstitious Rossini was always afraid of Friday the 13th. Ironically, he died on November 13—a Friday— in 1868. He will always be remembered for the two brilliant decades in which he composed works that entertained his devotees, influenced his contemporaries, and inspired generations of composers who followed him. His works are still widely performed today, a sure sign of his lasting and important influence on the world of music. In Rossini's hometown of Pésaro, at Via Rossini 34, there is the Casa di Rossini, a small museum that houses memorabilia from the great composer's life and career. And also in Pésaro, the Teatro Rossini on Piazza Lazzarini has an annual opera festival every August in Rossini's honor.

59

Cimabue
(Bencivieni di Pepo)
c. 1240–1302

All changed, changed utterly:
A terrible beauty is born.
　　　　　—W. B. YEATS
　　　　　Easter 1916

*C*imabue (pronounced chima-BOO-ay) is an Italian word that combines of two smaller words: *cima*, meaning "the top" or "on top of" and *bue*, which means "ox" or "bull." Thus, *cimabue* means "on top of the bull." But as is often the case with the Italian language, it is the *spirit* of the word or words that is important to our understanding, not necessarily the literal translation. Thus, we must ask ourselves, what is on top of the bull? His head, of course.

Therefore, the word *cimabue* has come to mean "bullheaded." And that colorful translation gives us an important clue as to the nature of the great thirteenth-century painter who is the subject of this chapter, Bencivieni di Pepo, otherwise known as Cimabue.

Cimabue, usually distinguished as the "father of Italian painting," was the bridge between what Giorgio Vasari describes as the "rude Greek manner" of Byzantine art, and what we now know as modern Western painting (as it flowered during the Renaissance) with its realistic and expressive depictions of people and spatial dimensions.

The period of Cimabue's activity (from around 1272 through his death in 1302) followed a long epoch—the Middle Ages—during which artists were reluctant to sign their names to their works. The maverick Cimabue, on the other hand, was usually so proud of his efforts that he boldly claimed credit for his paintings and mosaics. But Cimabue's pride was tempered with a genuine depth of self-criticism. Vasari, in his biographical essay on Cimabue, cites a thirteenth-century writer's assessment (translated by Julia Conaway Bondanella and Peter Bondanella) of the "bullheaded" Florentine painter:

> Cimabue of Florence was a painter who lived during the author's own time, a nobler man than anyone knew, but he was as a result so haughty and proud that if someone pointed out to him any mistake or defect in his work, or if he had noted any himself (as happened many times, since an artisan may err because of a defect in the materials he uses or because of some shortcoming in the tool with which he works), he would immediately destroy the work, no matter how precious it might be.

Regarding the details of Cimabue's life, even Vasari is unsure about certain basic facts, including the dates of the painter's birth and death. Nonetheless, most scholars today accept 1240 as the year of his birth. Vasari tells us that Cimabue's family was a "noble" one and that "while he was growing up, he was judged by his father and others to have a fine, sharp mind, and he was sent to Santa Maria Novella to a master, a relative who was teaching grammar there to the novices, so that he could be trained in letters." The nascent artist did not *wish* to be trained in letters, however, and instead spent all of his time drawing figures of men, horses, and houses in his notebooks. It so happened, Vasari continues, that when Cimabue was young, a group of Greek painters were hired by

the rulers of Florence to "revive . . . the art of painting which was at
that time not so much in disarray as completely lost." The eager
Cimabue was hired by the visiting Greeks to help them with their
work decorating and restoring the Gondi Chapel and thus,
"Cimabue made a beginning in the art which pleased him."

Cimabue's first major work that still survives is the 12′7″ by
7′4″ fresco for the Church of Santa Trinità in Florence, *Virgin and
Child Enthroned.*

In her book *Art History*, Marilyn Stokstad has written of this
work:

> Cimabue employed Byzantine formulas in determining
> the proportions of his figures, the placement of their fea-
> tures, and even the tilts of their haloed heads. Mary's
> huge throne, painted to resemble gilded bronze with
> inset enamels and gems, provides an architectural frame-
> work for the figures. To render her drapery and that of
> the infant Jesus, Cimabue used the Italo-Byzantine tech-
> nique of highlighting a background color with thin lines
> of gold where the folds break. The vantage point sus-
> pends the viewer in space in front of the image, simulta-
> neously looking down on the projecting elements of the
> throne and Mary's lap while looking straight on at the
> prophets at the base of the throne and the splendid
> winged seraphim stacked on either side. These interest-
> ing spatial ambiguities, as well as subtle asymmetries
> throughout the composition, the Virgin's thoughtful,
> engaging gaze, and the well-observed faces of the old
> men are all departures from tradition that enliven the
> picture.

The impact and power of Cimabue's fresco is most evident
when viewed from a distance. Cimabue's artistic sense of space and
distance was so highly developed that he was able to work "in close"
on the piece, and yet never lose sight of the overall "long distance"
view of it he had in mind. "Cimabue's concern for spatial volumes,
solid forms, and warmly naturalistic human figures," Stokstad concludes, "contributed to the course of later Italian painting."

In addition to his *Virgin and Child Enthroned*, Cimabue is best
known for his *Crucifixion*, completed around 1290, in the church of
Santa Croce in Florence. (This gripping and sad work was almost
completely destroyed by the floodwaters that swept through
Florence in 1966.)

Legend has it that Cimabue was the discoverer and teacher of the painter Giotto, a student who greatly eclipsed his master (see chapter 68). Toward the end of his life, Cimabue worked in Pisa, and that is where he is assumed to have died in the year 1302.

Cimabue's legacy is one of monumental change: He is considered to have been directly responsible for the birth of the modern, softer, and more naturalistic style of art today solidly associated with Western Renaissance art. Cimabue may very well have been bull-headed, but like most geniuses, he knew what he wanted to do; thanks to his resolute "stubbornness, the world has gained the works of Giotto and all the other Renaissance masters.

60

The Bellinis
1400–1516

Your children are not your children.
They are the sons and daughters of Life's longing for itself.
They came through you but not from you
And though they are with you yet they belong not to you.
— KAHLIL GIBRAN
The Prophet, "On Children"

The influence of the painting Bellini family—father Jacopo and his sons Gentile and Giovanni—was twofold: They defined the Venetian school of Renaissance painting, and they directly influenced and inspired the great artists Giorgione and Titian. In *The Story of Painting*, the art historian Sister Wendy Beckett observes that "the two generations of Bellinis became the most influential group of artists in northern Italy, and just as the early Renaissance is bound up with fifteenth-century Florentine culture, the Bellinis were responsible for the distinctly Venetian heritage of the High Renaissance of the late fifteenth to early sixteenth centuries."

The three Bellinis were all talented and successful painters, yet if the family was said to have had a single star, it would have to have been Giovanni, who, as historian Will Durant describes him, "was the first Venetian to reveal the glory of color; and at the same time [attain] to a grace and accuracy of line, a delicacy of feeling, a depth of interpretation, that, even in the lifetime of his brother [Gentile], made him the greatest and most sought after painter in Venice." The Bellinis appeared at a fertile time in Italian history. The printer Aldo Manuzio was developing his italic typeface; Michelangelo was completing his *David*; Botticelli was painting some of his most acclaimed works; and many other sculptors, artists, architects, and scientists, including Raphael, Leonardo da Vinci, Giorgione, and Titian, were producing masterpieces that would help to define the era. The Bellinis made a distinctive contribution to this flowering of culture, as their individual biographies show.

- **Jacopo Bellini (c. 1400–70):** worked throughout northern Italy, notably in Padua, Verona, Ferrara, and Venice. Much of his work has been lost, but his legacy survives in his extraordinary lead-point sketchbook, in which he experimented with perspective and composition, and which greatly influenced his son Giovanni. Jacopo's notebook contained hundreds of drawings, including mythological characters, biblical scenes, images from antiquity, and imaginative drawings of whimsical and fanciful subjects. Jacopo probably taught the painter Carpaccio who was later also influenced by Gentile Bellini. In Padua, Jacopo was so impressed by fresco panels he had seen being painted for the Eremitain friars that he offered the hand of his daughter Nicolosia to the seventeen-year-old painter of the murals, Andrea Mantegna. Mantegna would become an important Renaissance painter and engraver in his own right and would also influence his brothers-in-law Gentile and Giovanni Bellini.

- **Gentile Bellini (c. 1429–1507):** A year older than his brother Giovanni, Gentile moved with his family from Venice to Padua when he was twenty-three and was commissioned to paint scenes on the shutters of the pipe organ in the city's cathedral. These paintings were somewhat harsh in style and tone; when Gentile began working back in Venice during the 1470s, a new softness appeared in his work. In 1747, Gentile traveled to Constantinople and worked at the court of the Ottoman ruler Mohammed II. He returned to Venice in 1480 and completed work in the Signory with his brother Giovanni. His series entitled *The Piazza of San Marco* and *The Miracle of the True Cross* are his greatest paintings, containing meticulous renderings of Venice and its citizens. When he died in 1507 at the age of seventy-eight, Gentile was working on a painting of St. Mark, Venice's Patron saint. Giovanni Bellini completed the canvas and went on to achieve greater acclaim and praise than his older brother.

- **Giovanni Bellini (c. 1430–1516):** Described by Sister Wendy Beckett as the "bridge to the future" of Italian Renaissance art and "one of the most supreme painters of all the ages," Giovanni is the most renowned of the Bellinis. One of his favorite subjects was the Madonna and Child, depicted in fourteen of his surviving works. Prominent among them is *The Madonna of the Meadows*, which Bellini completed between 1500 and 1505. In this canvas, Virgin and the infant Jesus dominate the center of the painting, and are surrounded by the figure of a raven, an egret fighting with a snake, a farmer plowing his fields, and the towers of a distant city. Giovanni thus symbolically declares that the Virgin reigns over such secular concerns and that while death may be in her infant's future (the black raven waits patiently), for now he is protected from all harm. Other leading works by Giovanni Bellini include *The Agony in the Garden, St. Francis in the Wilderness,* and *St. Jerome Reading.* Whereas his father and brother were known for their skill as draftsmen, Giovanni built his style around the lavish use of color and the creation of lush, evocative landscapes: These qualities were especially influential on the following generation of Venetian painters.

Regardless of the personal achievements of the individual members of the Bellini family, their most significant impact can be seen when they are considered as a group. Jacopo (and Mantegna) influenced his sons; Gentile and Giovanni went on to influence Giorgione, Titian, and many others. The Bellinis defined the new Venetian school of painting, a tradition marked by a move away from the Florentine emphasis on an "architectural-sculptural" sensibility into a style featuring softer edges and spectacular colors. This powerful impact on Renaissance art earns them inclusion in *The Italian 100.*

61

Giorgione
c. 1477–1510

Since he appreciated the good qualities of craftsmanship, Giorgione always used to pick out the most beautiful and varied subjects he could find to put in his works. And nature gave him such a gracious spirit that, in either oil or fresco, he created living forms and other images so soft, so harmonious, and so carefully shaded off into the shadows that many of the most skillful artists of those times agreed he had been born to infuse life into his figures and to reproduce the freshness of living flesh more than any other artist who had ever painted, not only in Venice, but anywhere.

> — Giorgio Vasari, *The Lives of the Most Eminent Painters, Sculptors, and Architects* (translated by Julia Conaway Bondanella and Peter Bondanella)

Giorgione's most famous work, *The Tempest,* which now resides in the Galleria dell' Accademia in Venice, is an enigmatic study of seemingly incongruent events. On the viewer's right, a mostly nude woman sits beneath a tree by the side of a river, a tiny white shawl covering her shoulders and an infant nursing at her breast. A short distance away from the woman stands a young man wearing short trousers, a white shirt, and a dark red vest. He holds a tall staff in his right hand, and his head is turned as he nonchalantly watches the woman nursing. Not far from the riverbank, a handful of white

213

houses faces a bridge over the nearby river, and in the distant sky, a
bolt of lightning streaks from a lowering cloud.

The Tempest has intrigued scholars over the centuries, causing
them to speculate about the identity of the man and woman, their
possible relationship, and the meaning of their apparent indiffer-
ence to the approaching storm. The questions have a special
urgency because so little is known about Giorgione's life, and it is
hard to resist the belief that *The Tempest* contains biographical clues.
(An interesting development occurred when art historians x-rayed
the work and discovered that Giorgione had painted a *second*
woman in the scene, this one stepping into the stream.)

It is known that Giorgione was born Giorgio Barbarelli around
the year 1477 in Castelfranco Veneto, Republic of Venice, Italy.
Giorgio Vasari describes him as "nothing but gentle and well-
mannered all his life," and one of the few portraits of him that survive (a self-portrait in oil) shows a handsome young man with a
well-defined nose, full mouth, wide eyes, and long hair. Since
"Giorgione" translates as "big George," it is also believed that he
was a large man, and some sources indicate that he was a bit of a
womanizer.

In 1490, when Giorgione was thirteen or so, he traveled to
Venice to study under the great master Giovanni Bellini. Bellini
greatly influenced Giorgione's style, and his work clearly reflects
this. As Will Durant suggests, the great Leonardo also played a role
in Giorgione's artistic development: "From Leonardo—passing
through Venice in 1500—Giorgione may have acquired a taste for a
mystic, dreamy softness of expression, a delicacy of nuance, a
refinement of manner that made him, for a tragically brief
moment, the summit of Venetian art."

In 1507, when Giorgione was twenty-nine, he received a commission to paint a mural on the side of a Venetian warehouse.
Nothing remains of this work but a few indistinguishable patches of
faded color, and yet eyewitness accounts from the period are in
unanimous agreement that Giorgione's painting established him as
a master of the fresco and one of the greatest painters of the day.

Giorgione is now credited as being the progenitor of the High
Renaissance style of painting, a style that utilized a soft technique
with a subtle, mysterious atmosphere or quality. Art historian
Marilyn Stokstad writes that "[Giorgione's] importance to Venetian
painting is critical," not least because of his influence on Titian,
who served as one of his assistants.

Giorgione's career was extremely short: he died in 1510 when he was only thirty-three, after contracting the bubonic plague. At the time of his death there were more than a dozen painters rendering works after Giorgione's style, and this has created some doubt as to whether works attributed to Giorgione were actually created by his hand or painted by his disciples. The few surviving paintings considered indisputable Giorgiones include (in addition to *The Tempest*), *The Three Philosophers*, *Sleeping Venus*, *Boy with an Arrow*, and *Shepherd with a Flute*. (Giorgione was a lute player and loved music as well.) As many as seventy works in all have been considered as possibly belonging to Giorgione's catalog. As scholars continue to explore these issues and study Giorgione's powerful artistic legacy, perhaps they will even unlock the secrets of *The Tempest*.

Giorgio Vasari
1511–74

Caught up in a technological society, man tends to feel himself
increasingly dehumanized; thus, he once more reaches for the
lives of others to assure himself of the commonalities of existence.
—LEON EDEL

In his book *The Renaissance*, Will Durant freely admitted, "[T]his
and every book on the Italian Renaissance owes half its life [to]
Giorgio Vasari." Most art critics agree that Giorgio Vasari, while a
gifted architect, was only a fair painter. He more than made up for
the mediocrity of his frescoes, however, by his skill at biography.
Thanks to Vasari, we today have comprehensive, detailed, contem-

porary accounts of the lives of 161 of the "most eminent painters, sculptors, and architects," as the title of his definitive multivolume series on the history of art so confidently proclaims. Thanks to Giorgio Vasari, we know the story of Michelangelo's "alteration" of *David*'s nose (see chapter 9). And thanks to Vasari, we also know of Raphael's "amorous" nature and how the only way Agostino Chigi could motivate the great painter to complete a *loggia* (gallery) for his palace was to move Raphael's mistress (with whom he was obsessed) into the room where the great painter was working and allow him to indulge at will in, as Vasari described it, "the pursuit of his carnal pleasures."

Giorgio Vasari was born in Arezzo, Italy, on July 20, 1511. Vasari's grandfather was a painter and his father, Antonio, made ceramic pieces. ("Vasari" means "makers of vases.") Giorgio's first teacher was his uncle through marriage, the famous painter Luca Signorelli (known for his anatomical precision and groundbreaking nudes. In 1524, when he was thirteen, Giorgio was sponsored by the powerful cardinal of Cortona, Silvio Passerini, who was delighted by the adolescent's ability to recite entire passages of Virgil's *Aeneid* by heart. Giorgio was given housing by the cardinal and began studying with the legendary master Michelangelo. Historians generally agree that Vasari's "studies" at this time consisted mainly of running errands for Michelangelo, but the boy was in daily contact with the outstanding genius of the time, and Michelangelo's influence could not help but rub off on him. Vasari's admiration and appreciation of Michelangelo is evident in this effusive passage from his *Lives* (translated by Gaston De Vere), which also serves as further testimony to Michelangelo's "divine" stature:

> [T]he most benign Ruler of Heaven . . . became minded to send down to earth a spirit with universal ability in every art and every profession, who might be able, working by himself alone, to show what manner of thing is the perfection of the art of design in executing the lines, contours, shadows, and high lights, so as to give relief to works of painting, and what it is to work with correct judgment in sculpture, and how in architecture it is possible to render habitations secure and commodious, healthy and cheerful, well-proportioned, and rich with varied ornaments.

As he got older, Vasari began associating with the elite of Florence. Because of his friendly, ingratiating manner, he was soon on excellent terms with popes, dukes, and other illustrious rulers of the renowned city that art historian Michael Sonini describes as "the artistic center of the world." In 1546, at the urging of Pope Paul III, the thirty-five-year-old Vasari began compiling his history of art, which he described as "a treatise with an account of the men who had been illustrious in the art of design from Cimabue down to our own times."

Four years later, in 1550, Vasari published the first edition of his *The Lives of the Most Eminent Painters, Sculptors, and Architects.* (The book's original Italian title was *Vite de' più eccelenti pittori, scultori, ed architetti Italiani.* Interestingly, this original title uses "*eccelenti,*" which means "excellent," but through the centuries, the word has been customarily translated as "eminent." Also, Vasari included "Italian" in his title but that descriptive affiliation has since also been deleted.)

Vasari's sources were mainly first-person oral interviews with living artists and the people who knew them. Of his first edition, Sonini writes, "Since Vasari never stopped painting, designing buildings, and producing theatrical spectacles while he was writing the *Lives,* the speed in which the first edition was completed is amazing. He seemed to have transcended the limitations of his resources."

Even when the *Lives* was completed, Vasari continued to travel and compile biographical and historical information on art and artists. As an architect, he remodeled Florence's Palazzo Vecchio and built the now-legendary Uffizi Gallery. In 1568, when he was fifty-seven, he published the second edition of his magnum opus. This edition was huge: It now contained thousands of pages and comprised 161 meticulous biographies, plus much other historical material. One translated and annotated edition runs to almost twenty volumes. Vasari's *Lives* has served as the definitive (although at times contradictory and anachronistic) source for information on Renaissance art and artists.

Giorgio Vasari essentially invented the discipline that is today known as art history. If this "maker of vases" had done nothing during his life but write his *Lives,* he would have still been honored as one of the most influential Renaissance figures. When we add to his library work his design of the Uffizi and other architectural achievements, as well as the countless frescoes still on display in the Vatican and elsewhere, it is clear that he richly deserves inclusion in *The Italian 100.*

63

Raphael
(Raffaello Sanzio da Urbino)
1483–1520

Let anybody only try with human will and human power, to
produce something that may be compared with the creations
that bear the names Mozart, Raphael, Shakespeare. God did
not retire to rest after the well-known six days of Creation, but
is evidently as active as on the first.

—JOHANN WOLFGANG VON GOETHE

The artist and architect known simply as Raphael was an authentic Renaissance genius who was able to create paintings that still
enchant, delight, and inspire today. In his *History of Art*, H. W.
Janson evaluated Raphael's contribution:

219

As an innovator, Raphael seems to contribute less than Leonardo, Bramante, and Michelangelo, the three artists whose achievements were basic to his. *Yet he is the central painter of the High Renaissance; our conception of the entire style rests more on his work than on any other master's.* The genius of Raphael was a unique power of synthesis that enabled him to merge the qualities of Leonardo and Michelangelo, creating an art at once lyric and dramatic, pictorially rich and sculpturally solid. [emphasis added]

Raphael's accomplishments are all the more astonishing because they came about in a relatively short period, when one considers the six- or seven-decade careers enjoyed by some of the other great Renaissance artists: Raphael was only thirty-seven when he died.

Raphael was born on April 6, 1483, in Urbino, an arts center about seventy miles east of Florence, to Giovanni Santi, a painter Vasari called "of no great excellence." Though he lacked exceptional talent, Giovanni Santi inculcated in his son a love of and appreciation for art and humanistic philosophy. From an early age, Raphael manifested unusual artistic ability, and in or around 1495, he traveled to Perugia to serve an apprenticeship under the great painter Pietro Perugino. By the age of seventeen he was already called a "master," and after essentially learning all that he could in Perugia, he traveled to Florence, arriving there by the autumn of 1504.

In Florence, Raphael's primary teachers were Leonardo da Vinci and Michelangelo. The young painter made enormous strides in technique and style, drawing on Leonardo's use of *chiaroscuro* (the contrast between light and dark), and *sfumato* (delicate use of shading instead of lines to delineate features and forms). From Michelangelo, he learned how to depict the human anatomy in the most dramatic and eloquent manner. Michelangelo later proudly remarked of Raphael's mature work, "Here is an example of what profound study can bring forth."

In 1508, Raphael was called to Rome by Pope Julius II to paint a series of frescoes for certain of the Vatican apartments (known as the *Stanze*). Raphael continued to work in Rome, painting ever increasingly sophisticated frescoes and dozens of madonnas before his untimely death. According to Vasari, this artist whose work expressed such spiritual intensity fell victim to his earthly passions:

Meanwhile, pursuing his amours in secret, Raphael con-

tinued to divert himself beyond measure with the pleasures of love; whence it happened that, having on one
occasion indulged in more than his usual excess, he
returned to his house in a violent fever. The physicians,
therefore, believing that he had overheated himself, and
receiving from him no confession of the excess of which
he had been guilty, imprudently bled him, insomuch that
he was weakened and felt himself sinking; for he was in
need rather of restoratives.

After making his will, Raphael died on his birthday, April 6, in
1520. He was so esteemed that his funeral was held in the Vatican.

Everyone familiar with Raphael's prolific work inevitably com-
piles a list of personal favorites, and these are some of the author's:

- *Coronation of the Virgin* (Oddi Altarpiece): Christ crowns his
  mother as the twelve Apostles gaze rapturously into Heaven.

- *The Marriage of the Virgin*: A remarkable exercise in perspective
  and design: The viewer's eye is drawn to the distant temple,
  which is engraved with Raphael's name.

- *The Deposition*: The crucified Christ is carried away for burial as
  his mother swoons in agony.

- *Madonna of the Baldacchino*: Angels hover above the Virgin Mary,
  who sits on a throne with the infant Jesus on her lap.

- *The Ceiling of the Stanza di Eliodoro*: An enormous fresco that took
  Raphael three years to execute.

- *The School of Athens*: This fresco in the stanza della Segnature may
  be Raphael's most famous work, depicting Plato and Aristotle
  surrounded by fifty figures who represent centuries of Greek
  thought and philosophy.

- *Galatea*: Raphael's attempt at painting the ideal of beauty.

- *Madonna of Foligno*: The coloration is so brilliant and the Virgin
  and her son appear in the sky in such vivid detail, the painting
  has a nearly photographic quality.

- *The Burning of the Borgo*: The exquisitely detailed rendering of the
  fleeing crowd makes the terror of the event almost palpable.

- *St. Cecilia*: A powerful and dramatic scene of the heavens opening for the saint and her followers.

● *The Transfiguration*: Christ is risen in Raphael's last work left unfinished at his death and completed by his assistant Giulio Romano.

Raphael's epitaph sums up the impact of this magnificent artist:

RAFFAELLO SANTI, THE SON OF GIOVANNI OF URBINO.
EMINENT PAINTER. RIVAL OF THE ANCIENTS.
LOOKING UPON HIS LIFELIKE IMAGES
YOU CAN THUS BEHOLD
THE UNIFICATION OF NATURE AND ART.

64

Sandro Botticelli
1445–1510

Botticelli's pictures have *mood*. This was something new in the history of painting. . . . Eroticized melancholy is everywhere in Botticelli, in angels, Madonnas, saints, boys, nymphs. It is extruded as subtle tints of rose, sepia, grey, pale blue. . . . Botticelli's personalities have a fixity and dreamy apartness. They offer themselves to the eye and yet rebuff our intimacy. Within their nervous carved lines, they have a heaviness or density of consciousness. Their dispassionate faces are like the barred backdrop of the *Primavera*, a cultivated closure.
— CAMILLE PAGLIA
Sexual Personae

Leonardo da Vinci's masterpieces the *Mona Lisa* and *The Last Supper* are probably the world's best-known works of art, followed closely by Michelangelo's *David* and his Sistine Chapel ceiling frescoes. These works have achieved a level of recognition that extends to every stratum of society and into virtually every culture. There is another Renaissance painting in this category, though the title of the work and the name of the artist might not come so quickly to most people's minds.

The central figure of the painting is a nude, red-headed beauty who rises from the sea in the cradle of a huge white seashell. On her right a pair of burly male figures representing the zephyrs propel her toward the shore as a lovely maiden, on her left, offers her a long red cloak to cover her nakedness.

This enchanting image has been used in advertisements, on record albums, on postcards, on book covers, and, most recently, as a digitized graphic in a computer commercial. Art lovers identify it immediately as *The Birth of Venus*, by Sandro Botticelli.

The Birth of Venus is without question Botticelli's best-known painting, and yet it is but a small example of the extensive and truly influential body of work produced by one of the most unique "characters" of the Renaissance.

Sandro (Alessandro) Botticelli was born in Florence in 1445, the son of Mariano Filipepi, who, according to Vasari, "brought [Alessandro] up with care, and had him instructed in all those things that are usually taught to children before they are old enough to be apprenticed to some calling." But the young Sandro was restless and excitable and did not take too well to traditional schooling. His father tried to impress upon him the importance of reading, writing, and arithmetic, but the young Sandro wanted no part of these disciplines and truly taxed his father's patience. Mariano finally gave up and apprenticed Sandro to a goldsmith named Botticello. For some reason, Sandro Filipepi took Botticello's name and became known from then on as Sandro Botticelli.

Sandro studied with Botticello until he was around sixteen, after which he moved to the studios of the great Renaissance painter Fra Filippo Lippi. Lippi greatly influenced Sandro's early work, which included *The Adoration of the Kings* and the *Chigi Madonna*. Before long the young painter's genius was recognized, and he was able to establish a studio of his own and obtain a commission from the Medicis, an astonishing achievement considering that Sandro was only twenty years old at the time. Botticelli did a number of works for the Medici family between 1475 and 1485, including the breathtaking *St. Augustine in His Study* and *The Adoration of the Magi*, *The Madonna of the Magnificat*, *Primavera* (*Spring*), and *The Birth of Venus*. In 1481, Botticelli was commissioned by Pope Sixtus IV to work on the newly completed Sistine Chapel, an acknowledgment that he was regarded as one of Italy's true masters.

Most critics concur that Botticelli did his greatest work in the period from 1482 to around 1494 when he was producing altarpieces, portraits, drawings, and other works, including illustrations for Dante's *Divine Comedy*.

Unfortunately, Botticelli's principal patrons, the Medicis, were banished from Florence in 1494, and Sandro came under the influence of Girolamo Savonarola, the fanatical Dominican friar who effectively ruled the city for the next four years. Savonarola was deposed and executed in 1498, but the priest's extreme fundamentalism and violent opposition to "pagan" influences inevitably damaged Botticelli's career. Botticelli did not work much in his later years and died in 1510 at the age of sixty-six, physically disabled and financially impoverished.

Botticelli's most famous painting, *The Birth of Venus*, did far more than simply create an image that would endure as a popular icon. His vision contributed to a change in the fifteenth century's philosophical approach to art, representing what H. W. Janson has called the "opposite of the orderly system of medieval scholasticism." Ostensibly a pagan rendering, *The Birth of Venus* acknowledged the new Neo-Platonic thinking of Botticelli's day and allowed an interpretation in which Venus could be seen as a symbol for "rebirth," the zephyrs could play the role of attending angels, and the Baptism of Christ could be mirrored in the relationship between "Spring" and the newborn Venus. Thus classical and Christian symbolism were united, opening a rich intellectual dimension for artists to explore.

65

Donatello

c. 1386–1466

[Donatello] treats the human body as an articulated structure, capable of movement, and its drapery as a separate and secondary element, determined by the shapes underneath rather than by patterns imposed from without. [Donatello's] *St. Mark* looks as if he could take off his clothes.

—H. W. JANSON
The History of Art

[Donatello's] sculpture is like an encyclopedia of types of work, with nearly every piece breaking new ground.

—MARILYN STOKSTAD
Art History

Donatello was born Donato di Niccolò di Betto Bardi around 1386 in Florence. In his early teens, Donato was apprenticed to one of the many sculptors working in Florence at the time and also assisted Lorenzo Ghiberti in creating the bronze doors of the Baptistery. He displayed talent at working as a sculptor in Florence's cathedral at the age of twenty.

An overview of Donatello's brilliant career reveals a number of "firsts":

- From 1411 through 1413, Donatello executed his *St. Mark*, the first in his series of standing figures that helped define the Renaissance style.

- In 1417, Donatello created the bronze plaque *St. George Slaying the Dragon*, which used perspective for the first time in a carved relief.

- Donatello's statue of *David* (c. 1432) was the first completely freestanding, life-size nude bronze sculpture in the history of European art.

- Donatello's bronze monument entitled *Gattamelata* (1447–53) was the first life-size equestrian sculpture created since classical times.

Donatello was a passionate (some say difficult) man. Giorgio Vasari relates that Donatello once sculpted a bust for a Genoese merchant, who complained that he had been charged too much. (The truth was that the merchant was displeased with the way he had been rendered.) In reply, the great sculptor smashed the bust into tiny pieces, telling the man that he was only intelligent enough to discuss the price of beans.

The power of Donatello's work is such that it continually evokes visceral reactions from late-twentieth-century viewers who are far from unaccustomed to provocative works of art. The *David*, for example, now in the Museo Nazionale del Bargello in Florence, has been interpreted as an unabashedly homoerotic work by Camile Paglia, in *Sexual Personae*:

> Donatello's *David* is astonishingly young. . . . The hand on hip and cocked knee create an air of sexual solicitation. From the side, one is struck by the peachy buttocks, bony shoulderblades, and petulanty protruding boy-belly. The combination of child's physique with female body

language is perverse and pederastic.

The six-foot-high *Mary Magdalene*, created nearly thirty years later, evoked an equally intense though quite different response from the art historian Marilyn Stokstad, who commented in her 1995 book *Art History*, "[Donatello] shows the saint known for her physical beauty as an emaciated, vacant-eyed hermit in a ragged animal skin. Few can look at this figure without a wrenching reaction to the physical deterioration of aging and years of self-denial. Nothing is left for her but an ecstatic vision of the hereafter."

Though Donatello began his career in Florence—studying under Ghiberti and working for the Medici family between 1433 and 1443—he was soon in demand throughout Italy, working in Siena, Padua, and Rome. In his final years, he returned to Florence. Vasari reports that his patron, Cosimo de' Medici, thought so highly of the aging artist and took such good care of him that Donatello never had to worry about money. Reportedly, he kept his money in a basket that hung from the ceiling and instructed his friends to take whatever funds they might need. He died on December 13, 1466.

Apart from his direct impact on Renaissance style, Donatello influenced Western art and sculpture in another way. One of his pupils was a Florentine sculptor named Bertoldo di Giovanni, who went on to become a teacher of sculpture himself. Though Bertoldo's own sculpture never rivaled Donatello's, he passed on the master's teachings to a student who would achieve true greatness in the art—Michelangelo Buonarroti.

66

Masaccio

1401–28

Masaccio showed by perfect works that those who are led by
any guide except Nature, the supreme mistress, are consumed
in sterile toil.

—LEONARD DA VINCI

Masaccio's life was one of stark contrasts. He had a reputation
for clumsiness, personal carelessness, and absentmindedness, and
yet he manifested the utmost precision in employing Brunelleschi's
newly discovered laws of perspective in his paintings. His work
evinced the maturity of a master craftsman, and yet he died when
he was only twenty-six. Though the great Michelangelo recognized
the excellence of his work, Masaccio's fame and the acknowledgment of his influence has been largely posthumous.

Masaccio was born Tomasso di Giovanni di Simone Guidi on December 21, 1401, in Castel San Giovanni di Altura, in the Duchy of Milan. His father, a notary, died when Tomasso was five. At the age of sixteen, Tomasso left home and went to Florence, where his personal mannerisms and occasional witlessness quickly earned him the sobriquet "Masaccio," an abbreviation of Tomasso ("Masa") combined with the Italian pejorative suffix "-acchio," yielding a name that translates as "Big Clumsy Tom," "Sloppy Tom," or "Bad Tom." Giorgio Vasari described the young artist in the following terms:

> He was very absent-minded and unpredictable, like a man who has devoted his whole life and will only to the details of art, caring very little about himself and even less about others. And because he never wanted to think in any way about worldly affairs or concerns, not even about how he dressed himself, he was unaccustomed to collecting anything from his debtors unless he was in dire straits.

Vasari also made the point that Masaccio earned his nickname "not because he was a bad man, for he embodied goodness itself," and noted that "he was so kindly in doing favours or kindnesses for others that no more could be expected."

Scholars and art historians generally agree that Masaccio did not have any extensive formal art training, other than his brief period at the Arte dei Medici e Speziali in Florence. Apparently, he absorbed a great deal by studying the works of Brunelleschi and Donatello, after which his innate genius enabled him to apply these influences in his own paintings. Horst Janson makes the point that "the Early Renaissance was already well established in sculpture and architecture by [1420], making Masaccio's task easier than it would have been otherwise; but his achievement remains stupendous nevertheless."

All of the surviving works by Masaccio are from the brief period from 1420 or so through the year of his death, 1428. Two of his most representative masterpieces are his fresco in the Church of Santa Maria Novella in Florence called *Trinity with the Virgin, Saint John the Evangelist, and Donors*, and his fresco in the Brancacci Chapel called *Tribute Money*.

● *Trinity with the Virgin, Saint John the Evangelist, and Donors*

Masaccio's *Trinity* is an astonishing example of the use of depth and perspective and was truly revolutionary in its use of the vanishing point to invoke a sense of three-dimensionality. The fresco shows the crucified Christ in a barrel-shaped vault.

Behind him, God the Father stands on a raised platform and supports his Son's cross. The Holy Spirit, in the form of a white dove, hovers above Jesus' halo, just beneath God's beard. Beneath the cross on Jesus' right is the Virgin Mary, and to his left, John the Evangelist. One level below Mary and John stand the "donors" of the fresco's title, two members of the Lenzi family, whose burial vault was recently discovered beneath the fresco. Below Jesus' cross is a sarcophagus, on top of which lies an exposed skeleton, with an inscription reading, "What you are, I once was; what I am, you will become."

The most stunning aspect of this mural is the vault in which the scene occurs. Masaccio painted the architecture so precisely to scale that the viewer has the impression of looking far into the depths of an actual vault. The technique Masaccio employed for this fresco is now known as *trompe l'oiel*, which means "fool the eye," and it has never been employed to more striking effect.

- *Tribute Money*

This fresco, one of a series done for the interior of the Brancacci Chapel in Florence, is Masaccio's most important and influential work. It shows Christ instructing Peter to catch a fish, which will ultimately contain the coin demanded by the tax collector. The composition contains two vanishing points and was so superbly executed that throughout the Renaissance artists from all over the region came to study it, including Fra Filippo Lippi, Botticelli, Leonardo, Verrocchio, Michelangelo, and Raphael. According to Marilyn Stokstad: "*Tribute Money* is particularly remarkable for its integration of figures, architecture, and landscape into a consistent whole. The group of Jesus and his disciples forms a clear central focus, from which the landscape seems to recede naturally into the far distance. To create this illusion Masaccio used linear perspective in the depiction of the house. The lines of the house converge on the head of Jesus, which Masaccio reinforced by diminishing the sizes of the barren trees and reducing Peter's size at the left."

Masaccio abandoned his work on the Brancacci interior in 1427, leaving Filippino Lippi, Fra Filippo Lippi's son, to complete his frescos. He died the following year; Vasari hints that he may have been poisoned, but this has never been confirmed. Masaccio is now regarded as the outstanding Florentine painter of the fifteenth century, and as such he richly deserves to be ranked in *The Italian 100.*

67

Benvenuto Cellini
1500–71

I remember some of the delightful and some of the indescribably terrible things that have happened to me, and when I think back to them I am startled to realize that I am really fifty-eight years old and, with God's help, am prosperously growing older.
—BENVENUTO CELLINI

In a letter to Cellini, the great Michelangelo asserted, "I have known you all these years as the greatest goldsmith of whom the world has ever heard." The gold salt-cellar Cellini made for King Francis I is a masterpiece of exquisite detail and sublime beauty, and his bronze statue *Perseus with the Head of Medusa* evoked shouts

232

of enthusiasm when it was first unveiled in Florence.

Unfortunately, most of Cellini's works have been lost.

Cellini is known today primarily for his autobiography, originally titled *The Life of Benvenuto, The Son of Giovanni Cellini, Written by Himself in Florence*, now known simply as *The Life of Benvenuto Cellini*. Cellini's *Life* is the most accurate and detailed account of Renaissance life that has survived. The book has delighted generations of readers, possessing all the dramatic excitement of a novel and featuring a cast of characters ranging from popes and kings to prostitutes and musicians. Cellini translator George Bull states correctly that in the past century or so, Cellini's *Life* has universally been accepted as the most famous of all autobiographies, noting that it is "a revealing historical document, shedding light on matters as diverse as prison conditions in Rome, the behavior of Florentine exiles, or the relationship between Francis I and his mistress." (Benjamin Franklin's autobiography is probably the second most famous.) Cellini's *Life* has also served as a valuable resource for scholars seeking to illuminate the realities of sixteenth-century life.

Benvenuto Cellini was born in Florence on November 3, 1500. He acquired his first name, which means "welcome," because his parents had expected a girl and were pleasantly surprised by the birth of a male child. Cellini wrote his autobiography during the years 1558 through 1566 and died in 1571. During his life he was, as historian Will Durant describes him, "a ruffian, a master craftsman and a murderer."

Cellini's father—himself an architect and a musician—wanted his son to become a professional flutist, but Benvenuto loathed the instrument and instead moved to Rome when he was in his late teens. In Rome he apprenticed, and later worked, as a goldsmith. His father was terribly distraught at the absence of his son, and after two years of the elder Cellini's pleading, Benvenuto moved back to Florence.

While back in Florence, the reckless twenty-one-year-old Cellini stabbed a youth during a quarrel. Thinking he had killed the boy, he fled back to Rome, a circumstance that provided him with the opportunity to study the greatest works of Michelangelo, Raphael, and others. Cellini's exposure to the brilliant creations of these masters inspired him to greater heights; as a result, he became the finest goldsmith in sixteenth-century Rome. During this period, Cellini also enjoyed the privileges of papal sponsorship. Despite his early distaste for music, he played the flute in Pope

Clement's private orchestra and was later dubbed "stamp master" or the papal mint, producing beautifully designed coins and medallions for the papacy.

Cellini had a volatile personality and could easily become enraged. He wrote that when he was aggravated, he "felt a fever," and in his autobiography he claimed to have been in over one hundred fights (almost exclusively knife fights) throughout his life. He also asserted that he had been in the right in every one of these confrontations—except one. Cellini looked to this "record" as proof that God was on his side. This faith in God's munificence was unshakable—until, that is, God did not return his lost love Angelica to him, as Cellini had requested that He do. With the help of a sorcerer from Sicily, Cellini turned to asking for help from demonic powers, since his God had let him down.

In 1527, Cellini fought in defense of Rome when the city was sacked by the armies of Emperor Charles V. In his autobiography he claims to have fired the shot that killed the duke of Bourbon. Even though he later enjoyed the patronage of popes Clement and Paul III, Cellini eventually decided to abandon his goldsmith's shop in Rome and flee to Paris in 1537. His French sojourn did not last long, however, and he returned to Rome within a year, completely unaware that he was wanted there for allegedly embezzling papal jewelry. Cellini was imprisoned on this charge but escaped within two years and returned to France in 1540 at the request of French monarch Francis I. Francis gave Cellini a castle to use as his workshop. Some of the tenants living in the castle refused to leave, and Cellini had them forcibly evicted. When one of the displaced tenants sued Cellini (and won), Cellini crippled the man by stabbing him in both legs. The tenant wisely left Cellini alone following this incident.

Cellini was less than a gentleman in many situations. He would regularly have sex with his beautiful female sculpture models and then beat the women until he was exhausted if they did anything to annoy him. One of his models, Jeanne, gave birth to Cellini's daughter, but Cellini disowned the child after paying Jeanne a dowry, and the baby was later smothered by its nurse.

The brilliant sculptor's lawlessness earned him many enemies. Fearing for his own safety, he returned to Florence in 1545 at the age of forty-five, where he immediately gained the patronage of the powerful and influential Cosimo de' Medici. Cellini created his most acclaimed work—the aforementioned *Perseus*—for Cosimo. The statue was unveiled in 1554, four years before Cellini began dictating his autobiography to the fourteen-year-old son of Michele Goro of Pieve.

Two years after completing *Perseus*, the notorious Cellini was again imprisoned, this time for criminal immorality. After his release, he married in 1564, at the age of sixty-four, and fathered two children. During his life, Cellini fathered a total of eight illegitimate children—two during his early years in Florence, one in France, and five more in Florence prior to his marriage. He died in Florence on February 13, 1571, leaving behind a text that is probably the single most important and influential record of the Renaissance still extant. As translator George Bull correctly proclaimed in the introduction to his edition of Cellini's autobiography, "It is . . . the *Life* which has won Cellini his immortality."

68

Giotto
(Giotto di Bondone)
c. 1267–1337

> When nature wishes to grant anything she does so without avarice.
>
> —LORENZO GHIBERTI, talking about Giotto's talents

The great Italian painter Giotto di Bondone was so famous during his lifetime that he was actually referred to by name in Dante's great epic poem, *The Divine Comedy.* In the *Purgatorio*, Dante referred to Giotto's supplanting of his teacher, the great painter Cimabue:

> Once Cimabue thought to hold the field
> in painting, and now Giotto has the cry
> so that the other's fame, grown dim, must yield.

Being mentioned in *The Divine Comedy* would seem to be fame enough, but Giotto's celebrity was enormous in his time and permeated the age he lived in. Boccaccio wrote of him in his *The Decameron*:

> Giotto was a man of such genius that there was nothing in Nature . . . that he could not paint with his stylus, pen, or brush, making it so much like its original in Nature that it seemed more like the original than a reproduction. Many times, in fact, while looking at paintings by this man, the observer's visual sense was known to err, taking what was painted to be the very thing itself.

In later years, the great Florentine painter Lorenzo Ghiberti added, "Giotto saw in art what others had not attained. . . . He was the inventor and discoverer of many methods which had been buried for about six hundred years."

Giotto di Bondone can literally be credited with defining what we now know as modern Western art. When he began his career, painting was dominated by the traditions of Byzantine art, which featured refined but static forms—scenes were painted without any attempt to convey depth or movement, human figures were flat and awkward, and facial expressions bore little resemblance to those of living people. Giotto broke away from these restrictions, endowing both people and objects with lifelike solidity, conveying a sense of drama and movement in his compositions, and allowing the people in his paintings to express powerful emotions. Many scholars believe that Giotto's probing and compassionate view of his human subjects stemmed from his involvement with the Franciscan order.

Giorgio Vasari tells the (possibly apocryphal) tale of Giotto's meeting with his teacher Cimabue and offers an explanation for Giotto's uncanny ability to recreate reality in his art: "Wherefore Cimabue, going one day on some business of his own from Florence to Vespignano, found Giotto, while his sheep were browsing, portraying a sheep from nature on a flat and polished slab, with a stone slightly pointed, without having learnt any method of doing this from others, but only from nature."

This natural force is obvious in frescoes such as *The Kiss of Judas* (1304–6), for instance, where the faces of the Apostles leap out at the viewer, each manifesting a distinctive emotion, whether rage, sorrow, or confusion. Likewise, in *The Death of St. Francis* (c. 1325), now in the Church of Santa Croce in Florence, Giotto depicts with stunning accuracy the attitudes of those attending the great theologian at his deathbed. Though Giotto did not have the benefit of working with scientific rules of perspective, his acute perception of the natural word enabled him to convey a remarkably vivid sense of spatial relations.

Giotto di Bondone was born in Vespignano, near Florence, but we cannot be certain of the exact year. Many art historians use 1267 as the year of his birth, yet Vasari (who could occasionally be "less than accurate") said that Giotto was born in 1276. We know that he studied under the great Cimabue, and some historians believe that he was also influenced by the sculptors Nicola and Giovanni Pisano. (This would account in part for the quality of solidity so evident in his human figures.) Once he was established as an artist, Giotto worked throughout Italy, beginning in Assisi and moving on to Rome and Padua before returning to Florence. Among his great achievements during this period were a series of thirty-eight frescoes in Padua's Arena Chapel.

Around 1300, Giotto left Florence for Naples, where he created a number of works under the patronage of King Robert. But he soon returned to his hometown, taking the post of chief architect of the Florence cathedral: In this capacity he designed the cathedral's *campanile*, or bell tower, which is now known as Giotto's Tower.

Giotto di Bondone died in Florence on January 8, 1337. The advances he made in painting were pursued by his many pupils and contributed enormously to the growth of the mature Renaissance style of the fifteenth and sixteenth centuries. There is an indissoluble link between Giotto's fidelity to nature and Leonardo's guiding principle of "Knowing how to see."

69

Alessandro Scarlatti
1660–1775
Domenico Scarlatti
1685–1757

After silence that which comes nearest to expressing
the inexpressible is music.
—ALDOUS HUXLEY

The great Baroque composers Alessandro Scarlatti and his son
Domenico have been given a dual ranking in *The Italian 100*
because each was a major contributor to music and deserves to be
acknowledged for his specific influence.

Alessandro Scarlatti was responsible for some important developments in musical composition, including the use of classical
chromatic harmony (half tone harmony), an advancement that
foreshadowed (and undoubtedly influenced) the work of Mozart

and Schubert. He can also be credited with the establishment of the now traditional Italian operatic overture. Alessandro wrote the overtures for his operas in three distinct sections—allegro, adagio, allegro—(fast, slow, fast) a technique that in some ways referred back to the form of the sixteenth-century sonata. His innovations with the overture are now seen to be one of the primary influences on the development of the classical symphony. (The other two composition types that influenced the final shape of the symphony were the sonata and the dance suite of the eighteenth century.)

Alessandro also made changes in the design of the symphonic orchestra as well, adding horns to its makeup, using wind instruments in unique and novel ways, and allowing the strings to accompany the voices rather than simply play introductions. During his lifetime, Alessandro was especially noted for his cantatas, of which he wrote almost seven hundred. The celebrated eighteenth-century English music historian Dr. Charles Burney wrote of him, "[Alessandro Scarlatti] is the most voluminous and most original composer of cantatas that has ever existed. . . . Indeed, this master's genius was truly creative, and I find part of his property among the stolen goods of all the best composers of the first forty or fifty years of the present century." Twentieth-century music historian Gerald Gifford, commenting on Burney's evaluation of Alessandro's influence, notes "More recent writers have expanded this opinion to include the whole of Classical music."

Alessandro Gaspare Scarlatti was born in Palermo, Sicily, on May 2, 1660. He was sent to Rome as an adolescent and studied under the master composers Carissimi and Pasquini. When he was eighteen he married Antonia Anzalone, and the Scarlatti's eventually had ten children. According to surviving records, "il Scarlattino alias al Siciliano" (the Sicilian called Scarlatti") was commissioned in 1679 to compose a Lenten oratorio, although no other details exist regarding this work. In the same year, Alessandro composed his first opera (of an eventual total of 115, of which about 50 are extant), a work titled *Gli equivoci nel sembiante*. This work gained him the sponsorship of Queen Christina of Sweden; in 1680, he wrote the opera *L'honestà negli amori* for her.

In the years between 1700 and 1720, Alessandro produced a stunning range of works, including masses, cantatas, oratorios, serenades, orchestral music, and, of course, operas. He also wrote about music, most notably a treatise on accompaniment entitled *Regole per Principianti* (*Rules for Beginners*).

Alessandro died in Naples on October 24, 1775, and was

buried in the Montesanto church there. He was survived by his ten children, two of whom, Domenico and Francesco, followed in their father's musical footsteps. Of the two brothers, Domenico was by far the most brilliant.

The sixth of Alessandro and Antonia Scarlatti's ten children, Domenico was born in Naples on October 26, 1685, when his father was twenty-five. (The musical gods were unusually generous in 1685: Johann Sebastian Bach and Georg Friedrich Händel were also born in that year.) Domenico studied music with his father, and in 1703 two operas he had composed while in his teens— *Ottavia ristituta al trono* and *Il Giustino*—were produced at the Teatro San Bartolomeo in Naples. His opera *Irene* followed in 1704.

From 1714 through 1719, Domenico served as musical director of St. Peter's at the Vatican. He then moved on to Lisbon, Portugal, and became music director at the court of King John V and the music teacher of Princess Maria Barbara. In 1729, he accompanied the princess to the Spanish court at Madrid and remained there for the rest of his life. He was now a married man, having wed Maria Catalina Gentili of Rome in 1728 (at the relatively late age of forty-three). The couple ultimately had five children.

When Domenico was in his sixties, he produced the bulk of the works for which he is acclaimed today. Of the 555 sonatas he composed throughout his life, 350 were written in the four years between 1753 and 1757, when he died at the age of seventy-one. All but thirteen of his sonatas were written for the harpsichord. Domenico's harpsichord pieces are astonishing in their virtuosity. Harpsichordist and musicologist Ralph Kirkpatrick described Domenico's technique in The Encyclopedia Brittanica:

> Spectacular innovations in keyboard virtuosity—including hand crossing—are often accompanied by audacious dissonances, unconventional voice leading, and far-flung modulations. . . . Scarlatti imposed a variety of sonorities and textures that elevate his writing for the harpsichord to a level comparable to that of Frédéric Chopin and Franz Liszt for the piano.

Ironically, Domenico's influence was not truly felt in a significant way until the nineteenth and twentieth centuries, when complete editions of his sonatas were published. Since then, his music has been regarded as some of the most original and innovative work of the eighteenth century, and he is considered a major contributor to the stylistic development of the sonata.

Antonio Vivaldi

1678–1741

[Antonio Vivaldi was] the motive force behind the development of music in the early eighteenth century. . . . Whilst with
every ounce of his being he lived in his time and fulfilled its
claims on him, he created works which have survived that time
and will, all being well, tell unborn generations of the splendour and beauty of his native Venice.
—WALTER KOLNEDER
Antonio Vivaldi: His Life and Work

Vivaldi's body of work is astounding: According to his biographer
Walter Kolneder, he composed at least 825 authenticated musical
works during his creative years: 78 sonatas, 21 sinfonias, 457 concertos and other instrumental works, 48 stage works and operas, 100
(approximately) separate arias, 59 secular cantatas, 2 oratorios, and

60 sacred vocal works.

This is an impressive output, especially when one takes into account the belief of musicologists that there are likely many more Vivaldi compositions buried in archives, libraries, museums, and private collections throughout the world. Assuming that he began composing in 1703, when he was in his mid-twenties (the first print- ed Vivaldi compositions, collections of his trio and violin sonatas, appeared in the years between 1705 and 1710) and composed until just before his death in 1741, Vivaldi produced an average of one major work a month for almost four decades. This would be impressive enough under normal circumstances, but there were additional factors in Vivaldi's case that make his productivity and commitment to music truly remarkable.

Vivaldi, who had been ordained a priest in 1703, suffered from a chronic illness so debilitating that he could not even perform the Mass. In a November 16, 1737, letter to Marchese Guido Bentivoglio d'Aragona, Vivaldi explained his condition:

> I have not now said mass for twenty-five years, and I shall never do so again, not because of a veto or a command, as His Eminence can confirm, but of my own accord, and this on account of an ailment I have suffered since birth, which oppresses me greatly. When I had just been ordained a priest, I still said mass for rather more than a year and then gave it up, because three times I had to leave the altar without finishing mass on account of my illness.
>
> For this reason I spend my life almost entirely at home, leaving my house only in a gondola or a carriage, because with my chest complaint, known as heart seizure, I can- not walk. No nobleman invites me to his house, not even our doge, because they all know of my ailment. I can usu- ally leave the house immediately after breakfast, but never on foot. This is the reason that I do not say mass.

Sources differ on what exactly was wrong with Vivaldi. The Encyclopedia Brittanica suggests that he suffered from bronchial asthma. Vivaldi's use of the term "chest complaint" bolsters this view, but bronchial asthma usually causes severe wheezing and shortness of breath, which Vivaldi does not mention. Kolneder identifies Vivaldi's condition as angina pectoris, a condition caused by a narrowing of the coronary arteries. The spasms of severe chest pain associated with angina can be brought on by physical exertion and could certainly have afflicted Vivaldi during the performance of the Mass.

Antonio Lucio Vivaldi was born in Venice, Italy, on March 4, 1678. His father was a barber and amateur musician and probably gave Antonio his first instruction on the violin. When Antonio entered the priesthood as a young man, he became known as *Il Prete Rosso* (The Red Priest) because of his flaming red hair. He was ordained at the age of twenty-five and spent the next thirty-five years or so teaching, conducting, and composing mostly in his native city.

Even though Vivaldi was enormously popular during much of his life, his work suddenly fell out of favor during the 1730s. When he died on July 28, 1741, in Vienna, Austria, he was given a funeral that some experts today claim had the hallmarks of a ceremony rendered to the destitute. After his death, Vivaldi's music was essentially forgotten until the mid-nineteenth century, when research was undertaken to compile a definitive catalog of the works of Johann Sebastian Bach. Bach had so admired Vivaldi's string concertos that he had transcribed ten of them for keyboard instruments. When musicologists uncovered this fact, they were moved to take a fresh look at Vivaldi. A great many of his forgotten works were "dusted off," so to speak, and enjoyed a new surge of popularity.

The four Vivaldi violin concertos known collectively as *The Four Seasons*, for instance, may now be some of the most recognizable music in the world. The opening allegro section of Vivaldi's "Spring" concerto is now as recognizable as the opening bars of Beethoven's Fifth Symphony. In recent years, classical music stations trying to broaden the base of their appeal have turned increasingly to Vivaldi's music, and in 1981 Alan Alda wrote, directed, and starred in *The Four Seasons*, an entire movie based on the four sections of Vivaldi's *Four Seasons*, using the music as the soundtrack.

As far as his musical legacy is concerned, Vivaldi had an enormous impact on the development (and perfection) of the concerto form and greatly influenced eighteenth-century music. As one present-day admirer stated to the author, "I've never heard anything of his I didn't like."

71

Titian
(Tiziano Vecellio)
1477–1576

Nobody cares much at heart about Titian; only there is a
strange undercurrent of everlasting murmur about his name,
which means the deep consent of all great men that he is
greater than they.

— JOHN RUSKIN
The Two Paths, Lecture 2

For all his genius, Titian was a no-nonsense man who treated
painting as an enterprise. In a classic example of his pursuit of paying work, we have his May 31, 1513, letter to the Venetian doge and
Council of Ten requesting a commission to paint a fresco on the
wall of the Hall of the Great Council:

Illustrious Prince! High and mighty lords! I, Titian of
Cadore, have from childhood studied the art of painting,
desirous of a little fame rather than of profit. . . . [I]f it
seem good to your Excellencies, I am anxious to paint in
the Hall of the Great Council, employing therein all my
powers; and to begin with a canvas of the battle on the
side of the Piazetta, which is so difficult no one has yet
had the courage to attempt it. I should be willing to
accept for my labor any reward that may be thought
proper, or even less.

Regarding the relation between art and commerce during the
Renaissance, historian Valerio Lintner observes that "the salient
point here is the relationship between art and the money and
power which rendered it possible. The artists of the period were
basically craftsmen, at best from the middle classes. It is true that
some of them . . . ended up being rich and prosperous; it is also
true that others, such as Leonardo, Raphael and Titian, lived their
lives in the style of gentlemen."

In 1477, Tiziano Vecellio was born in Cadore, a tiny town on the
banks of the Piave River in northeastern Italy. Giorgio Vasari, in *The
Lives of the Most Eminent Painters, Sculptors, and Architects*, reports that
Titian as a boy had "a fine spirit and a lively intelligence" and that at
the age of ten, he was sent to live with an uncle in Venice, where he
was apprenticed to the celebrated artists Gentile and Giovanni
Bellini. In Bellini's studio, Titian worked with the painter Giorgione,
each greatly influencing the other. Giorgione died of bubonic plague
at the age of thirty-two, however, and Titian moved to Padua, where
he painted three frescoes for the School of the Saints. He returned
to Venice in 1513 and painted frescoes in the Ducal Palace. (His letter of application, quoted above, was quite effective.) Will Durant,
discussing Titian's "formative" years, noted that "Titian developed
leisurely, like any organism dowered with a century of life. But as
early as 1508 he showed the spiritual penetration and technical
power that were to put him above all his rivals in portraiture."

Even though he learned a great deal studying under the two
Bellini brothers, there is no question that Titian's early works were
more profoundly influenced by Giorgione, to whom he eventually
apprenticed when he was in his twenties. Even today there is controversy over the attribution of a number of paintings produced by
Giorgione and Titian during the first ten or fifteen years of the sixteenth century, such is the facility with which Titian absorbed his
teacher's techniques, especially Giorgione's brush technique and use

of color. Important works from this first period of Titian's career include *Sacred and Profane Love* (c. 1515); *The Assumption* (completed 1518); *The Worship of Venus* (c. 1519); and *The Bacchanal* (c. 1519).

Painted when Titian was in his early thirties, *The Bacchanal* is an example of Titian's "secular" interests and is illustrative of the well-defined duality of the man and artist. In Titian, the Renaissance produced an artist who could paint glorious religious masterworks and altarpieces, and could also delight in the glories of the naked human body and the pleasures of drinking and eating. Will Durant noted that "Titian could pass from Bacchus to Christ, from Venus to Mary, and back again, with no apparent loss to his peace of mind."

Titian's middle period (beginning around 1520, after the completion of *The Bacchanal*) is marked by a a succession of passionate and powerful works such as *Bacchus and Ariadne* (1523), *The Entombment* (c. 1525), and *Venus of Urbino* (1538). *Venus of Urbino*, now hanging in the Uffizi Gallery in Florence, especially illustrates Titian's brilliant ability to convey sensuality and to lovingly depict the nude female form.

Titian's final period (from c. 1545 until his death in 1576) was most notable for the artist's stylistic control of color and light. He painted with thick, confident brushstrokes that gave his works an almost three-dimensional richness. Important paintings from this period include *The Entombment* (1559); *Venus and Adonis* (c. 1560); and *The Rape of Europa* (1562). Titian's final painting, *The Deposition* (also known as *Burial of Christ*), begun in 1576, belonged to a body of late work that has been described as haunting and bold. *The Deposition* remained unfinished at the time of Titian's death.

Titian, with his meticulous detailing combined with a body of work that encompassed lush nudes and glorious religious vistas at the same time (if not in the same painting), influenced many later painters, including Rubens and El Greco, who included portraits of Titian, Raphael, and Michelangelo in the corner of his painting *The Purification of the Temple*.

This great artist lived an exceptionally long life, and he continued painting until the end. In 1576, with a remarkable confidence in his endurance and in his enduring ability to carry on, he agreed to paint a work—*The Deposition*—for the church of Santa Maria Gloriosa de' Frari in Venice. Titian was ninety-nine years old when he agreed to the work and in exchange, the church promised that he could be buried there. Alas, his defiance of death did not make him immune to the terrible ravages of the plague, and on August 26, 1576, Titian died, leaving his final painting unfinished.

72

Antonio Stradivari

c. 1644–1737

'Tis God gives skill
But not without men's hands: he could not make
Antonio Stradivari's violins
Without Antonio.

—GEORGE ELIOT
Stradivarius

In the center of Cremona, Italy (a city of 75,000 that boasts one hundred violin shops and over two hundred violin makers), less than a five-minute walk from the Via Dante, there is a museum called Museo Stradivariano. This museum is a mecca for the lovers of stringed instruments. Museo Stradivariano houses designs, wood-working tools, early models, and elaborate acoustic diagrams from the instrument-making workshop of the man many call the greatest violin maker ever, Antonio Stradivari. Also in the museum, safely ensconced in glass showcases, are actual instruments made by Stradivari and his staff, including violins, violas, cellos, viols, and guitars. Like living things, these instruments must all be allowed to breathe: In order to prevent them from warping and otherwise deteriorating, all of these brilliant creations must be taken out daily and played by the museum's director, Professor Mosconi. It is the lucky tourist indeed who happens to visit the museum at the time of the day the Stradivarius violins are played.

What is so special about a Stradivarius? And why is the musical tone, breathtaking power, and beautiful sound of a Stradivarius so unique that it is now universally considered to be the definitive example of the absolutely perfect stringed instrument? To this day, we still do not know the answers to these questions, other than to acknowledge that the sounds that emanate from a Stradivarius are unlike the sounds that come from any other violin. For almost three centuries, instrument makers have been trying to duplicate them. So far, none has succeeded in reproducing the precise features that elevate a Stradivarius to the pinnacle of violins.

Some theorize that the secret lies in the high mineral content of the wood Stradivari used to make his violins, cellos, and other stringed instruments. Others look to the special varnish that Stradivari applied to his instruments. To this day, no one has been able to accurately determine the varnish's formula. And still others suggest that the delicate layer of pozzolana ash (a silica-based material that forms a cementlike finish when mixed with slaked lime) Stradivari applied to his instruments affected the tone in a unique manner.

So far, there is more guesswork than certainty when it comes to truly understanding the nature of the Stradivarius instruments.

Antonio Stradivari was born in Cremona around the year 1644 (although one of his biographers, Bacchetta, asserts that Antonio was born either at the end of 1648 or the beginning of 1649). As a young man, Stradivari was apprenticed to another great violin maker, Niccolò Amati. In 1666, Stradivari began to make his own violins and place his own label on them. These early efforts were similar to Amati's smaller violins. In 1648, however, Stradivari began making larger violins, and he also began to experiment with the dimensions and specifics of the instruments until he essentially completely redesigned the violin. He continued throughout his life to improve his design and build violins and other stringed instruments, working with two of his sons, Francesco and Omobono.

Stradivari's greatest instruments were made between 1679 and 1736. The following is a listing of his twenty-five most famous violins.

VIOLIN	DATE OF CONSTRUCTION
Hellier	1679
Sellière	pre-1680
Tuscan	1690
Betts	1704
Ernst	1709
La Pucelle	1709
Viotti	1709
Vieuxtemps	1710
Parke	1711
Boissier	1713
Dolphin	1714
Gillot	1715
Alard	**1715**
Cessol	1716
Messiah	1716
Sasserno	1717
Maurin	1718
Lauterbach	1719
Blunt	1721
Rode	1722
Sarasate	1724
Deurbroucq	1727
Kiesewetter	1731
Habeneck	1736
Muntz	1736

(Stradivari's Alard violin of 1715 [bold type] is regarded as the finest violin he ever made.)

Each instrument Stradivari made bore the following label:

Antonius Stradivarius Cremonesis.
Fecit Anno [year].
(A X S)

In addition to redesigning the dimensions and components of the violin, Stradivari also changed musical history by inventing the violin bridge. The bridge is the small piece of wood that allows the strings to be raised off the body of the instrument, enhancing tonal control and permitting precise plucking or bowing. Stradivari's bridge design is still in use today on all manner of stringed instruments, including guitars, cellos, and violas.

Stradivari lived a long life. He married twice and had a total of eleven children. He built his last instrument when he was ninety-two, still working in the house he had purchased in 1680 and in which he had his workshop. He died in his hometown of Cremona a week before Christmas, on December 18, 1737, at the age of ninety-three. His contribution to the art of music making and the science of instrument making greatly influenced the future of both disciplines and elevated performing to another level.

Today, about 600 of Stradivari's instruments survive. (It is thought that he made over 1,500 instruments of all types during his working life.) They are, of course, almost priceless, although some do change hands now and then between private collectors and museums for enormous sums of money. Interestingly, the most valuable Stradivaris are currently cellos: It is estimated that Stradivari made only about fifty during his lifetime, and those still extant are exceedingly precious.

No one who has ever thrilled to the sound of a fine violin will dispute Antonio Stradivari's right to inclusion in *The Italian 100*.

73

Giacomo Puccini

1858–1924

Few composers have established an abiding popularity with a
worldwide public during their lifetimes to the same degree as
did Giacomo Puccini. . . . [I]t is safe to say that today Puccini's
importance both as a composer and as a figure in the history of
Italian opera is, quite simply, unassailable.

—WILLIAM ASHBROOK
The Romantic Era

Puccini was born in Lucca, Italy, December 22, 1858, into a family
that boasted four generations of musicians and composers, beginning with his great-great-grandfather, also named Giacomo. Despite
this great tradition, young Giacomo showed no interest in music,
nor did he display any talent for performance or the art of compos-

ing. He also did poorly in school and showed no particular ambition. At one point, his first music teacher gave up in despair, declaring that there was absolutely no hope that young Giacomo would continue the family tradition.

His devoted mother refused to give up and sent him to Lucca's Instituto Musicale. There he was taught by Carlo Angeloni, a professor who had endless patience and unflagging enthusiasm for the young Puccini.

Giacomo, who actually possessed a natural affinity for music despite his early lack of motivation and discipline, learned quickly and soon became an excellent pianist and organist. In 1875, at the age of eighteen, he took up the post of church organist in the nearby village of Mutigliano.

In 1877, Puccini composed a cantata called *Juno*, which he entered unsuccessfully in a music competition in Lucca. In 1880, thanks to financial assistance from a great-uncle and King Umberto I's wife, Queen Margherita, Puccini entered the Milan Conservatory and studied there for three years. His graduation composition was a piece called *Capriccio sinfonico*, which was met with unanimous praise from the critics. The *Capriccio* highlighted two of Puccini's greatest gifts; the ability to compose appealing melodies and a talent for dramatic orchestration.

At the time of his graduation in 1884, Puccini entered another competition, this time producing his first one-act opera, *Le Villi*. Again he failed to win, but the opera was still produced at the Teatro del Verme in Milan, making its debut on May 31, 1883. Puccini's first operatic effort was widely praised, mainly because of his bold decision to include a dance segment in the work.

The renowned publisher of music scores, Giulio Ricordi, was so impressed with *Le Villi* that he commissioned Puccini to write a full-length opera. Ricordi provided a libretto by Ferdinando Fontana (who had also written the text for *Le Villi*) for an opera called *Edgar*. This work, however, was not a success and has not survived. Puccini blamed the failure of *Edgar* on the weakness of the libretto and resolved that his next opera would have a compelling and powerful story worthy of his skills.

He found his story in *Manon*, the 1731 novel by Abbé Prévost that had already been set to music by Jules Massenet in 1884. Puccini's version, entitled *Manon Lescaut*, transformed him into a worldwide success literally overnight. After hearing *Manon Lescaut* (which premiered in Turin on February 1, 1893, the same month as the premiere of Verdi's final opera, *Falstaff*), the English playwright and music critic George Bernard Shaw declared, "Puccini looks to me more like the heir of Verdi than any of his rivals."

Following *Manon Lescaut*, Puccini produced his three most popular operas. These three works are still beloved by opera fans the world over and are performed everywhere on a regular basis. The first of the classic trio, *La Bohème*, premiered at the Teatro Regio in Turin on February 1, 1896, when Puccini was thirty-seven years old. Combined with the proceeds of *Manon Lescaut, La Bohème* made Puccini a wealthy man. In 1900, he built a glorious villa at Torre del Lago in Italy. He composed there on a black upright Steinway piano piled high with manuscripts and scores, sitting on a wooden swivel chair rather than a piano bench. Here he completed *Tosca* (which opened on January 14, 1900, in Rome) and *Madama Butterfly* (February 17, 1904, Milan), adding further to his immense popularity.

In 1909, the Puccinis' maid, Doria, committed suicide because Puccini's wife believed (incorrectly) that he and Doria were having an affair. (An extremely handsome man, Puccini was notoriously fond of women.) This tragic event delayed Puccini's next opera a bit, but in 1910, *La Fanciulla del West*, based on a play by David Belasco called *The Girl of the Golden West*, premiered on December 10 at the Metropolitan Opera in New York. (Belasco had also written the original one-act drama *Madam Butterfly*, which Puccini transformed into his popular opera.)

Puccini next tried a change of pace with *Gianni Schicci*, a one-act comic opera that premiered at the Met on December 14, 1918, combined with two earlier Puccini one-acters, *Il Tabarro* and *Suor Angelica*. Puccini's final opera, *Turandot*, was left unfinished in 1924 when the composer died of throat cancer in Brussels, Belgium, at the age of sixty-five. The opera's last act was ultimately completed (at the request of Arturo Toscanini) by the Italian composer Franco Alfano and staged for the first time in 1926.

Puccini had enormous influence on the development of modern musical theater. Musicologist William Ashbrook explained his "unflagging popularity" by stating that "he understood, as only the most accomplished composers can, the art of insinuating his complex musical personality into the public's consciousness." Opera fans who visit Lucca can tour the Casa di Puccini. This is the house where the great composer was born, and it now serves as a museum dedicated to his life and work. Mementos in the museum range from Puccini's Steinway to personal items such as his overcoat. Fittingly, the Casa di Puccini is also a school of music.

74

Federico Fellini
1920–93

All I can say is this: I am a man like so many others, living
through my own experience, a man who looks at things around
him humbly, respectfully, with naive curiosity, and above all
with love. This love produces the tenderness and pity which I
feel towards everyone I meet, I am not a pessimist and I don't
want to be one, but my preference is for those who suffer most,
who are the victims of evil, injustice and deceit.
> — FEDERICO FELLINI, from a
> 1957 letter to Jesuit priest
> Dr. Charles Reinert

Federico Fellini was born in Rimini, Italy, on January 20, 1920. His father was a salesman, his mother a housewife. (Fellini's parents reportedly had hopes of their son becoming an attorney.) He had a brother, Riccardo (who played the part of "Riccardo" in Fellini's 1953 film, *I vitelloni—The Young and the Passionate*), and a younger sister not involved in the film business. Fellini's elementary education was in religious boarding schools and in his later years, he remarked that the only thing he remembered about those early years was the strict discipline and repressive atmosphere of those schools.

Fellini began making films in 1940 when he was twenty, first working as either a writer, an assistant, or a collaborator on such movies as *Il pirata sono io*; *Senza pietà*; *Il miracolo*; *Europa 51*; and *Fortunella*. After World War II, he wrote screenplays for Roberto Rossellini's *Open City* and *Paisan*.

In 1950, he made his debut as director with *Variety Lights*, but it wasn't until the incredible success of his 1956 masterpiece *La Strada* that he garnered worldwide recognition. Fellini's films became known for several key elements, including a garish surrealism (often involving circus characters and Daliesque visuals); merciless social satire; explorations of the torment endured by creative artists; and depictions of man's solitude in the modern world. His work offered a bleak pessimism that could easily veer from nihilistic torment to giddy euphoria within the sensibility of a single character (often portrayed by his wife and muse, Giullietta Masina). Of Masina (the direct inspiration for his 1965 film, *Juliet of the Spirits*), Fellini said, "[S]he made me cross a certain threshold; she made me pass through a certain gate and enter a landscape, a territory that I still have not completely described but that I very much hope, should imagination again steer me in such a direction, to be able to translate into images." Masina also starred, with Anthony Quinn, in *La Strada*.

Fellini's later work and major successes included *Nights of Cabiria* (1957); *La Dolce Vita* (1960); *8 1/2* (1963); *Juliet of the Spirits* (1965); *Fellini Satyricon* (1969); *The Clowns* (1971); *Fellini's Roma* (1972); and *Amarcord* (1974). Some say his work declined in his later years, but critics still consider his final films brilliant examples of the satirical and autobiographical style he perfected in his early years. Fellini's last works include *City of Women* (1981); *And the Ship Sails On* (1983); *Ginger and Fred* (1986); and *Intervista* (1987).

Fellini's work was a dizzying blend of fantasy and dream

sequences combined with childhood memories and sardonic observations. In *8 1/2*, for example, we see the director Guido (Fellini's alter ego) trying desperately to marshal his creative forces and complete his new picture, but then suddenly and without warning, we are back in Guido's childhood; or we are in a surrealistic fantasy (one memorable scene is when Guido floats above a beach like a kite and we see the scene through his eyes); or in some other dream landscape that transports us into Guido's interior reality. "Our dreams are our real life," Fellini once said.

And then there is the sheer visual virtuosity of Fellini's work. Fellini's influence on world cinema has been enormous: Today, the word *Felliniesque* immediately summons to mind the themes and images so specific to the work of this great Italian artist. Scores of books have been written about Fellini's work, and the critical establishment continues to find fresh insights and new ways of interpreting his deeply symbolic films.

During his lifetime, Fellini won Academy Awards for *La Strada*, *Nights of Cabiria*, *8 1/2*, and *Amarcord*. He also won many awards around the world for his screenplays, as well as the Golden Palm Award in 1960 for *La Dolce Vita* and Silver Lion Awards for *I vitteloni* and *La Strada*.

Fellini died on Halloween, October 31, 1993, in Rome. A few years before his death, after the completion of *Ginger and Fred*, Fellini dutifully toured the world, making media appearances to promote his new film. In *Fellini: A Life*, Hollis Alpert relates a particularly revealing (and characteristic) Fellini moment:

> [On CNN], a pretty young blonde interviewer informed him that she had heard he was a genius. "Are you a genius?" she demanded. He stared at her in astonishment. "What would you like me to say?" he asked, as though suddenly finding himself in his own movie. She smiled, waiting helplessly. "It would be nice to think so," he told her, tolerantly.
>
> She wasn't finished. "What would you like to be if not a director?" she asked.
>
> He sighed, but did his best. "An actor," he said, "a singer, a painter, a circus performer, a musician, a writer, and a doctor in a mental hospital. I am very fortunate. As a director I can be all of these."

75

A. P. Giannini

1870–1949

Courage is the thing. All goes if courage goes!

—Sir J. M. Barrie

A. P. Giannini had the kind of courage and determination of which legends are made. The son of Italian immigrants, Amadeo Pietro Giannini can be credited with founding the bank that would grow to be one of the largest and most successful financial institutions in the world. The transformation of his Bank of Italy into the Bank of America National Trust and Savings Association—the largest bank in the United States and the largest privately held bank in the world—is a fascinating and inspiring story. The most dramatic episode in this saga is Giannini's courageous rescue of his bank's assets from the ravages of the 1906 San Francisco earthquake.

A. P. Giannini was born on May 6, 1870, in San Jose, California, the son of Genoese immigrants. He started out when he was thirteen working as a fruit and vegetable vendor.

After graduating from the Washington Grammar School, Giannini completed a five-month business course and then went to work at the L. Scatena wholesale fruit and vegetable company. By the age of seventeen, Giannini was traveling on buying trips for the company. Because of his outgoing and charismatic personality, it wasn't long before an increase in Scatena's business could be directly attributed to the "live wire" Giannini. By the time he was in his twenties, Giannini was a well-known business figure in San Francisco and on the surrounding ranches and farms.

He soon married and became a father. (His son Mario was active in the family bank both before and after Giannini's death.) Though he continued to prosper, he did not have his sights set on becoming one of the most influential bankers in the history of American finance. "I don't want to be rich," he remarked, "No man actually owns a fortune; it owns him." According to Marquis James's history of the Bank of America, *Biography of a Bank*, Giannini organized the Bank of Italy for one reason: "[H]e was indignant at the neglect of North Beach, San Francisco's Italian colony, by other banks." Ethnic pride, then, was the catalyst for the development of one of the most successful business endeavors undertaken in the United States.

In 1904, Giannini opened his Bank of Italy in San Francisco with money borrowed from his stepfather. He immediately began making loans to farmers and small retailers (often turned away by the larger financial institutions of the day) and actively sought out small depositors instead of courting the business of corporate clients.

By 1906, his San Francisco bank had $2 million in gold and securities on deposit. When the earthquake struck early on the morning of April 1, Giannini knew he would face complete financial ruin if he allowed his bank's assets to burn in the countless fires that were already erupting throughout the city. Giannini acted fast: He harnessed two horses to a fruit and vegetable wagon and raced through the chaotic streets of the city. When he arrived at his bank he saw that the building was still intact. He then single-handedly loaded all $2 million of the bank's assets into the back of the wagon, hiding the gold and bonds under baskets of fruits and vegetables, and then dashed to safety. The Bank of Italy (and over 28,000 other structures and homes) ultimately burned, but Amadeo Giannini saved his business—and the funds of his customers.

When order was restored in the city, Giannini reopened the Bank of Italy. He set up temporary "facilities" (a plank laid across two barrels), in a warehouse by the waterfront and immediately began making loans to people who wanted to rebuild their homes and businesses. The Bank of Italy was the only bank in San Francisco open for business so soon after the earthquake, and this was directly due to A. P. Giannini's personal bravery and his refusal to accept defeat.

The Bank of Italy grew rapidly after 1906, but even as a major banker, Giannini held to his original principles: He insisted on maintaining a strong gold reserve to safeguard his depositors' funds, and he also continued to be extremely liberal in his lending policies. In 1909, Giannini began systematically buying up smaller banks throughout California and converting them to branches of the Bank of Italy. Bank of Italy customers could do business at any of these branches; Giannini thus invented the branch banking system that is taken for granted today but was unheard of before his innovation. In 1919, he formed the Bancitaly Corporation, which became the Transamerica Corporation in 1928 and the Bank of America in 1930. The Bank of America was one of the few banks to survive the Great Depression, and by 1934 it was one of the biggest commercial banks in the world.

In addition to creating the branch banking system, Giannini also made a major contribution to the growth of the motion picture industry. During the first two decades of the twentieth century, Giannini willingly lent money to struggling filmmakers, including Charles Chaplin, Mack Sennett, and Darryl Zanuck. Thus, this Italian entrepreneur also had a powerful impact on the development of popular culture in the United States.

As Giannini's personal wealth increased, he turned increasingly to philanthropy. In 1927, for example, he donated $1.5 million to the University of California to establish the Giannini Foundation for Agricultural Economics. He kept on working until 1945, when he retired at the age of seventy-five "to swim, to listen to music." He died four years later, on June 3, 1949. Much of A. P. Giannini's modest fortune went to a foundation—The Bank of America –Giannini Foundation—devoted to medical research, continuing his lifelong commitment to improving the lives of ordinary people.

76

Giuseppe Garibaldi

1807–82

I offer neither pay, nor quarters, nor provisions; I offer hunger, thirst, forced marches, battles and death. Let him who loves his country in his heart and not with his lips only, follow me.
—GIUSEPPE GARIBALDI

Italians have a saying, "alla garibaldina," which, loosely translated means, "as Garibaldi would do." This has come to mean acting impulsively, following one's heart instead of one's intellect.

Giuseppe Garibaldi's contribution to the modern nation of Italy was his activity as a staunch military leader in the struggle of the Italian states to throw off foreign domination and unite under

261

the royal House of Savoy. Garibaldi was a leading figure of the Risorgimento (the nineteenth-century movement for Italian unity) and, along with Camillo de Cavour and Giuseppe Mazzini, ranks as one of Italy's most important champions. Garibaldi's influence on modern Italy was so powerful that the Italian national anthem is now called "Garibaldi's Hymn." The red shirts he and his followers wore became so famous that there is a type of women's blouse known as a "garibaldi."

Giuseppe Garibaldi was born July 4, 1807, in the Mediterranean seaport of Nice. Having long been part of the Kingdom of Sardinia, Nice had a large Italian population. However, the city had been annexed by France in 1793, and Garibaldi was baptized Joseph Marie, the French form of his Italian name. Until 1814, when the French emperor Napoleon was deposed and Nice was returned to Sardinia, Joseph Marie Garibaldi was a French subject.

When Garibaldi was sixteen, his parents reluctantly allowed him to become a merchant sailor. During his years at sea, he was waylaid by pirates three times and robbed of everything he owned, including in one instance, the clothes on his back. He joined the navy of the Kingdom of Sardinia-Piedmont when he was in his twenties and came under the influence of Giuseppe Mazzini, the fiery advocate of Italian nationalism. After participating in a failed attempt to free Piedmont in 1834, Garibaldi fled to South America and remained there until 1848. In South America he learned the techniques of guerrilla warfare while fighting alongside Brazilian and Uruguayan rebels. He also married a Brazilian woman, Anita Rebeiro da Silva.

When the Revolutions of 1848 erupted, Garibaldi returned to Italy and fought magnificently in defense of Mazzini's Roman Republic when Rome was invaded by French troops serving Pope Pius IX. When the republic fell, Garibaldi led his troops in a daring retreat across central Italy; he escaped his enemies, but his wife, Anita, lost her life during this action. Garibaldi left for the United States in 1850 and lived in New York for four years, working as a candle maker and taking American citizenship.

When he returned to Italy, Garibaldi was convinced that Italy could only be united under a monarchy. In May 1860, he led 1,000 volunteers, known as the Red Shirts, in the conquest of Sicily and proclaimed himself dictator of the island in the name of King Victor Emmanuel. Through the summer of that year his forces captured Naples and advanced to the Volturno River. Though he could have ruled southern Italy himself, Garibaldi ceded his conquests to

Victor Emmanuel. The Kingdom of Italy was established in 1861, and Garibaldi retired to the island of Caprera.

Garibaldi's fame was so immense that in 1861, President Abraham Lincoln offered Garibaldi a high command position in the Union Army. Garibaldi said he would accept the position on two conditions: The first was that he be given the position of commander-in-chief, and the second was that President Lincoln declare that the Civil War was being fought to bring an end to slavery. Since the president is the commander-in-chief of the armed forces, Garibaldi was offered the rank of major-general; and Lincoln not surprisingly declined to issue a statement of policy dictated by Garibaldi. Thus the great revolutionary sat out the American Civil War.

He was back in action in 1862, however, leading an expedition to free the Papal States from French occupation and thus complete the unification of Italy. But Victor Emmanuel did not want to jeopardize his relations with France and thus ordered his troops to stop Garibaldi, who was captured but then pardoned. Garibaldi made another futile attempt on Rome in 1867 and then fought in the Franco-Prussian War of 1870–71, which finally brought about the liberation of the Papal States.

From around 1872 until his death on June 2, 1882, Garibaldi lived mostly on Caprera. In his final years he suffered great pain from his battle wounds and from rheumatism, but he maintained an interest in Italy's political affairs and was a member of the Italian Parliament. After his death, the citizens of Rome erected a statue of Garibaldi and engraved it with his battle cry *Roma o Morte* (Rome or Death). There is also an imposing monument to his memory in New York's Washington Square Park.

As Jasper Ridley wrote in *Garibaldi*:

> He did not deny that he enjoyed the excitement of war, but he never fought except for what he believed was the cause of human freedom. He declared at the Congress of Peace in Geneva that just as he would leap into their lake to save someone from drowning, so he would go to the aid of any nation which cried out to be rescued from oppression; and both in his life-saving activities and in waging war he put his principles into action. . . . He [once said] that human beings are divided into two types, "the selfish ones, who never sacrifice anything for the common good, and the true patriots, who freely sacrifice

what is most dear to them for the benefit of others. The latter are always misunderstood, insulted and dragged through the dirt, while the former rule the world."

There have been wiser politicians and greater generals than Garibaldi; but none have been more lovable or more loved.

77

Charles "Lucky" Luciano
1897–1962

I hate this "crime doesn't pay" stuff. Crime in the United States
is perhaps one of the biggest businesses in the world today.
— PETER KIRK
The Bootleggers and Their Era

The details of Lucky Luciano's life read like the most lurid fiction.
In 1906, when he was ten, he was already mugging people, shoplift-
ing, and extorting money. As a teenager, he peddled heroin. In
1929 he was kidnapped by four hoods, severely beaten, and stabbed
several times with an icepick; then his throat was slit, and he was
left for dead on a Staten Island beach. Amazingly, Luciano survived
and went on to become the most powerful organized crime figure

in the 1930s in the United States, the "boss of all the bosses" and the man who continued to run the National Crime Syndicate even from a jail cell.

The organized crime cartel known as the Mafia surfaced in the United States in 1890 in New Orleans, when the society shot and killed the city's police chief, David Hennessey. The organization's roots, however, were in Sicily, and they were centuries old. According to *A Picture History of Crime*, "Crime historians place the beginnings of the Mafia in the late 13th century when Sicily was struggling to free itself from the domination of the French. A secret society was instrumental in the fight and their slogan was 'Morte Alla Francia Italia Anela!' (Death to the French is Italy's Cry!) The word "mafia" is an acronym taken from the slogan."

Charles "Lucky" Luciano was born Salvatore Lucania in Lercara Friddi, Sicily, on November 24, 1897. He emigrated to New York with his parents when he was nine years old and shortly thereafter got involved in an impressive range of criminal activity, starting out with the Five Points Gang on New York's Lower East Side. His budding career came to a temporary halt in 1916, when he was arrested for drug dealing and served a six-month jail term.

When he got out of prison, Luciano teamed up with two other hoods, Frank Costello and Meyer Lansky. In 1920, he joined the powerful Masseria crime family, headed by Giuseppe Masseria. (By this time he had earned the nickname "Lucky" because of his great success at shooting craps.) Luciano took over the prostitution "department" of Masseria's crime empire, taking a fifty percent cut of everything the prostitutes made. This was payment for Luciano's "protection," and the women who protested this arrangement ended up with their legs or arms broken or their faces disfigured, or worse. By 1927, when he was only thirty years old, Luciano was a millionaire several times over and controlled the majority of the prostitutes in New York City.

By 1930, Masseria had christened himself "Joe the Boss" and was facing competition from Salvatore Maranzano, head of a rival crime family. Luciano, ever the pragmatist, realized that it was in his own best interests to eliminate Masseria and then forge a mutually advantageous "peace agreement" with Maranzano.

On April 15, 1931, Luciano and Masseria were having lunch together in a Brooklyn restaurant. Luciano excused himself and got up to use the men's room. While he was in the bathroom, four gunmen—Vito Genovese, Albert Anastasio, Joe Adonis, and Bugsy Siegel—stormed the restaurant and killed Masseria. Luciano, who had ordered the hit, met with Maranzano two days later (with Al Capone's blessing and on his turf) and worked out an agreement that had Maranzano running things as the new "boss of bosses." Six months later, Luciano had Maranzano killed and then took over as the chief of the American underworld.

Luciano had big plans. In 1934, he and Meyer Lansky formed the National Crime Syndicate, controlling and expanding their prostitution business as well as all other facets of the rackets. But two years later the law caught up with him again when New York Special Prosecutor Thomas Dewey succeeded in getting Luciano sentenced to a thirty-to-fifty-year prison sentence for extortion and promoting prostitution. Undeterred, Luciano continued to run his crime empire from his prison cell. When the United States entered World War II in 1941, it turned out to be another break for Luciano. By 1942, shipments of war supplies were being delayed by disgruntled members of the longshoreman's union. In one of the stranger episodes in American history, government officials visited Luciano in prison and asked him to use his influence to stop the sabotaging of the docks. Luciano graciously issued a few orders, and the problems stopped. In return for his help, Luciano was granted a parole in 1945. He was deported to Italy the following year and lived for a time in Rome. But he soon turned up in Havana, Cuba, a convenient base for the direction of his criminal activities in the United States. Cuba soon bowed to U. S. pressure, though, and Luciano was again deported to Italy and remained there for the rest of his life. On January 26, 1962, he died of a heart attack at the Capodicino Airport in Naples, at the age of sixty-four. At this point, he was finally allowed back in his adopted country, and his remains were buried in Queens, New York.

Lucky Luciano is notorious for being the most powerful boss in the history of American crime. His influence reached through prison bars and across oceans. It is probably fair to say that much of the organizational structure of today's crime families is due in large part to the criminal genius of Lucky Luciano.

78

Lee Iacocca
1924–

I was eleven before I learned we were Italian. Until then, I
knew we came from a real country but I didn't know what it
was called—or even where it was. I remember actually looking
on a map of Europe for places named Dago and Wop.
— LEE IACOCCA
An Autobiography

In 1986, while he was still president of the Chrysler Corporation,
Lee Iacocca was the commencement speaker at Duke University in
1986. One of the things he told the graduates was the following:

> Think for yourselves. Let me repeat it. Think for your-
> selves. This isn't the first time you've heard it, but it's the
> best advice you'll ever get from me or anybody else. . . .

Remember, everything worthwhile carries the risk of failure. I have to take risks every day. I'd rather not, but the world doesn't give you or me that option.

Iacocca has thought for himself since his high school days, when (according to his yearbook profile) he was "a raconteur extraordinary, and not only can he quip with the best, but he can pun with the worst." Iacocca focused on engineering and science in high school and excelled in his studies. His yearbook profile (which Iacocca's unauthorized biographer Peter Wyden said was "uncannily predictive") also noted that "If knowledge really is power, he is omnipotent. This, together with the ability he has developed in managing and directing school affairs, will prove a great asset in his career of engineering."

Lee Iacocca is the corporate genius who persuaded the United States Federal Government during the late 1970s that his dying car company was too big to fail and that therefore the government should make the largest federal loan guarantee ever to a private company—$1.2 billion—to prevent Chrysler Motors from going bankrupt. Iacocca argued that if Chrysler failed, the nation's unemployment rate would go up by half of one percent overnight; tens of thousands of jobs would be lost; and the nation's balance of payments would suffer as Japanese manufacturers gained an even greater share of the U.S. auto market. Iacocca also cited the Treasury Department's estimate that if Chrysler failed, the United States would have to spend $2.7 billion in the first year alone on unemployment benefits and welfare payments.

Iacocca's dramatic testimony before Congress gained support for his cause, and in 1979 the Loan Guarantee Act was passed, guaranteeing $1.2 billion in loans to Chrysler, payable in ten years. On July 13, 1983 (the same day that he had been dismissed by the Ford Motor Company five years earlier), Iacocca handed over a check for $813,487,500, the balance due on Chrysler's $1.2 billion loan package. This final payment was early: Iacocca paid off his company's debt a full seven years before the loan's final due date. Lee Iacocca single-handedly changed the way business and government interact. The federal government had certainly guaranteed loans for struggling companies before, but never on such a scale and never in the face of so much opposition from the business community and the media. Iacocca persuaded the government to take a chance and ensured that the risk paid off.

Lido Anthony Iacocca was born on October 15, 1924, in

Allentown, Pennsylvania, the son of Nicola and Antoinette Iacocca, who had come to America twenty-two years earlier from Naples. After graduating from high school, Iacocca entered Lehigh University in Bethlehem, Pennsylvania, and completed a four-year degree in industrial engineering in just three years, graduating in 1945.

In 1946, armed with a master's degree from Princeton, Iacocca got his first job, signing on with the Ford Motor Company as a student engineer. Twenty-three years later, he became president of the company. But in 1978, after eight years at the helm, Iacocca was fired by Henry Ford II after Ford became convinced that he was disloyal, a charge steadfastly disputed by Iacocca. Iacocca immediately took the position of president of Chrysler, where he served until his retirement in 1993, restoring the company to solvency and guiding its 1992 acquisition of American Motors. Iacocca's success at Chrysler attracted so much publicity that an "Iacocca for President" movement took root during the 1980s. Iacocca never offered himself as a candidate, although many felt he could have been the first Italian American elected to the White House. Iacocca himself stated in the June 1986 issue of *Life* magazine, "I believe that if I wanted to be President, I could be President."

Following his retirement, Iacocca pursued many interests, including the Statue of Liberty–Ellis Island Foundation, an organization devoted to raising money for the restoration of the great landmarks. During Iacocca's tenure as chairman of the foundation, donations exceeded the $265 million needed for the job, such was his persuasiveness and charisma. When he spoke on behalf of the foundation, he was commemorating his parents' arrival at Ellis Island, their first glimpse of the Statue of Liberty, and their hopes for a better life in America.

Lido Iacocca's most important legacy is that of a leader. He was thrust into a battle for the survival of his company—and for the jobs of thousands of American workers—and he led the way to victory, using personal charisma, determination, and the undying belief in that most sacred of Italian moral tenets—that hard work rewards.

79

Arturo Toscanini

1867–1957

He changed the whole concept of conducting.
— CONDUCTOR GEORGE SZELL
on Arturo Toscanini

*N*ew York World music critic Samuel Chotzinoff, in his 1955 biography, *Toscanini: An Intimate Portrait*, describes the experience of seeing Toscanini conduct:

> I haunted the green room of Carnegie Hall after every Toscanini concert. Though I was entitled, as a music critic, to a pair of seats, I subscribed to a second-tier box, one practically over the stage, from which I could see the con-

271

ductor at very close range. For Toscanini had cast his spell over me, as he did over everyone who had access to him. Yet seeing him at close range did nothing to explain the mystery of his power. He did not, in fact, *exercise* power. He *radiated* it, effortlessly, unconsciously, like some absolute monarch of a long, unbroken, unopposed line of absolute monarchs. Nor could familiarity reveal the secret of his personal fascination. There was no one in any way like him, no one to whom I could compare him.

Arturo Toscanini was born to Claudio Toscanini, a tailor, and his wife, Paola, on March 25, 1867, in Parma, Italy, less than one hundred miles from the birthplace of his idol, Giuseppe Verdi. (Toscanini once told Chotzinoff, "[Verdi] was born a *contadino* [peasant]. He remained a *contadino* all his life. Like me.")

Toscanini entered the Parma Conservatory at the age of nine and graduated nine years later as a cellist. Even at the age of eighteen, Toscanini had already acquired a prodigious knowledge of music, which was astonishingly displayed a year later, in 1886. At that time, Toscanini was a cellist with a traveling opera company. On June 26, in Rio de Janeiro, Brazil, the troupe's conductor abruptly resigned. The nineteen-year-old Toscanini stepped in and conducted that evening's performance of Verdi's *Aida*—without using a score. For the next decade, Toscanini conducted throughout Italy, and in 1898, he became the chief conductor of the La Scala Opera House in Milan. He conducted the first performances of a number of famous operas, including Leoncavallo's *Pagliacci* and Puccini's *La Bohème*.

Toscanini left Italy for New York in 1908 and became the chief conductor at the Metropolitan Opera House. The Maestro's fiery temper and fierce devotion to the integrity of the score was a new experience for the divas who had been used to getting their own way at the Met. A soprano once told Toscanini, "Maestro, you must conduct in the tempo I sing. I am a star." The conductor replied, "[T]he stars are in heaven. Here we are all artists, good artists and bad artists. You are a bad artist."

After seven legendary seasons, Toscanini resigned from the Metropolitan after an acrimonious disagreement with the director, Giulio Gatti-Cassazza. Toscanini returned to Italy and served as artistic director of La Scala from 1921 to 1929. After Benito Mussolini came to power as Italy's dictator in 1922, Toscanini, a staunch democrat, often defied the regime and was threatened and harassed by the Fascists. When he was offered the post of principal conductor of the New York Philharmonic Orchestra in 1929, he left Italy again and did not return until Mussolini was gone. In 1937, Toscanini was appointed conductor of the NBC Symphony, an orchestra established especially for the seventy-year-old maestro. For the next seventeen years Toscanini conducted legendary performances of the works of Brahms, Beethoven, Hayden, Stravinsky, and other composers. The NBC Symphony Orchestra was disbanded upon his retirement in 1954, at the age of eighty-seven.

Toscanini and his wife, Carla, had three children, one of whom, Wanda, eventually married the legendary concert pianist Vladimir Horowitz.

The Maestro died at his home in Riverdale, New York, on January 16, 1957, at the age of eighty-nine. According to one of his biographers, Toscanini had wanted to live to the age attained by Verdi. He beat his idol by a year. His funeral was held in St. Patrick's Cathedral in New York City, officiated by Cardinal Spellman. Toscanini's body was then flown to Milan, where it lay in state at La Scala, until his burial there a month later.

Arturo Toscanini was one of the most visible and renowned musical figures of the twentieth century. He attracted a cult following that included both connoisseurs of music and ordinary people who only knew that they loved what they heard when they listened to a Toscanini performance. As his biographer George Marek expressed it, "For me the outstanding feature of his performances of great works was always the impression it gave me that I was hearing the work as the composer must have heard it in the solitude and silence of his own soul."

80

Gaetano Donizetti

1797–1848

If I am not in complete sympathy with the libretto I shall send it back. I want love, violent love, without which these subjects are cold.

—GAETANO DONIZETTI

The name of Gaetano Donizetti is often mentioned in the same breath as the names of Giuseppe Verdi and Gioacchino Rossini; all of whom can be credited with defining Italian opera in the nineteenth century, as well as influencing generations of composers who followed.

Donizetti's opera *Don Pasquale* (1843) is universally considered to be one of the three masterpieces of *opera buffa* (comic opera) of the nineteenth century, the other two being Rossini's *The Barber of Seville* and Verdi's *Falstaff.*

Gaetano Donizetti was born in Bergamo, in Italy's Lombardy region, on November 29, 1797. (For a period in the eighteenth and nineteenth centuries a rumor persisted that Donizetti's grandfather was a Scottish soldier named "Don Izett" who had moved to Italy and transformed his name into "Donizetti" to blend in with the natives.) Gaetano was one of six children, but only he and his brother Giuseppe pursued a musical career.

When Donizetti was only eight, his talents were so obvious that he was sent to study with the German composer Johannes Simon Mayr, then residing in Bergamo. Mayr, who was enjoying great acclaim in Italy at that time, recognized in the young Gaetano a genuine natural talent. Throughout his life, Donizetti acknowledged the critically important influence Mayr had on his work and on the development of his composing skills.

When he was eighteen, Donizetti traveled to Bologna, where he studied counterpoint under Rossini's teacher, Padre Mattei. He returned to Bergamo three years later with the hopes of becoming a professional opera composer. He got his chance in 1818, when he was commissioned to write his first full-length opera, *Enrico di Borgogna*, which premiered in Venice in November. *Enrico* was fairly well-received, and it allowed Donizetti to continue composing professionally. Four years later, in 1822, his breakthrough opera, *Zoraide*, had its premiere in Rome. A review of the opera in Rome's *Notizie del giorno* contained the following comments:

> A new and very happy hope is rising for the Italian musical theatre. The young maestro Gaetano Donizetti, a pupil of the most famous professors of music, has launched himself strongly in his *opera* truly *seria, Zoraide di Granata*. Unanimous, sincere, universal was the applause that he justly collected from the capacity audience, which decreed a triumph for his work. Every piece was received with particular pleasure.

Donizetti soon had more work than he could ever have imagined. In the eight years between 1822 and 1830, he composed twenty-six operas, an average of more than three a year. In 1830 alone, he composed five operas, one of which, *Anna Bolena*, was a huge success. Even the leader of the Italian Risorgimento, Giuseppe Mazzini, praised *Anna Bolena* in an exceptionally flattering review. Two years later, Donizetti completed *L'Elisir d'Amore* (*The Elixir of Love*), one of his most beloved works. This work was met with unanimous acclaim and is still performed with regularity today.

Donizetti's later works touched on a wide range of subjects, including Italian history (*Lucrezia Borgia*), English history (*Rosamonda d'Inghliterra*, 1834, and *Maria Stuarda*, also 1834); and the work of Sir Walter Scott (*Lucia di Lammermoor*, 1835, believed to be his best opera). In addition to his vast operatic output (numbering more than sixty works in all), Donizetti wrote church music, chamber music, piano pieces, and songs.

As musicologist Charles Osborne correctly notes, "Donizetti is important as the leading Italian opera composer of the 1830s and 1840s, spanning the gap between Rossini and Bellini." And Donizetti biographer William Ashbrook comments on the composer's range and significance:

> [Donizetti's] versatility as a composer is demonstrated in his mastery of all the operatic genres then current: farce, *opera buffa, opera seria* (which he played a very significant part in developing towards the Romantic *melodramma*, which became the dominant form of Italian opera through much of the nineteenth century), *opera semiseria*, French *grand opéra*, and French *opéra comique*.

The hallmarks of Donizetti's extensive repertoire include flowing, exuberant melodies that have captivated such notable modern singers as soprano Joan Sutherland and tenor Luciano Pavarotti. (Sutherland's performances of the title role in *Lucia di Lammermoor* were the hallmark of her career.) Donizetti's precise melodic lines, requiring sophisticated vocal agility, stand as outstanding examples of the exquisite *bel canto* (Italian for "beautiful singing") style and evince a lyrical purity prized by singers and audiences for the past century.

Though Donizetti mastered the comedic charm of *opera buffa*, his life was often marred by misfortune. His wife gave birth to two stillborn children and died herself after the second delivery. Donizetti had a variety of ailments, and by early 1843, it became clear that Donizetti was suffering from tertiary syphillis. He became periodically incoherent and would unexpectedly explode into violent rages. He attempted to continue working, but within the next couple of years, his condition got so bad that he was incapable of composing any more. Sometime in 1846 he suffered a stroke that left him paralyzed. He remained in a coma until his death on April 8, 1848, at the age of fifty.

81

Enrico Caruso
1873–1921

This Neapolitan will make the whole world talk about him.
—ARTURO TOSCANINI, on Caruso

Caruso's voice was such a transcendently beautiful instrument that he was allowed to leave the Italian army after less than two months of military service (the legal requirement was three years) so he could go home and pursue his singing career. The official release indicated that he was being dismissed so that he could go home and support his family, but the truth is that his commanding officer, Major Nagliati, believed that Caruso's voice was such a rare and unique gift, it was likely that the young tenor would be of more service to his country as a singer than as a soldier. (Enrico's brother had to take his place in the army.)

Enrico Caruso was born on February 27, 1873, in Naples, Italy.

He would ultimately be one of twenty children born to his parents, Marcellino and Anna Caruso. All seventeen of the children born before him had died in infancy. Enrico's arrival ended this frightful series of misfortunes. His brother, Giovanni, born in 1876, and his sister, Assunta, born in 1882, both survived into adulthood.

As a youth, Enrico often sang at baptisms, weddings, church services, and other functions, usually for little or no money, such was the joy he received from singing. "It was as natural for me to sing as to play," Caruso would say years later. His parents, understandably, were anxious about Enrico's future. His father wanted him to become a mechanical engineer; his mother simply wanted him to have a good education. Enrico wanted to sing.

He attended a school run by Father Giuseppe Bronzetti and made what can generously be called his "debut" when he appeared as the janitor Don Tommaso in an opera called *I briganti nel giardino di Don Raffaele* (*The Thief in the Garden of Don Raffaele*), a light opera written by his teachers.

After his extremely brief stint in the Italian army, Caruso made what is considered to be his *professional* debut on March 15, 1895, in an opera called *L'Amico Francesco* (*The Friend of Francesco*). The opera was a vanity production put together by a wealthy Neapolitan composer named Domenico Morelli who paid for everything himself—the hall, the singers, the costumes, the advertising—just so his music could be heard. The opera was a complete failure, and Caruso only sang in two performances. Two local impresarios, however, heard the young tenor and were impressed enough to offer him work at the Cimarosa opera house the following season.

In 1895 and the years following, Caruso appeared in several major operas throughout the world, including *La Traviata, Faust, Rigoletto, Aida, Carmen, La Bohème, Tosca, La Giocanda,* and *Manon Lescaut,* in venues including Cairo, St. Petersburg, Moscow, and Buenos Aires. The critical and the public response to his powerful voice and stage presence were unanimously positive, and on the day after Christmas in 1900, Caruso sang *La Bohème* at La Scala in Milan. From there, he went on to London, Rome, Lisbon, and Monte Carlo and made his American debut on the stage of the Metropolitan Opera on November 23, 1903, singing *Rigoletto.*

Following his triumph in New York, Caruso was established as an international phenomenon. He toured the world, often making huge sums of money, including a record-breaking $15,000 for a single appearance in Mexico City in 1920. But performing was not his only source of income. On April 11, 1902, Caruso recorded ten arias (from *Rigoletto, Manon Lescaut, Tosca, L'Elisir d'Amore, Iris, Aida, Germania,* and *Mefistofele*) in Milan. Fred Gaisberg, the manager of London's Gramophone and Typewriter Company, wrote of the afternoon in his memoirs:

> One sunny afternoon, Caruso, debonair and fresh, sauntered into our studio and in exactly two hours sang ten arias to the piano accompaniment of Maestro Cottone. . . .Not one *stecca* [wrong note], blemish, or huskiness marred this feat.

This marked the beginning of a facet of Caruso's career that would make him enormously wealthy and that would also preserve his singing for future generations.

Caruso's dedication to singing overcame all obstacles. On December 11, 1920, for example, during a performance of *L'Elisir d'Amore* at the Brooklyn Academy, his throat began to hemorrhage and he coughed up a quantity of blood, staining his costume. "Caruso would not stop," his doctor recalled, and the opera continued. Caruso's last performance was in *La Juive* at the Met on Christmas Eve, 1920. He was gravely ill with pleurisy, yet he sang anyway.

The next several months were torture for Caruso. He had several agonizing surgical procedures, yet continued to waste away. On the morning of August 2, 1921, Caruso's son, Enrico Jr., had a terrifying dream in which he saw his father lying in bed covered with a white sheet. His father, lying thousands of miles away in Naples, had just died. The great tenor was only forty-seven years old.

Many music lovers considered Benjamino Gigli the equal of Caruso as an operatic tenor and anointed him Caruso's successor. But in a letter to the *New York Times,* Gigli expressed the following sentiments:

> I believe that to speak of [a successor to Caruso] is a sacrilege and a profanity to his memory; it means violating a tomb which is sacred to Italy and the entire world. The efforts of every artist today aim to gather and to conserve the artistic heritage received from the great singer, and everyone must strive to do this, not with vain self-advertisement, but with tenacious study for the triumph of the pure and the beautiful. He struggled for this, and we for the glory of his art must follow his example with dignity.

82

Niccolò Paganini
1782–1840

[I] heard an angel sing.
—COMPOSER FRANZ SCHUBERT, after hearing Paganini play

Composer and violin virtuoso Niccolò Paganini warrants a position on *The Italian 100* just for his musical compositions alone; twenty-four caprices (among other works) that inspired and influenced the composers Liszt, Schumann, Brahms, and Rachmaninoff. Adding to this his groundbreaking innovations in the technique of playing the violin and his establishment of the definitive benchmark for violin-playing excellence, his ranking is doubly secure.

The English writer Colin Wilson, author of *The Outsider*, wrote of Paganini:

In every age, there are certain men and women who become legends, because they seem to embody the dreams, or nightmares, of their contemporaries. Perhaps the most interesting are those who manage to embody both—like the god Dionysius, half miracle-worker, half demon. Niccolò Paganini is one of the few musicians to have occupied this dubious eminence.

The legends that have survived about Paganini are truly astonishing. According to one, his mother was told in a dream that she would give birth to the greatest violinist ever to live. Another story claims that Paganini drank and gambled so heavily that he had to sell his violin to pay his debts, while still in his teenage years. Paganini is also said to have perfected his brilliant playing technique while serving three years in prison for murder. The most dramatic tale of all alleged that Paganini achieved his musical skills by selling his soul to the devil.

Niccolò Paganini was born in Genoa on Sunday, October 27, 1782. His father was a clerk and a musician who played the mandolin. Supposedly, he was so impressed by his wife's prophetic dream that he insisted that Niccolò begin learning the violin as soon as he could hold the instrument. Niccolò made his professional debut in Genoa when he was eleven, rousing the audience with his own variation of the patriotic French song "La Carmognole." He studied with the teachers Rollo and Ghiretti, and when he was in his mid-teens, he ran away from home and performed throughout the Tuscany and Lombardy regions. After this tour, young Niccolò apparently did begin to indulge in both drinking and gambling. When he was nineteen, he moved in with a Tuscan noblewoman who had fallen in love with him; he remained under her protection for the next three years, allegedly practicing nonstop and inventing new techniques for his instrument. Interestingly, this interlude is also the one during which he was supposed to have been in prison.

Whatever the real story of his late teens may be, Paganini returned to the stage when he was twenty-three, traveling throughout Europe and stunning audiences everywhere with his unbelievable skills. He was a consummate showman by now, timing his entrance onto the stage to precisely the moment when he knew the audience was at a fever pitch of anticipation. "There was a divine, a diabolic enthusiasm. The people have all gone crazy," wrote a reviewer after Paganini's debut performance in Paris. He loved to show off his brilliance by cutting three of his violin's four strings with a scissors and then performing the piece "The Witches' Dance" entirely on the remaining string. Paganini also used this "one-string" highlight for other works. A poster from his 1832 appearance at London's Covent Garden reads, "Recitative e Variazione Brillante, upon Three Italian Airs, composed and to be performed on ONE STRING ONLY (the Fourth String) by SIGNOR PAGANINI."

Paganini had a truly unique and dramatic performing stance: He stood with his right leg jutting forward and the weight of his body on his left hip. His head hung over the violin, which he held at a much lower angle than most violinists, and his dark complexion combined with his hooked nose and thin build to give him a decidedly diabolic look, all of which made for a mesmerizing stage presence. After attending a performance by Paganini, the writer J. M. Schottky observed, "His clothes flop loosely about his limbs, and when he takes a bow he moves his body in such a singular way that every instant you expect the upper part to separate from the lower part and both collapse in a heap of bones."

Paganini's technical contributions to violin technique included the perfection of double stops; use of the bow to produce left-hand pizzicato and staccato; harmonics; the use of a low bridge for chordal playing; and an unprecedented demonstration of the violin's power.

There is a story about Paganini and the composer Hector Berlioz that illustrates the immense confidence Paganini had in his own talent. Paganini owned a Guarneri del Gesù violin and a Stradivari viola. After hearing him play, Berlioz wrote the orchestral work *Harold in Italy* specifically for Paganini and his Stradivari viola. Paganini read the score, but refused to play it: "This is not at all what I want!" he exclaimed. "I am silent a great deal too long! I must be playing the whole time!"

Paganini was only forty-eight when he died. In his last decade, he had to have all of his bottom teeth as well as part of his lower jaw removed due to an infection. He also had other, more serious health problems that scholars now believe included tuberculosis and syphilis. In his last few years he also lost a great deal of money owing to the failure of one of his business ventures, the Casino Paganini, which had opened in Paris in 1836 and boasted a ballroom, restaurant, gaming club, and concert hall.

Paganini fathered a son with singer Antonia Bianchi when he was in his early thirties, and there is evidence that he was a dutiful father. Paganini separated from Bianchi in 1827, when he was thirty-five. Little is known of Paganini and his son's later relationship and it is apparent that Paganini died alone in Nice (part of the Kingdom of Sardinia) on May 27, 1840, probably from cancer of the larynx. The final legend about Paganini claims that he spent his last few hours playing the violin, giving the greatest performance of his life.

Al "Scarface" Capone
1895–1947

Prohibition has done nothing but make trouble for all of us.
—AL CAPONE

The eighteenth amendment to the U.S. Constitution was enacted on January 16, 1920. It prohibited the sale of alcoholic beverages anywhere in the United States. Its passage came about after a long campaign by churches, women's groups, temperance organizations and, other self-appointed guardians of public morality, and it was hailed by its proponents as the "Noble Experiment."

Although it reduced alcohol consumption among the working classes, the Nobel Experiment was an overall failure, as middle- and upper-class Americans took to illegal drinking with unbridled enthusiasm. Prohibition's major effect was to promote bootlegging, and until the Eighteenth Amendment was repealed in 1933 (by the passage of the Twenty-First Amendment) the bootleg liquor business made Al Capone one of the most powerful crime figures in history. By 1926, six years after Prohibition was enacted, bootlegging was estimated to be a $3.6 billion-a-year enterprise, creating a gigantic underground web of commerce operated by organized crime cartels. In 1927, a year in which U.S. physicians earned around $3,000 annually and public school teachers less than $1,000, Capone's criminal enterprises—which included liquor, gambling, drugs, and prostitution—grossed an estimated $105 million.

How powerful and influential was Al Capone? In *The Bootleggers and Their Era*, Kenneth Allsop stated that "the President in status and several hundred industrialists in material possessions were mightier and more influential Americans than Capone, yet not by so great a margin, and, in concentrated autonomy, were much less so."

At the peak of his career, Capone essentially owned Chicago, and his overall power reached far beyond the confines of the city. Paul Sann, in his book *The Lawless Decade*, noted that "[Capone was] mayor, governor and machine boss all rolled into one. He gave the orders; the people's elected servants carried them out and kept their mouths shut. His authority was so great it could not be measured." Capone's influence extended into journalism, politics, unions, Hollywood studios, shipping companies, and countless other areas. It is impossible to estimate the number of murders and assassinations he was responsible for.

Paradoxically, Capone was neither feared nor hated by ordinary citizens. He was a renowned philanthropist who gave freely to everyone from the homeless to churches. Capone was often perceived as a smart businessman who was just giving people what they wanted, and many people blamed the government for, in effect, "creating" people like Capone by instituting Prohibition.

Capone drove a sleek and powerful Cadillac that was built especially for him in 1928 at the staggering cost of $30,000. The car weighed close to four tons and had an armor-plated body, a steel-encased gas tank, bulletproof windows (one and a half inches thick) and a rear-gunner's window in the back. It also boasted hidden compartments for all manner of guns and ammunition and, ironically, a police siren. Chicagoans would stare as Capone's car drove past, hoping for a glimpse of the legendary gangster. Capone seemed to enjoy the attention; later, when he was being led out of a courthouse and the flashbulbs began to pop, he remarked proudly that someone would have thought that Mussolini was walking by.

Al Capone was born Alphonso Caponi on January 6, 1895, in a small village near Rome. His parents, Gabriel and Theresa, emigrated to the United States in 1896 when Al was a year old, and the family settled in a Brooklyn slum. As was common in poor immigrant families, Al was taken out of school when he was fourteen and sent to work. In 1917, at the age of twenty-two, he was drafted into the U.S. Army. He initially claimed he received the two three-inch scars on his left cheek that earned him the nickname "Scarface" from shrapnel wounds while fighting in France, but he was actually rejected by the Draft Board after appearing as ordered and got the scars in a knife fight with Frank Galluccio over an offensive remark Capone made to Galluccio's sister.

When Prohibition began, Capone moved to Chicago and began working for the racketeer John Torrio, setting up bootlegging operations. Ruthlessly eliminating rivals (including Torrio), he eventually took control of the entire operation and built his criminal empire. The federal government finally caught up with Capone in 1931, when he was convicted of tax evasion and sentenced to eleven years in prison.

Capone was released from Alcatraz in 1939, when it became clear that he was terminally ill with syphilis. He retired to his estate in Miami Beach, where he lived as an invalid until his death in 1947 at the age of fifty-two.

84

Frank Sinatra

1915–

He is [one of] what in traditional Sicily have long been called *uomini rispetta*—men of respect: men who are both majestic and humble; men who are loved by all and are very generous by nature, men whose hands are kissed as they walk from village to village, men who would *personally* go out of their way to redress a wrong.

—GAY TALESE, on Sinatra

Frank Sinatra is unquestionably one of the best-known Italian Americans in the world. As the *Rolling Stone Album Guide* succinctly put it: "Combining a jazz player's technique, an actor's sense of language, and the instinctual, provocative style of a natural star, Frank Sinatra transformed American pop culture."

Francis Albert Sinatra was born on December 12, 1915, in his parents' Monroe Street apartment in Hoboken, New Jersey. He was baptized on April 2, 1916, and spent his childhood years in Hoboken. He was an unruly child and was expelled from high school after attending for only forty-seven days. Inspired by Bing Crosby movies, Frank decided he wanted to be a singer. Around the age of seventeen, he started singing in public, and in 1935, at the age of twenty, his mother, Dolly, got him a job singing at the Union Club on Hudson Street in Hoboken, where he made a total of forty dollars for singing five nights a week. Four years later, he became the featured male vocalist with the Harry James orchestra and then sang with the Tommy Dorsey band. In 1940, he achieved stardom with his first recorded single, "I'll Never Smile Again," which was the number-one song on *Billboard*'s first chart (the week of July 20, 1940). Sinatra's popular appeal during the 1940s was enormous. In December 1942, he appeared at the Paramount Theater in New York with Benny Goodman and his band. This landmark show catapulted Sinatra to unprecedented stardom, made his name a household word, and brought back into vogue the word *swoon,* a term that had not been used for over seventy-five years. Teenage girls became hysterical when Sinatra appeared onstage. They shrieked, fainted, and wet their pants before he even sang a note. These fans—who came to be called "bobby-soxers" because of their fondness for the short white socks they all wore—transformed Sinatra from a popular singer and actor into an adored idol and national pop-culture icon.

Sinatra went on to record a string of hit records, while also making it big in 1940s movie musicals such as *Higher and Higher, Anchors Aweigh, On the Town,* and *Step Lively.* His popularity during the 1950s faded, however, due to a string of mediocre records that some (especially his nemesis, Columbia director of artists Mitch Miller) blamed on his well-publicized romantic troubles with the actress Ava Gardner, then his wife. In the mid-1950s, Sinatra said, "Nowadays I hear records I made three or four years ago and I wish I could destroy the master records. It was all because of emotion. No doubt about it." At the time, however, Sinatra blamed Miller for his decline, claiming he was forced to record second-rate songs with gimmicky effects.

In 1953, with his recording career in the doldrums, he lobbied for the role of Maggio in *From Here to Eternity,* taking a mere $8,000 instead of his usual $150,000 a picture. The popular and critical reaction to Sinatra's performance (and to the film) was overwhelmingly positive. The Capitol Theater in New York showed the movie almost round-the-clock, and the reviews were unanimously enthusiastic. The *Los Angeles Examiner* wrote that "Frank Sinatra is simply superb," while *Time* magazine proclaimed, "[Sinatra] does Private Maggio like nothing else he has ever done before." *The New Yorker* called Sinatra "a first-rate actor," and *Newsweek* wrote that "Sinatra can act when the mood is on him and when the writing is good." He won a Best Supporting Actor Oscar for his performance; his career was revitalized, and he went on to star in a string of successful films through the 1950s and 1960s, including such classics as *The Manchurian Candidate* and *The Detective.*

The 1950s also saw a rebirth of Sinatra's recording career. He teamed up with arranger Nelson Riddle, who was able to smoothly redefine Sinatra and position him as a sophisticated, mature song stylist. The "new" Sinatra recorded a number of hit albums, including *Songs for Swingin' Lovers, Come Fly With Me,* and *Only the Lonely.* These recordings are seminal Sinatra, showcasing his innovative lyrical phrasing, his engaging and sophisticated rhythmic playfulness, and, of course, his ability to communicate the "mood" of a song with the first few notes of his rendition. Sinatra's novel singing technique continues to influence vocalists today.

Sinatra continued to churn out hits through the 1960s, including "Strangers in the Night," and "Something Stupid" (sung with his daughter Nancy). Later in the decade, he recorded what may be the most famous song of his career, "My Way." A decade later, he recorded "New York, New York," a song that had originally been written for the 1977 Martin Scorsese movie of the same name and soon became the unofficial anthem of New York City.

Even after celebrating his eightieth birthday, Sinatra continues to be a vital presence, both commercially and artistically. Several retrospective boxed sets of his records have been released; rare versions of songs have been culled from the archives and packaged as collector's items; and in the 1990s, Sinatra recorded two albums of *Duets* with younger recording artists such as Stevie Wonder, The Pretenders' Chrissie Hynde, and U2's Bono, who said of Sinatra, "Rock-and-rollers love Sinatra because he's got swagger and attitude."

Frank Sinatra's career has spanned a large portion of the twentieth century, and his appeal has extended across generations. As a proud Italian American, he has been a visible symbol of Italian culture and a global ambassador of music and style. Some have faulted him for unsavory acts and associations, and there is some justification for this criticism. But Frank Sinatra's music and movies exist independent of his personal life, and since he has essentially defined popular music for several decades, he must be ranked as one of the most influential Italians on the cultural scene.

85

Martin Scorsese
1942–

Martin Scorsese is a kind of cinemaholic, a man who thinks about movies—who runs them in his brain—more than he thinks about anything else, a driven perfectionist who fuses his obsessions with sin, redemption, violence, sensuality, rock & roll, and camera movement into exhilaratingly dark psychodramas of the soul.

—OWEN GLEIBERMAN, FILM CRITIC

I always felt that Fellini and Bertolucci and Marty are like the Renaissance painters, that sort of Italian touch. It's sort of a flowing painting, a movie is a flowing painting.

—*TAXI DRIVER* ACTOR PETER BOYLE

In 1974, Martin Scorsese made a documentary called "Italianamerican" as part of the *Storm of Strangers* television series sponsored by the National Endowment for the Humanities. To shoot this forty-five minute film, Scorsese simply turned on a camera in his parents' apartment in New York's Little Italy living room and let them talk about their lives. The film is alternately funny, touching, and insightful. It is also a simple, yet very powerful look at the early-twentieth-century immigrant experience and what it meant to the families—of all nationalities—who left their native lands to begin a new life in America.

Martin Scorsese was born in Flushing, New York, on November 17, 1942. He attended Roman Catholic elementary and high schools and enrolled in the Cathedral College seminary with the intention of becoming a priest. (According to his parents, Catherine and Charles Scorsese, the seminary "threw him out" after a year because he didn't know his Latin.)

From an early age, Scorsese loved movies and went to one almost every day. "I had asthma as a kid," he explained, "[and] couldn't play rough. I'd go to the movies." These early "screenings" were profoundly influential on Scorsese: "I just have a feeling of how I loved films so much when I saw them as a child, and growing up and how much they influenced me and my growing." As early as the age of ten, Scorsese was intuitively drawing storyboards and writing scripts for enormous Roman epics to be produced by his own company, MarScor Productions.

In 1964, Scorsese graduated from New York University as a film major, and in 1966, he enrolled in NYU Film School's graduate program. After completing his first feature film, *Who's That Knocking at My Door?* (1968), Scorsese moved to Europe, where he directed commercials and won the prestigious film award the *Prix de l'Age d'Or* for his short film *The Big Shave*.

From 1969 to 1970, Scorsese taught film studies at New York University (while also serving as assistant director on the landmark concert film, *Woodstock*) and in 1971, he moved to Hollywood. His morality tale *Boxcar Bertha* was released in 1972. The powerful *Mean Streets* followed in 1973 (featuring newcomers Harvey Keitel and Robert De Niro); the impact of this film was so enormous that one of the most exacting critics of the day, *The New Yorker*'s Pauline Kael, called it "a true original of our period" and "a triumph of personal filmmaking." For more than two decades Scorsese has continued to make extraordinary films that his close friend, director Steven

Spielberg, has described as being "about things that a lot of us are afraid to admit we even think about." Here is an overview of some of his most memorable works:

- *Mean Streets* (1973): Scorsese's view of Little Italy street life. The film focuses on a fledgling mobster who is driven to become the protector of a self-destructive neighborhood loser. Scorsese is on record as admitting he can no longer watch this film, such is its emotional impact on him.

- *Alice Doesn't Live Here Anymore* (1975): In this post-feminist film twenty years ahead of its time, a woman trapped in an abusive relationship takes to the road after her husband is killed in a truck accident. The critical and popular reaction to *Alice* was mixed, mainly because the audience and the critics were both surprised and a bit taken aback by what Mary Pat Kelly described as a movie that "seemed out-of-frame for Martin Scorsese" (coming so quickly after the edgy and violent *Mean Streets*). The performances in the movie were universally praised, however (especially Burstyn's and Harvey Keitel's), and the film inspired a very successful TV show, *Alice*, which unfortunately transformed a potent, sensitive drama into a brash, lightweight comedy. Ellen Burstyn won an Academy Award for her performance as Alice Hyatt.

- *Taxi Driver* (1976): A disturbed loner tries to find some direction for his life while driving a taxi in New York and becomes enmeshed, with fatal results, in the city's seamy underside. *Taxi Driver*, written by Paul Schrader, is an unsettling look at obsession. The film gained unwanted notoriety when, in 1981, an assassination attempt was made on President Ronald Reagan's life by a deranged young man who had become obsessed with actress Jodie Foster after seeing her as the teenage prostitute in *Taxi Driver*. When the film was originally released five years earlier, however, the critical reaction was most positive, and most critics reviewed it as yet another example of the classic and enduringly popular film noir genre. As the years went by, *Taxi Driver* gradually achieved cult status. (Scorsese himself appears twice in the film: first as a passerby outside the Palantine campaign headquarters and later as a passenger in Travis Bickle's cab.)

- *New York, New York* (1977): A saxophone player and a singer hook up after World War II and begin a romance. Unlike other romantic films of this type, though, there is no happy ending. A decided change of pace after *Taxi Driver, New York, New York* was a box-office flop, but video release has created a cult audience for the film.

- *Raging Bull* (1980): The violent and painful life and times of boxer Jake LaMotta. *Raging Bull* was voted the best film of the 1980s by dozens of critics in *Premiere* magazine, and Robert De Niro won an Oscar for his portrayal of La Motta. De Niro, Joe Pesci, and *Raging Bull* also won Golden Globe Awards, Los Angeles Film Critic Association Awards, and National Board of Review Awards. Scorsese believed he was in a death spiral after the failure of *New York, New York* and thus put everything he had into this film. The result is an unequivocal milestone in American filmmaking.

- *The King of Comedy* (1983): A struggling comic kidnaps a talk show host in order to get a spot on his show. This dark anticomedy is one of the most incisive and trenchant comments on media, celebrity, and the entertainment industry ever made.

- *The Color of Money* (1986): Scorsese's sequel to *The Hustler.* Pool genius (Paul Newman) Fast Eddie Felson (now a liquor salesman) takes on a protégé (Tom Cruise) and gives him "life lessons." Newman's performance earned him an Academy Award, and most critics considered the film a worthy sequel to the 1961 classic.

- *The Last Temptation of Christ* (1988): A powerful and emotional exploration of what Jesus Christ might have gone through if he wasn't *really sure* that he was both God and man. *The Last Temptation of Christ* (which was based on the novel of the same name by Nikos Kazantzakis) included scenes that acknowledged Christ's human sexuality. The film caused worldwide controversy even before it was released. Religious groups picketed theaters showing the film, and many theologians publicly denounced it as blasphemous, although many of them admitted that they had not even seen the film. *Last Temptation* remains a controversial film even today, although its video release has allowed those who did not see it in a theater to see for themselves what all the rhetoric and outrage was about.

- *GoodFellas* (1990): Mob life as seen from the inside; one of Scorsese's most powerful achievements. Joe Pesci won an Oscar as Best Supporting Actor.

- *Cape Fear* (1991): Remake of the 1962 classic about a convict out to get the lawyer who put him away.

- *The Age of Innocence* (1992): Scorsese's brilliant take on the classic Edith Wharton novel.

- *Casino* (1995): The story of how organized crime built Las Vegas and turned it into an archetype for the American dream gone sour. Sharon Stone won a Golden Globe Award and an Academy Award nomination for her work, adding her name to the roster of stars who have turned in award-winning performances in Scorsese films.

With all these major works to his credit, Scorsese has been remarkably consistent about which of his films he considers to be his finest work. In 1991, he told his biographer Mary Pat Kelley, "The movie *Italianamerican,* a film I made about my parents in 1974 is, I think, the best film I ever made."

86

Francis Ford Coppola
1939–

So what if my telephone is turned off again at home? Or my electricity is shut off? Or my credit cards canceled? If you don't bet, you don't have a chance to win. It's so silly in life not to pursue the highest possible thing you can imagine, even if you run the risk of losing it all, because if you don't pursue it you've lost it anyway. You can't be an artist and be safe.
—FRANCIS FORD COPPOLA

Francis Ford Coppola is one of those artists who has set the standards for being obsessed with his work. At various points in his career, he has gone broke, almost had a nervous breakdown, endured the collapse of his studio, American Zoetrope, and seen pet projects like *One From the Heart* receive scathing reviews and even worse box-office numbers. And yet Coppola must be included in the elite group of artistically brilliant *and* financially successful twentieth-century filmmakers, a group that includes Martin Scorsese (another Italian American featured in this volume), George Lucas, and Steven Spielberg.

Coppola is included in *The Italian 100* because of the increased awareness and enormous exposure giving to Italian American life—both its best and worst elements—in the 1972 film many consider his magnum opus, *The Godfather.* Coppola's meticulous and loving attention to detail elevated the perception of this ethnic subculture for many viewers, even as it explored the darker side of the Italian American experience, organized crime. As Mario Puzo did in the source novel, Coppola lovingly recreated the elaborate family dinner scenes; the all-important religious events like weddings and baptisms; the rituals surrounding cooking and eating (notably the "Leave the gun; grab the cannolis" scene), and the formal, almost ceremonial customs of greeting and other manifestations of respect and honor so common among Italians of all social and financial strata.

As *Gone With the Wind* recreated the antebellum South in exacting detail and allowed "foreigners" to fully experience this world, so *The Godfather* offered a glimpse into the lives of Italian Americans in the 1940s. Though the focus of the film was one particular organized crime family, the appealing way in which the Italian lifestyle was depicted did a great deal to combat what have often been garish and caricaturish stereotypes. If moviegoers witnessed Italians committing criminal acts, they also saw them exhibiting personal loyalty, family devotion, and the ability to achieve wealth and outwit their opponents.

Francis Ford Coppola was born in Detroit, Michigan, on April 7, 1939. His family moved to the borough of Queens in New York City when he was a child. At the age of nine he contracted polio and was bedridden and partially paralyzed for almost a year. To amuse himself during this agonizing period, young Francis produced his first theatrical epics: puppet shows he wrote and performed himself. After high school, he attended Hofstra University, where he studied drama and wrote a handful of musicals. He then went on to graduate school at UCLA, where he studied film and worked with Roger Corman, the legendary director of low-budget action films. Corman was instrumental in Coppola's being hired to direct his first feature film, *Dementia 13*, in 1963. (The film critic who writes as Phantom of the Movies remarked that "*Dementia 13* is not without its atmospheric moments, especially the justly famous opening rowboat-murder scene.")

From there, Coppola moved into screenwriting (celebrity chronicler Earl Blackwell diplomatically called Coppola's career during this period "eclectic"), scripting *This Property Is Condemned* (1966), *Reflections in a Golden Eye* (1967), and *The Great Gatsby* (1974), as well as directing some less-than-successful films, including *Finian's Rainbow* (1968) and *The Rain People* (1969).

In 1970, Coppola's career took off when he won an Academy Award for coscripting the blockbuster *Patton,* and in 1972, *The Godfather* catapulted him to fame. The equally brilliant and financially successful sequel, *The Godfather, Part 2* followed in 1974, and the third part of the trilogy was released in 1990. This three-film epic remains Coppola's crowning artistic achievement.

In the late 1970s, the director began shooting what would become his most difficult and potentially ruinous project, *Apocalypse Now,* a Vietnam War film inspired by Joseph Conrad's novella *Heart of Darkness.* This project was so overwhelming in scope and so demanding on all concerned that Coppola suffered a near breakdown, and the film's star, Martin Sheen, had a heart attack during shooting. Eleanor Coppola, Francis's wife, kept a video diary of the shooting of the film; released in 1991 as *Hearts of Darkness: A Filmmaker's Apocalypse,* this acclaimed documentary offered a gripping and frightening explication of what Coppola went through to get the film completed.

In addition to the films already mentioned, Coppola's other work during the 1980s and 1990s included *The Outsiders* (1983); *Rumble Fish* (1983); *The Cotton Club* (1984); *Peggy Sue Got Married* (1986); *Gardens of Stone* (1987); *Tucker: The Man and His Dream* (1988); *New York Stories* (1989); and *Bram Stoker's Dracula* (1992).

Though Coppola's finest work exhibits a profound grasp of Italian life, there is an enormous difference between the work done by *Italian* directors and *Italian American* directors. A different sensibility prevails, a distinct energy found in the U.S. artists that contrasts with the more detached approach of the Europeans. A comparison of the works of Federico Fellini, Vittorio De Sica, Pier Paolo Pasolini, and Bernardo Bertolucci, with those of Coppola, Scorsese, Quentin Tarantino, and Brian DePalma makes this clear. It is also the case that at the present time, the greatest Italian filmmakers enjoy a more exalted rank in the history of world cinema. But years from now the work of the best Italian American directors is sure to survive and achieve classic status with new generations of film enthusiasts. Francis Ford Coppola will surely be included in this select group.

87

Italo Calvino
1923–85

Trying to assess Calvino's writing, I—a hybrid of chemist and writer—would say it is perhaps most concisely defined as a rejection of any given plan or pattern. This rejection happened to coincide in him with a wondrous ability to create new patterns. This is why I truly believe that, if there is one Italian writer or indeed one modern writer in this world who will never be imitated (or, at least never imitated well), it is Calvino, for he is inimitable.

— PRIMO LEVI, in the *New York
Times Book Review,* March 20, 1988

There is a short story in Italo Calvino's multilayered 1985 novel *Mr. Palomar* (in reality a collection of linked stories) called "The Naked Bosom," in which the eponymous Mr. Palomar comes upon a young lady sunbathing topless on a beach on which he happens to be strolling. As Mr. Palomar walks up and down the beach, repeatedly passing by where "the naked bosom" is on display, his mind goes through a thousand evaluations and interpretations of his actions.

First, he looks away, focusing instead on the horizon. He decides, however, that this is not the right thing to do "because the taboo against nudity is implicitly confirmed" by his action. The second time he passes the woman, he stares straight ahead, not looking away as his gaze encompasses the surf, the boats, the woman's bath towel and, finally, her bosom. At first he is satisfied that *this* was the right thing to do, but he then rejects it as demeaning to the woman because he is in essence transforming her into just one more *thing* instead of the special person she undoubtedly is.

The third time he passes he decides to acknowledge the woman's presence by allowing a tiny shift in his glance, thereby granting her bosom the respect it deserves as an important part of an irreplaceable person. But again he questions his motives, this time concerned that by looking at the woman's breasts he was communicating an "attitude of superiority," and by so doing "relegating the bosom again to the semidarkness where centuries of sexomaniacal puritanism and of desire considered sin have kept it."

The final time he approaches the woman (and we learn *why* this is the final time as the story concludes) he decides to be bold and allows his gaze to linger on the woman's bosom, thereby recognizing its specialness and importance in the grand scheme of things and granting the young lady the same respect he proffers to the sun, the sky, the water, the beach, and all the rest of glorious nature. "This should be enough," he muses, "to reassure once and for all the solitary sunbather and clear away all perverse assumptions." But as soon as he comes near, the woman jumps up, covers her breasts with angry indignation, and storms off, "as if she were avoiding the tiresome insistence of a satyr."

Mr. Palomar is stunned! How could she misunderstand him so? The story concludes with the considerate and thoughtful voyeur coming to a bitter realization (which is also the tale's moral): "The dead weight of an intolerant tradition prevents anyone's properly understanding the most enlightened traditions."

"The Naked Bosom" is quintessential Calvino: The central character, Mr. Palomar, experiences a completely self-contained crisis of decision in an interior landscape in which motives, desires, and countless layers of speculative interpretation are all entangled, and which no one but himself is aware of. John Updike once said that Calvino's writings "can no longer be called novels; they are displays of mental elegance." They are, ultimately, fusions of reality with the fantastic, a superb exemplar of the literary school that has recently been called "neorealism," since it is based in reality but coexists with the fantastic on a wide variety of levels.

Italo Calvino was Italy's outstanding literary figure of the post–World War II era and one of the most important Italian writers of the twentieth century. With the translation of almost all of his work into English (and other languages), he has attracted a global readership and has influenced new generations of writers eager to employ his experimental techniques and stylistic "blendings" in their own work.

Italo Calvino was born on October 15, 1923, in Santiago de las Vegas, Cuba, the son of two Italian agronomists who were working on the island. He left Cuba as an adolescent and traveled to Italy. During the Second World War he joined the Italian Resistance, an experience that influenced his first two works of fiction, *The Path to the Nest of Spiders* (1947) and *Adam, One Afternoon, and Other Stories* (1949).

After the war he settled in Turin, where he worked for a publishing company for a while and then edited the political magazine *Il Menabò*. In the 1950s, he produced the three tales that garnered him international acclaim and established him as one of Italy's brightest intellectual lights: "The Cloven Viscount" (1952), "The Baron in the Trees" (1957), and "The Non-Existent Knight" (1959) which are all included in the collection entitled *The Non-Existent Knight and the Cloven Viscount.*

Calvino's other works (in English translation) include *Cosmicomics* (1968); *t zero* (1969); *The Argentine Ant* (1971); *Smog* (1971); *The Watcher* (1971); *Invisible Cities* (1974); *The Castle of Crossed Destinies* (1977); *If on a Winter's Night a Traveler* (1981); *The Seasons in the City* (1983); *Difficult Loves* (1984); *The Uses of Literature* (1987); *Under the Jaguar Sun* (1988); *Italian Folktales* (1988); and *Six Memos for the Next Millennium* (1988). The last three works were posthumous collections—Italo Calvino died in Siena, Italy, on September 19, 1985, at the age of sixty-one.

Echoes of Calvino's unique narrative voice can be encountered today in writing throughout the world. He redefined fiction writing and was one of the world's truly great thinkers. He was also a writer who shunned the limelight and was reluctant to discuss details of his life. He expressed this in "By Way of an Autobiography," one of the essays collected in *The Uses of Literature*:

I realize that in this autobiography I have dwelt chiefly on the subject of birth, and talked about the later stages as of a continuation of my first seeing the light; and now I tend to go even further back, to the prenatal world. This is the risk run by every autobiography felt as an exploration of origins, like that of Tristam Shandy, who dwells on his antecedents and, when he gets to the point of having to begin to recount his life, finds nothing more to say.

88

Luciano Pavarotti
1935–

We don't have time to pause and see where we are. If someone asks an old singer how he is feeling he will either say he doesn't know or he will lie. Because every moment of every day is a new experience to be conquered. People my age don't ask who and why and what it is like to be great—we just do, and be the best we can. I love people. I genuinely love everybody.

—LUCIANO PAVAROTTI

Italy gave birth to opera in the early 1600s, and Italians have traditionally rewarded opera singers with the kind of adulation that Americans reserve for sports heroes and movie stars. In other parts of the world, however, the appeal of opera has always been limited to a fairly small segment of the population and stereotyped as a "highbrow" pursuit. It is the rare opera star whose fame (or notoriety) extends beyond the world of opera and opera lovers. During the first few decades of the twentieth century, only two performers achieved such overwhelming celebrity: Enrico Caruso during the 1910s and 1920s and Maria Callas during the 1950s and 1960s. In recent years, a third name has been added to this select list— Luciano Pavarotti, the Italian tenor who has become a worldwide cultural phenomenon.

Luciano Pavarotti was born in Modena, Italy, a small town in northern Italy between Verona and Bologna, on October 12, 1935. His father, Fernando, was a baker who had a fine tenor voice and sang in the local chorus; his mother, Adele, worked in a tobacco factory. When Luciano was a child, his father had hopes that he would become a professional singer, but his mother apparently had more modest ambitions for her son: She wanted him to become a bank teller.

Luciano took voice lessons throughout his youth, but he also paid attention to his studies, and in 1955, at the age of twenty-two, he graduated from the Istituto Magistrale Carlo Sigonio with a teaching certificate. He then taught school for a while and even sold insurance. He continued his voice training, though, studying with the renowned vocal teachers Arrigo Pola and Ettore Campogalliani.

In 1961, when he was twenty-six, two major milestones occurred in Pavorotti's life. The first was his operatic debut in Reggio Emilia, located only a few miles from his hometown. He sang the role of Rodolfo in Puccini's *La Bohème*, which would soon become one of his mainstays. The other landmark event of this year was his marriage to Adua Veroni on September 30. The Pavarottis eventually had three daughters, Lorenza, Cristina, and Giuliana.

Following his successful debut in *La Bohème*, Pavarotti toured Europe, performing in Venice, Palermo, Vienna, Amsterdam, London, Spain, and Dublin, singing roles such as Edgardo in *Lucia di Lammermoor*, the Duke in *Rigoletto*, Tonio in *The Daughter of the Regiment* and gathering accolades with each new performance. He made his American singing debut in 1966 in Miami, Florida, in *Lucia di Lammermoor*, then toured Australia with the great soprano Joan Sutherland. Following this tour, he debuted at La Scala in Milan, the world's most legendary opera house, and joined the ranks of opera's most honored and beloved tenors.

Pavarotti's repertoire over the past three decades has included nearly all the major tenor roles, although he may be best known for his virtuoso performances in the operas of Donizetti, many of which are noted for their difficulty and repeated high Cs. Some tenors have their arias transposed to a lower key in order to more easily hit the high notes. Not Pavarotti, though: He insists that the music be played in its original key, and he always hits each note with casual confidence, driving his audiences crazy. Lately, his voice has not been as strong or powerful as it was during his peak years, but he still can wow a crowd and bring them to their feet.

Pavarotti's career took an odd turn in 1982, when someone came up with the idea of putting him in a movie. His popularity was so enormous that it seemed like he could cross over into films and become a star in that medium as well. His debut project was *Yes, Giorgio*, in which Pavarotti plays a famous opera singer named Giorgi Fini whose voice fails him during a rehearsal. He then consults a pretty throat specialist, played by Kathryn Harrold—as Mick Martin put it in his *Video Movie Guide*, "They fall in love and the viewer falls asleep." After the movie bombed, Pavarotti reflected, "The failure of *Yes, Giorgio* taught me one thing: I am a singer not a lover—at least not in public."

Since then, Pavarotti has concentrated on his singing career, traveling the world eleven months out of the year, performing in opera houses everywhere and also appearing in documentary films. In his "spare time" the tenor known as Opera's Golden Voice teaches master voice classes and spends time with his family at their home in Rimini, Italy.

Pavarotti has been very successful commercially, generating excellent sales for any recording in which he participates. And as with any extremely popular musical star, Pavarotti's fame has resulted in a thriving underground traffic in "pirate" recordings. Technically illegal recordings of Pavarotti performances are in the hands of fans and collectors all over the world and are traded and sold within a discreet, yet highly knowledgeable network.

Since the mid-1960s, Pavarotti has been a major recording artist for London Records. His recorded discography includes all the major operas, as well as collections of arias, compilations of superb concert performances, duets with Joan Sutherland, selections of Christmas hymns, and collections of Neapolitan popular songs, as well as unique and interesting recordings such as *Pavarotti and Friends* and collaborations with contemporary artists.

Pavarotti is one of the most successful performance and recording artists of all time. His manager, Herbert Breslin, has claimed that Pavarotti is the highest-paid concert singer in the business and boasted in *Pavarotti: My Own Story* that his client's album of popular songs, *O Sole Mio*, outsold any record ever released by a classical singer. At one point, Breslin noted, Pavarotti had eight records on *Billboard* magazine's list of the top-forty classical recordings, an amazing twenty percent of the list. Pavarotti has appeared on television all over the world, including *The Tonight Show* and *Late Night with David Letterman* in the United States; after his *Live from Lincoln Center* concert aired throughout the United States, Public Broadcasting received over 100,000 letters praising his performance.

In 1981, he published his autobiography, *Pavarotti: My Own Story*, and in the early nineties he had a huge mainstream hit with an album and video called *The Three Tenors*, in which he sang with Plácido Domingo and José Carreras.

Luciano Pavarotti is a true crossover artist: He appeals to every age group (including, surprisingly, teenagers), as well as to people who do not usually consider themselves fans of opera.

Pavarotti has a warm and dynamic personality that his fans find irresistible. It is obvious to them that he loves what he is doing and that he revels in delighting them. Fittingly, Pavarotti concluded his autobiography with the following thought: "Singing by itself gives me enormous joy. But the greatest satisfaction comes from knowing that my singing makes many people happy."

89

Robert De Niro
1943–

Al Pacino
1940–

[H]e knows how powerful he is. It's total economy. Borders on rarefied. He knows exactly to the vowel what's too much.
—ROBIN WILLIAMS, talking about De Niro

There is only one way of surviving all the early heartbreaks in this business. You must have a sense of humor. And I think it also helps if you are a dreamer. I had my dreams all right. And that is something no one can ever take away. They cost nothing, and they can be as real as you like to make them. You own your dreams, and they are priceless. I've been a lavatory attendant, a theater usher, a panhandler, all for real. Now, as an actor, I can be a journalist today and a brain surgeon tomorrow. That's the stuff *my* dreams are made of.
—AL PACINO

These two important and powerful movie stars of Italian descent (who finally appeared in a movie together in 1995's *Heat*) exemplify the best of the acting profession. They each *inhabit* their roles, creating fully-defined and immediately recognizable characters that are so distinctive and compelling that they instantly become part of contemporary popular culture and cinematic history. Their presence in a film is a virtual guarantee of quality.

Robert De Niro's roles include such classic portrayals as the catatonic patient brought back to awareness in *Awakenings*; the psychotic cabbie Travis Bickle in *Taxi Driver*; the Vietnam vet Michael in *The Deer Hunter*; the young Vito Corleone in *The Godfather, Part 2*; Jake La Motta in *Raging Bull*; the obsessive Rupert Pupkin in *The King of Comedy*; the amoral Jimmy in *GoodFellas*; plus other superb performances in *Midnight Run*; *Mean Streets*; *1900*; *Angel Heart*; *Backdraft*; *Bang the Drum Slowly*; *The Mission*; *Mad Dog and Glory*; *Casino*; *New York, New York*; *Once Upon a Time in America*; *This Boy's Life*; and *The Untouchables*.

Robert "Bobby" De Niro was born on Manhattan's Lower East Side on August 17, 1943. Both his parents were painters, and his father, Robert De Niro, Sr., achieved fame for his abstract canvases. As a youth, Bobby was a loner and was even part of a street gang for a while. (His mother once told a reporter that her son's idea of high school "was not to show up.") When he was sixteen, he met the renowned acting teacher Stella Adler, and from that point on acting became his passion.

De Niro made his screen debut in 1968 in the early Brian DePalma film, *Greetings*. He first garnered critical attention with his performance in 1973's *Bang the Drum Slowly*, followed by his powerful, gritty role in Martin Scorsese's first feature film, *Mean Streets*. De Niro made his directorial debut in 1993 with *A Bronx Tale*, in which he also acted. De Niro has been nominated three times for an Academy Award, and won twice, for *The Godfather, Part 2* in 1974, and for *Raging Bull* in 1980.

De Niro has three children and is a partner in restaurants in New York City (TriBeCa Grill) and San Francisco (Rubicon, with Robin Williams). He was married for a time to model Toukie Smith, with whom he had two sons. (His other child is with his first wife, actress Diahnne Abbott.) His latest films include *Copland*, *The Fan*, *Heat*, *Sleepers*, and *Marvin's Room*. De Niro also appeared on the cover of the second issue of John F. Kennedy Jr.'s magazine, *George*, dressed as George Washington.

Al Pacino has had an equally remarkable career. His roles include the noble and dedicated cop Frank Serpico; Michael Corleone in all three *Godfather* movies; the gay bank robber in *Dog Day Afternoon*; the guileful real estate salesman in *Glengarry Glen Ross*; the Cuban-American drug lord in *Scarface*; the blind colonel in *Scent of a Woman*; the charismatic mayor in *City Hall*; plus other notable performances in *Bobby Deerfield, Carlito's Way, Frankie and Johnny,* and *Sea of Love.*

Alfred Pacino was born in the Bronx, New York, on April 25, 1940, to Sicilian parents. He spent a lot of time during his adolescence at the movies and claims never to have entered his house during his childhood without making a dramatic gesture: "Every time I came home, I fell down as if I were dead. I *always* made an entrance into my house."

Pacino attended the High School of Performing Arts but quit before his junior year. Prior to making it as an actor he held the usual variety of dead-end jobs, including working in the mail room at *Commentary* magazine, working as a movie usher, and serving time as a building superintendent.

He made his stage debut in William Saroyan's *Hello, Out There* in 1963 and his film debut in *Me, Natalie* in 1969.

Pacino has won an Obie (in 1968 for his performance in the off-Broadway play *The Indian Wants the Bronx*), and two Tonys (for 1969's *Does a Tiger Wear a Necktie?* and 1977's *The Basic Training of Pavlo Hummel*). He has been nominated several times for an Academy Award (including for *The Godfather, Serpico, The Godfather, Part 2; Dog Day Afternoon,* and *. . . And Justice for All*), and won the Oscar for best actor in *Scent of a Woman* (1992). *New York Times* movie critic Mel Gussow once described Pacino's roster of characters as "misfits, people out of the mainstream, besieged by and battling society's expectations of conformity. The essential Pacino character is a loner—isolated but with a burning intensity."

Pacino is passionate about his craft. He is constantly challenging himself—and questioning his artistic choices. Here he talks about what he goes through deciding on a role:

> To do anything is scary for me. To do a movie or a play, you're as good as the chances you take, so it's a chance to fail. Also, it's a little frightening to go into yourself and commit yourself, take the responsibility of it, take hold of the reins and say, "I'm somebody, I've got this to say and that to say, and here it is." The most exciting thing about

it is that opportunity to change, to go through an experience and come out of it different.

Robert De Niro and Al Pacino have portrayed a wide range of complex characters, and in doing so have contributed to a balanced perception of Italians and Italian Americans. It is important for the public to understand that for every Michael Corleone, there is a Frank Serpico. De Niro and Pacino have brought this truth home with all the power of their art.

Joe DiMaggio
1914–

[DiMaggio] was the ultimate ballplayer, not only for talent but for style and grace. This was the epitome of celestial craftsmanship in a ballplayer. DiMaggio has to this day a mystique, and like most mystiques, it's unexplainable. Is he shy? Is he aloof? Is he a snob? What is he? To the fan it never really mattered because there was Joe out on the ballfield.

— DONALD HONIG, quoted in the
documentary *When It Was a Game*

There are two stories about Joe DiMaggio, both involving autographed baseballs, that succinctly convey his impact on twentieth-century culture.

The first was told by the famous actress Lillian Gish, who lived for a time in the Elysée Hotel in midtown Manhattan. The Elysée was also DiMaggio's summer home during the years when he starred for the New York Yankees. Gish ran into DiMaggio at the hotel and asked him for an autographed baseball. Joe kindly obliged, and Gish then took the ball with her on a trip to Spain. When she was in Madrid, she placed the baseball on the windowsill of her hotel room. As soon as passersby learned that the ball had DiMaggio's signature on it, crowds gathered beneath the window just to catch a glimpse of it. People reacted as though the baseball were some sort of sacred relic that could only be displayed on rare occasions, and they regarded it with silent awe. Gish then moved on to Barcelona, and the same thing happened. Clearly few Spaniards followed American baseball in those days, but they had all heard of Joe DiMaggio. As Joseph Durso wrote in *DiMaggio: The Last American Knight,* "The mystique crossed international frontiers."

The second story concerns a ball owned by DiMaggio himself, probably the most unusual baseball souvenir in history. DiMaggio got the ball in December 1987, when he was invited to an exclusive state dinner at the White House in honor of the three-day summit conference on arms reduction attended by Soviet premier Mikhail Gorbachev and hosted by President Ronald Reagan. The guest list included luminaries from all spheres of American life, and DiMaggio was representing the world of sports.

With the help of Maureen Reagan, the president's daughter, DiMaggio got Reagan and Gorbachev to autograph a baseball for him. When the ball was returned to him, DiMaggio knew he had a valuable piece of history. When asked what he intended to do with his souvenir, DiMaggio replied, "I haven't made the decision yet. . . . I've already had requests to buy it. But there's no way in the world I'll sell it."

Reflecting on this incident, Joseph Durso pointed out that DiMaggio could actually have made the ball worth more "by adding the one other signature that would enhance it: Joe DiMaggio's." It speaks volumes about Joe DiMaggio's stature that *his* signature would increase the value of a ball signed by the world's most powerful political leaders.

Joseph Paul DiMaggio was born on November 25, 1914, in Martinez, California, to Giuseppe Paolo and Rosalie DiMaggio. Joe was the eighth of nine children. Giuseppe DiMaggio struggled to make a living as a fisherman, and Joe dropped out of high school when he was sixteen to help his family get through the Great Depression. He played ball whenever he could, and it was soon clear that the lanky youngster possessed an explosive bat, a sure

glove, and a powerful arm. He worked his way up through the
minors, and in 1936, the New York Yankees purchased him from
the San Francisco Seals of the Pacific Coast League.

DiMaggio's accomplishments on the diamond are overwhelming:

- He had a sixty-one-game hitting streak in the minor leagues at
  the age of eighteen.

- He led the American League in homeruns twice, in 1937 and
  1948.

- He had the highest batting average in the AL—.381—in 1939.

- He led the AL in slugging average twice, in 1937 and 1950.

- He had the most runs batted in in the AL in 1941 and 1948.

- He was voted the AL's Most Valuable Player three times, in 1939,
  1941, and 1947.

- In his thirteen seasons with the New York Yankees (he spent
  three years in the armed forces during World War II) he led the
  team to ten pennants and nine World Series titles.

- In 1941, he hit safely in fifty-six consecutive games, a record that
  baseball people believe will never be surpassed.

- He finished his career with a .325 lifetime batting average, 2,214
  hits, 361 home runs, and 1,537 runs batted in.

- He was elected to the Baseball Hall of Fame in 1955.

Statistics alone cannot account for his popularity. What fans—
and other players—admired most was DiMaggio's grace and elegance on the field, his personal dignity, his refusal to boast about
his triumphs or to make excuses when injuries hindered his performance—to countless people, he was the ideal man as well as the
supreme ball player.

DiMaggio's hold on the imagination of Americans grew even
more powerful in January 1954, when he married the glamorous
actress Marilyn Monroe. The public was enchanted by this story-
book romance, but the couple split up nine months later when it
became obvious that Marilyn could not live up to the rigidly conservative standards set by Joe. They remained close until her death in
1962, and DiMaggio sent roses to her crypt three times a week for
fifteen years, canceling the order only because fans kept stealing

the flowers. Marilyn was probably the one true love of Joe's life and he has always refused to speak publicly about her or their relationship.

Joe DiMaggio has kept busy in retirement with sports shows, sponsorships (Bowery Bank, Mr. Coffee, among others) and his grandchildren. (DiMaggio's first wife was showgirl Dorothy Arnold, whom he married in 1939. In 1941, Dorothy gave birth to DiMaggio's only child, Joe Jr., who later attended Yale University, married, and had two daughters.) He still appears regularly on Old Timers' Day at Yankee Stadium, and when he steps onto the field the fans—most of whom were born long after he retired—greet him with the kind of ovation reserved for living legends.

91

Sacco and Vanzetti

Nicola Sacco
1891–1927

Bartolomeo Vanzetti
1888–1927

[A]ny stigma and disgrace should be forever removed from their names.
— MASSACHUSETTS GOVERNOR MICHAEL DUKAKIS
in 1977, upon issuing a proclamation that
posthumously vindicated Sacco and Vanzetti

The seven-year-long criminal prosecution (from 1920 through 1927) of Nicola Sacco and Bartolomeo Vanzetti, two Italian immigrants accused of murdering two men during the robbery of a shoe factory, generated a worldwide outpouring of protests that seared their names into the annals of American history. Sacco and Vanzetti merit inclusion in *The Italian 100* because their condemnation and execution changed forever the relationship between the large population of Italian immigrants and the American power structure and judicial system.

On Thursday, April 15, 1920, Frederick Parmenter, a shoe factory paymaster, and Alessandro Berardelli, a factory guard, were shot and killed during a robbery in South Braintree, Massachusetts. Three weeks later, on May 5, Sacco and Vanzetti, two avowed anarchists, were arrested while trying to distribute radical antigovernment literature from their car. They were brought to trial in the Massachusetts Superior Court at Dedham on May 21 before Judge Webster Thayer, and less than two months later, on July 14, a jury pronounced both men guilty of the heinous crimes with which they had been charged. Judge Thayer sentenced them to death.

Four years later, as Sacco and Vanzetti's conviction was being appealed, a convicted murderer named Celestino Madeiros confessed that he and other members of the Joe Morelli gang had actually committed the South Braintree murders. However, this revelation proved worthless to Sacco and Vanzetti because the law at the time gave the presiding judge—Webster Thayer—the final say on whether or not to reopen the case. Thayer's refusal to do so convinced Sacco and Vanzetti's supporters, as well as many fair-minded Americans, that the two men were actually being persecuted because they were immigrants and political radicals. Sacco and Vanzetti's lawyer, William Thompson, scathingly summed up the judge's character in his appeal to the governor for a new trial: "[H]e is a narrow minded man, he is a half educated man, he is an unintelligent man, he is carried away with his fear of reds. . . . ."

Thompson's motion was denied, but the uproar over Sacco and Vanzetti's conviction became a worldwide phenomenon. Bombs were set off in New York and Philadelphia, and huge public demonstrations on behalf of the two Italians were staged in cities all over the globe. Nevertheless, on August 23, 1927, after countless appeals and continuances, Sacco and Vanzetti were put to death in the Massachusetts electric chair. Fifty thousand marchers, each wearing a red armband, accompanied their coffins to the cemetery.

In 1928, Upton Sinclair published his book *Boston*, which detailed the injustice done to the two Italians, and the cause of Sacco and Vanzetti remained very much alive. As late as 1959, hearings were still being held in Massachusetts on motions to clear Sacco and Vanzetti's names; finally, in 1977, the Commonwealth of Massachusetts officially exonerated the two Italians.

Sacco and Vanzetti's execution changed forever how Italian immigrants viewed their new homeland. Many Italians concluded that there was a conspiracy against the two outspoken radicals and the same thing could happen to any one of them, at any time. In *La Storia: Five Centuries of the Italian American Experience,* Jerre Mangione and Ben Morreale explain the importance of the Sacco-Vanzetti case to Italians:

> What is significant for the history of Italian Americans is not so much whether the men were guilty, but what the case tells us of the relationship that existed between those early immigrants and the rest of America. The Sacco and Vanzetti case was a crossroads for the Italian immigrants and their children. Significantly, it was during this period that some of the young and ambitious turned their energies to crime rather than politics or honest work as a way out of the ghetto.

The Sacco and Vanzetti case was a milestone event in the history of Italian Americans, even more significant than the mass lynching of Italian immigrants in New Orleans in 1891, because of the massive publicity it generated. It still resonates as one of the great moral crises in American history, and the issues it raised are still debated in many different forms. Significantly, in 1977, exactly half a century after the execution, the noted author Katharine Anne Porter published her impassioned memoir of the Sacco-Vanzetti case, *The Never-Ending Wrong.* It is only fitting to conclude with excerpts from the pre-sentencing remarks of the two doomed Italians:

> **NICOLA SACCO:** I know the sentence will be between two classes, the oppressed class and the rich class, there will always be collision between the one and the other.

> **BARTOLOMEO VANZETTI:** [M]y conviction is that I have suffered for things that I am guilty of. I am suffering because I am a radical and indeed I am a radical; I have

suffered because I was an Italian, and indeed I am an Italian; I have suffered more for my family and for my beloved than for myself; but I am so convinced to be right that if you could execute me two times, and if I could be reborn two other times, I would live again to do what I have done already.

92

Bernardo Bertolucci
1940–

I don't follow a script. I write one, mostly for producers, and then close it. I prefer to go on the memory of what I've written rather than film an illustration of words. All film for me is *cinema verité*, and that means capturing what happens naturally between two actors in front of the camera, unrehearsed and unprepared.

—BERNARDO BERTOLUCCI

In 1987, Bernardo Bertolucci's *The Last Emperor* won four Golden Globe Awards: Best Dramatic Picture, Best Director, Best Screenplay, and Best Original Score. *The Last Emperor* also received three Academy Award nominations: Best Actor, Best Screenplay Adaptation, and Best Director. The film that won these accolades from the movie industry establishment was directed by the same man who had been charged with obscenity in 1972 for his film *Last Tango in Paris*, which can be seen in retrospect (now that the controversy has faded) as a defining moment in twentieth-century cinema.

Many believe that *Last Tango* contains Marlon Brando's greatest performance (much of which was improvised), but this same film was banned in Bertolucci's Italian homeland. By the standards of the 1990s, the nudity and sexual activity in the film are hardly shocking, and even in its day it did not go that far beyond the limits of what was being done by other directors. Much of the controversy surrounding the film derived from scenes such as the one that implies (though it does not depict) anal sex between Brando and his costar, Maria Schneider. Nevertheless, *Last Tango in Paris* enjoyed what Parisians call a *succès de scandale*.

When the film was released in the United States, *Time* magazine ran stills that showed Schneider in the nude, and the magazine received a great deal of angry mail as a result. Many of those who went to see the film undoubtedly expected to be titillated, and they may have been surprised to find themselves watching a profound and troubling portrait of a disintegrating soul. Film critic Roger Ebert wrote:

> Bernardo Bertolucci's *Last Tango in Paris* is one of the great emotional experiences of our time. . . . Bertolucci begins with a story so simple (which is to say, so stripped of any clutter of plot) that there is little room in it for anything but the emotional crisis of its hero.
>
> What is the movie about? What does it all mean? It is about, and means, exactly the same things that Bergman's *Cries and Whispers* was about, and meant. That's to say that no amount of analysis can extract from either film a rational message. The whole point of both films is that there is a land in the human soul beyond the rational—beyond, even, words to describe it.

Entertainment Weekly said that *Last Tango in Paris* presented "an unblinking dissection of the male ego, and it's not a pretty picture." Bertolucci managed to strip away all the artifice of a traditional "relationship" movie and portray visceral emotion, raw pain, and the kind of sex that serves as an anesthetic—and ultimately a form of suicide, in this case—when a person's inner landscape becomes too horrifying a place to inhabit.

Bernardo Bertolucci was born in Parma, Italy, on March 16,

1940. His father was a film critic and poet, and when Bernardo was twenty-one, his father got him a job working as an assistant to the great Italian director Pier Paolo Pasolini. Bertolucci made his first film, *The Grim Reaper*, in 1962, and then directed *Before the Revolution* (1964); *Partner* (1968, based on Dostoevsky's *The Double*); *The Spider's Strategem* (1970); and *The Conformist* (1971, based on an Alberto Moravia novel). At this point, Bertolucci was a skilled and admired director but was not well known to the general public. And then he made *Last Tango in Paris*, and his reputation and influence skyrocketed. *Last Tango in Paris* enabled Bertolucci to make the ambitious films that followed, including, among others, *1900* (1976), *The Last Emperor* (1987), *The Sheltering Sky* (1990), and *Little Buddha* (1993).

Until he made his 1996 film, *Stealing Beauty*, starring newcomer Liv Tyler, the director had eschewed locations in his Italian homeland, favoring locales in Asia and the Orient. When asked in 1996 why he left Italy, Bertolucci told the *New York Daily News*, "I had in some ways finished it. I left my country at the beginning of the horrible '80s. I am not a political leader, all I could do was leave and go look for something different. I went east because I was looking for a world where consumerism hasn't yet created all the devastation we see in our world."

Bertolucci has been called the successor to Luchino Visconti and Jean-Luc Godard, and his work continually inspires and influences younger directors, who look to his work as cinematic textbooks on visual composition and uniquely expressive narrative technique. His projects have attracted many outstanding young American actors, including Debra Winger, John Malkovich, Joan Chen, Keanu Reeves, Campbell Scott, Chris Isaak, Bridget Fonda, and others, as well as such established stars as Peter O'Toole.

Though Bertolucci has achieved mainstream success, his work continues to challenge moviegoers as he explores subjects such as incest (in 1979's *Luna*), with the aim of generating discussion, understanding, and enlightenment.

Vittorio De Sica
1901–74

> For me it is above all a moral position from which to look at
> the world. It then became an aesthetic position, but at the
> beginning it was moral.
> — ITALIAN DIRECTOR ROBERTO ROSSELLINI, offering
> his definition of cinematic neorealism

There are many ways in which the work of an influential artist (writer, director, painter, musician, and the like) can be acknowledged or referred to in the work of other artists. Filmmakers in particular find innovative ways of paying tribute to those who have inspired them.

The director Brian DePalma, included in his 1987 movie *The Untouchables* a scene that mirrored the famous "baby carriage down the steps" sequence in Sergei Eisenstein's 1925 classic, *Battleship*

Potemkin. A similar homage occurs in Robert Altman's acclaimed 1992 dark comedy about Hollywood, *The Player,* when two characters encounter one another at a showing of Vittorio De Sica's *The Bicycle Thief.* Parts of De Sica's 1948 masterpiece are shown, and the movie is mentioned later with the awed respect befitting its legendary status.

The Bicycle Thief (released in 1948 as *Ladri di Biciclette,* often translated as *Bicycle Thieves*) is set in 1940s Rome and tells the story of a wretchedly poor man named Antonio who is offered a job posting advertising bills on the walls of buildings. The only requirement is that he have his own bicycle, a condition he cannot meet, since he has just pawned his bicycle in order to buy food for his wife and son. At his wife's suggestion, however, Antonio pawns their bed sheets and redeems his bicycle.

Antonio reports for work, but then tragedy strikes: While he is occupied putting up a poster, his precious bicycle is stolen. From here, the film focuses on Antonio and his son Bruno's desperate attempts to find the thief and retrieve the bicycle. The police are indifferent; a psychic urgently tells Antonio that if he does not find his bicycle immediately, it will be lost forever.

After a frustrating day of false leads and intensive searching, the exhausted Antonio comes upon a building outside of which dozens of bicycles are parked. As the workers from the building come out and retrieve their bicycles and head home, Antonio keeps his eye on one bicycle that no one seems to be claiming. After everyone seems to have left and the bicycle still remains, Antonio impulsively steals it and rides away, only to get stopped by a mob before he gets too far. A police officer arrives and pities him, though, when he sees Bruno approaching, mercifully letting Antonio go. But it is too late for Antonio: He has been publicly humiliated and he has lost his soul. His poverty has transformed him into one of the "bicycle thieves" he loathed and pursued throughout the film, and the movie ends with Antonio weeping over his sorry plight.

With masterly efforts such as *The Bicycle Thief,* De Sica helped create the Italian neorealist school of filmmaking, defined as follows in *The Illustrated History of the Cinema:*

> Cinema's task was no longer simply to "entertain" in the usual sense of the word, but to confront audiences with their own reality, to analyze that reality, and to unite audiences through a shared confrontation with reality. . . . The theorists, especially Zavattini [De Sica's scriptwriter],

insisted that there was a natural affinity between the cinema and "reality," despite the fact that a camera will record whatever is in front of the lens and that the processed film will then (depending upon the skill of the filmmaker) convince a spectator of the reality of what he is seeing. But it was never quite so simple and Zavattini frequently made it clear that, for him, the entire question remained ambiguous, that cinematic "realism" was merely a convention, and that the neo-realist method was only one possible approach to cinema.

Born in the aftermath of the collapse of Mussolini's government and Italy's defeat in World War II, neorealism was an attempt to present the unvarnished truth to the Italian people and awaken forces that would revitalize the struggling Italian nation. These new post-fascist films were seen as a way to counteract and negate years of propaganda and show Italian social and cultural reality the way it really was. The films were not very well received by the Italian people, however, because they were simply *too* real: People did not want to see in a movie the sad and bleak reality of their lives in the postwar years. But the films had a powerful impact on sophisticated audiences in other nations and redefined world cinema in the postwar period.

Vittorio De Sica was born in 1901 in the Ciociara region of Italy, about halfway between Rome and Naples. He began acting in films at the age of seventeen and also appeared on the stage in musicals and comedies. He began directing films in 1940. De Sica also acted in many films during his life, taking acting jobs (often comic roles) as a means of financing the films he wanted to direct. In 1957, De Sica was nominated for an Oscar as Best Supporting Actor for his performance in *A Farewell to Arms.*

Other important and influential De Sica films include *Teresa Venerdi* (1941); *The Children Are Watching Us* (1944); *Shoeshine* (1947); *Miracle in Milan* (1951); *The Gold of Naples* (1954); *Indiscretion of an American Wife* (1954); *Umberto D* (1955); *It Happened in the Park* (1956); *Two Women* (1961); *Marriage Italian Style* (1964); and *Yesterday, Today and Tomorrow* (1964). De Sica worked often with the Italian acting luminaries MARCELLO MASTROIANNI [95] and SOPHIA LOREN [96].

Not every moment of De Sica's film career has been memorable or influential: In addition to his work as a director, he has also acted in over 150 films, few of which had any real lasting merit. A stunning exception is *General Della Ruvere* (1959), directed by Roberto Rossellini, in which De Sica portrays a con man enmeshed in German intrigues during the latter part of World War II. But as a director, his work has almost always been superb; in fact, he has won two Academy Awards for Best Foreign Film. His first was in 1949 for the indisputable masterpiece *The Bicycle Thief;* his second, over two decades later, was for his visually stunning and emotionally wrenching 1971 classic, *The Garden of the Finzi-Continis,* which details the plight of Italian Jews under fascism.

De Sica died in 1974 at the age of seventy-three, leaving behind a body of films that are brilliant cinematic diaries of a place and a time but also explore universal subjects and themes in a manner that continues to inspire both filmmakers and filmgoers.

Luchino Visconti

1906–76

Enough now.
                —LUCHINO VISCONTI'S LAST WORDS

Luchino Visconti, director of the first neorealist film, *Ossessione*, is today regarded as the key figure in the Italian school of neorealist cinema, inspiring and influencing other important neorealist directors such as Vittorio De Sica and Roberto Rossellini. In addition, Visconti's work serves as a "cinematic textbook" for other directors, showing them how to produce stunning visual techniques and how to brilliantly adapt primary literary sources to film. Commenting on Visconti's visual style, film critic Roger Ebert wrote:

The photography [in Visconti's *Death in Venice*] is almost the first I have seen that is fully worthy of the beauty of Venice; the pink-and-gray city rises from waters of a glasslike smoothness, so that the water and the quality of light itself seem to suggest the presence of the plague-bearing siroco wind.

Luchino Visconti was born to a noble and distinguished family on November 2, 1906, in Milan, Italy. His father was Giuseppe Visconti, the duke of Modrone (which automatically granted the newborn Luchino the title of duke of Modrone as well). The heritage and historical associations of the Visconti family are impressive and important: Giuseppe Visconti's ancestors were descended from King Desiderius, the father-in-law of the eighth-century Lombard king Charlemagne. Luchino's paternal grandfather, Senator Guido Visconti, duke of Modrone, appointed Toscanini artistic director of Milan's La Scala theater in 1897. The effect of all this history on the young Luchino was significant. As Visconti biographer Monica Stirling described this artistic millieu in which Luchino grew up, "This little universe of history and of art, home, and beauty welcomed Luchino Visconti into the world, fed him on honeydew, wove a circle around him thrice, but opened, rather than closed, his eyes to holy dread."

Luchino was a very independent young man, loathing "even the mildest constraint except when self-imposed," according to Stirling. He seemed to always be in trouble at school and was once expelled for having pastries delivered to him daily, a delightful escapade that continued until the baker sent his bill to the school. In his teens, Visconti was drafted for military service, a period which he greatly enjoyed for one simple reason: He was stationed in the cavalry and was required to take care of the horses. After he left the military, his love of horses endured, and he bought his own stallions when he was in his twenties.

In 1936, when he was thirty, Visconti met the famous French director Jean Renoir and was hired to serve as Renoir's assistant on the films *Une Partie de Campagne* and *Les Bas-fonds*. Visconti was deeply influenced by Renoir and the French realist school of cinema, but his genius was such that he was able to take the "poetic realism" of Renoir's films (which Visconti diligently studied) and transmute the style into something new. Film scholar Peter Cowie notes that "[W]hen his first film, *Ossessione*, appeared in 1942 it was sufficiently unlike any other film to excite tremendous comment.

For many critics, *Ossessione* was the blueprint for Italian Neo-realism."

It would be six years before Visconti released another film. World War II and its consequences increasingly made normal living a trial and such "nonessential" industries as filmmaking were severely hampered. Visconti's second film, *La Terra Trema* (1948), told the story of Sicilian fishermen and was another groundbreaking effort. Visconti's fidelity to the tenets of neorealism inspired him to not translate some of the impossible-to-understand dialect of the characters, causing an edgy restlessness throughout the film that contributes to the moody and somber tone.

As he moved through his career, Visconti often drew from a distinguished body of literary work for his films, including *The Postman Always Rings Twice* by James Cain (*Ossessione*); "White Nights" by Dostoyevsky (*Notti bianche*); *The Outsider* by Albert Camus (*Lo straniero*); and *Death in Venice* by Thomas Mann (*Death in Venice*).

Visconti was also a consummate theater director, and during his career he guided such important stage productions as Ernest Hemingway's *Fifth Column*; Jean-Paul Sarte's *Vicious Circle*; Erskine Caldwell's *Tobacco Road*; Dostoyevsky's *Crime and Punishment*; Tennessee Williams's *Glass Menagerie* and *A Streetcar Named Desire*; Shakespeare's *As You Like It* and *Troilus and Cressida*; Arthur Miller's *Death of a Salesman, The Crucible, A View from the Bridge*, and *After the Fall*; Anton Chekov's *The Three Sisters* and *The Cherry Orchard*; Eurypides' *Medea*; August Strindberg's *Miss Julie*; Thomas Wolfe's *Look Homeward Angel*; and Harold Pinter's *Old Times*. He extended his directorial talents to the opera house as well, staging works that included Bellini's *La Sonnambula*; Verdi's *La Traviata, Simon Boccanegra, Don Carlo, Macbeth, Il Trovatore*, and *Falstaff*; Mozart's *The Marriage of Figaro*; Puccini's *Manon Lescaut*; Strauss's *Der Rosenkavalier* and *Salome*; and Donizetti's *Il Duca d'Alba*.

In addition to *Ossessione* and *La Terra Trema*, Visconti's greatest accomplishments, the films that are considered classics today are *Rocco and His Brothers* (1960), *The Leopard* (1964), *Senso* (1968), *The Damned* (1969), and *Death in Venice* (1971).

Visconti died on March 17, 1976, shortly after completing his last film, *The Intruder*. In a biography of Visconti, Gaia Servadio wrote:

> Those who went to see him while he was filming *The Intruder* and were embarrassed at seeing him confined to a wheelchair were immediately put at their ease by a joke

or two: "You'll see me directing my next film from a stretcher!" They were also amazed to see the change in his face when he started work, shaping a scene or correcting a move; this last lordly exercise of his mastery erased the wrinkles of his suffering. He died working, as he had wished to.

Visconti's student Franco Zeffirelli once said, "As time goes by, I find myself missing Luchino Visconti more and more. . . . There seems to be no one around today of his heroic stature."

At Visconti's request, his burial place was kept secret. Thus his legions of admirers were deprived of the opportunity to pay their respects at his funeral. Instead, they expressed their admiration for this great artist in the "Mourning Posters" that appeared all over Rome on March 19, the day Visconti was buried:

LUCHINO VISCONTI
a man of culture who by his great work
has for more than 30 years followed
the history of art, of the cinema and the theater
of our country, of Europe, of the world
and we remember him
as a militant anti-Fascist of the Resistance
who always showed loyal and profound solidarity
with the working class and their struggle

95

Marcello Mastroianni

1924–96

They come for you in the morning in a limousine; they take you to the studio; they stick a pretty girl in your arms. . . . They call that a profession? Come on!

—MARCELLO MASTROIANNI

In Marcello Mastroianni's acclaimed 1987 drama *Dark Eyes*, he plays an Italian named Romano who finds his soulmate—a married Russian woman named Anna—during a chance encounter at a spa. Romano falls deeply in love with Anna and then follows her to her small hometown in Russia, where she lives with her much older husband. After a night of passion, Romano persuades Anna to wait for him while he returns to Italy to tell his wealthy wife that he's leaving her. Upon his return, however, he learns that his wife has lost all her money, and his guilt is so overwhelming that he resigns

329

himself to never seeing his one true love again.

Eight years later, Romano tells this poignant tale to an Italian-speaking Russian gentleman he meets on a ferry. As he speaks, the scenes of his tragic affair are shown in flashback. Mastroianni does not simply *tell* the story, he literally *inhabits* the unhappy persona of Romano, providing a glimpse into the tortured soul of a man who genuinely knew true love—if only briefly—and then lost it forever. (Or so he believes—the film delivers a startling revelation and ends ambiguously.) Mastroianni's performance is a textbook example of acting excellence and earned him an Academy Award nomination.

World Almanac's *Who's Who in Film* describes Mastroianni as "darkly handsome" and remarks that he projects an "often cynical, world-weariness onscreen but retains an air of dignity whatever befalls him." *Who's Who in Film* also points out that Mastroianni seems to "personify the modern European male," and concludes, "There have been few actors before him who have so dominated movies."

This surprisingly self-deprecating star worked with such legendary Italian directors as Federico Fellini, Luchino Visconti, and Michelangelo Antonioni. Along with Sophia Loren, he was the most famous Italian actor of the twentieth century, and his performances have influenced generations of younger actors.

Marcello Mastroianni was born on September 28, 1924, in Fontana Liri, Italy. His family were originally farmers, but when Marcello was five, they moved to Turin in northern Italy. Marcello served in World War II as a draftsman but was sent to a labor camp by the Germans when they occupied Italy during the latter stages of the war. After the war ended, Mastroianni attended the University of Rome. He supported himself by working as a clerk and began acting in regional and collegiate theater at night. He was ultimately discovered by Luchino Visconti and joined the great director's acting troupe, appearing in Italian-language versions of such classic American plays as Tennessee Williams's *Streetcar Named Desire* and Arthur Miller's *Death of a Salesman*. Mastroianni made his first film appearance in 1947 in an Italian version of *Les Miserables*. He worked steadily over the next decade, becoming extremely popular in Italy and then finally earning international acclaim and success in the 1959 classic *La Dolce Vita*, directed by the renowned Italian director Federico Fellini.

Mastroianni won a British Film Academy Award for his work in Pietro Germi's 1962 film *Divorce—Italian Style*, after which he appeared as Fellini's alter ego in the influential and innovative film

8 1/2. Mastroianni then won a second British Film Academy Award for his performance (alongside Sophia Loren) in Vittorio De Sica's 1963 comedy, *Yesterday, Today and Tomorrow.*

During his career, Mastroianni appeared in over forty films, including such classics as *City of Women, Ginger and Fred, Intervista,* and *Henry IV.* And even though he was generally able to resist the lure of Hollywood, he did act in a handful of American films, starring in movies such as *A Fine Romance* and *Used People* (costarring with Shirley MacLaine and Kathy Bates, respectively). Mastroianni was married for a time to former Italian actress Flora Carabella, with whom he had a daughter. He was romantically involved with American actress Faye Dunaway until 1971, when she left him for another man. He had a second daughter with French actress Catherine Deneuve, his costar in the film *It Only Happens to Others.* After his divorce from Carabella, Mastroianni did not marry again.

Mastroianni died on Thursday, December 19, 1996, in Paris, France, of pancreatic cancer. He was seventy-two. Catherine Deneuve and their daughter, Chiara, 24, were both at his side.

To those who marvel at Mastroianni's ability to inhabit his characters and wish to know his secret, he has offered the following insight:

> Method acting is pure nonsense. All an actor must do is cultivate intelligence. For instance, if you have to play someone who's mad, there's no use going to an asylum to watch a madman. The madness you see is his; the gestures, the looks are his, not yours. To play a madman as I did in [Pirandello's] *Henry IV,* you must search within yourself, [and] above all, *invent.*

96

Sophia Loren

1934–

My nose is too long, my chin too short, my hips too broad. But together, all these irregularities seem to work.

—SOPHIA LOREN

Along with her frequent costar Marcello Mastroianni, Sophia Loren is probably the most beloved and popular Italian film star of the twentieth century. In addition to her worldwide fame, Sophia Loren has also been perceived internationally as the archetype of the voluptuous, sexy, sultry Italian woman, an iconic role model whose influence has extended to dozens of younger actresses from the 1960s through the 1990s.

Sophia Loren represents sex appeal in its most enticing form, and yet she is also an intelligent and versatile actress whose career has included hilarious comedies and poignant tragedies.

Loren's longtime friend Ines Bruscia has said of her, "For Sophia, work is a religion." She has appeared in over seventy films since her debut as an extra in 1950, and she has had the unique experience of playing both herself *and* her mother in the 1980 made-for-TV movie *Sophia Loren: Her Own Story.*

Sophia Loren was born Sophia Scicolone on September 20, 1934, in Rome's Clinica Regina Margherita, a charity ward for unmarried women. In her 1979 autobiography, Loren wrote:

> I was a skinny, pale, ugly little thing but my mother tells me that despite my unattractiveness and her humiliating and precarious condition, it never crossed her mind to put me in the orphanage which was run by a nearby convent for the accommodation of babies from my mother's ward.

After a short stint with her parents—her father acknowledged that Sofia was his but refused to marry her mother—she spent most of her childhood with her grandparents, living in a slum in the small seaside town of Pozzuoli, just southwest of Naples.

As a young girl, Sofia lived through the Nazi occupation of Naples during World War II. She witnessed firsthand the Four Days of Naples, when the populace launched an all-out offensive against the occupying troops, blowing up tanks with homemade bombs and ambushing soldiers with knives and clubs, ultimately forcing the withdrawal of the Germans from Naples.

When Sofia was fifteen, she won a beauty pageant in which she was named one of the Queen's Twelve Princesses, and after that, she enrolled in a drama school in Naples. Wanting to be a teacher, she considered her acting lessons a harmless avocation that she greatly enjoyed, until one day her professor made an announcement that would change her life. The professor informed her of an open casting call for extras for a new movie being filmed in Rome, Mervyn Le Roy's *Quo Vadis.* Loren got the part (her mother was also hired as an extra), and thus began a career that now spans close to five decades.

Since Loren's humble debut in 1950 at the age of sixteen, she has worked steadily in films throughout the world. Some of her more memorable efforts include *The Gold of Naples* (1954); *The Pride and the Passion* (1957); *Desire Under the Elms* (1958); *Houseboat* (1958); *That Kind of Woman* (1959); *Heller in Pink Tights* (1960); *It Started in Naples* (1960); *Two Women* (1961); *El Cid* (1961); *Boccaccio '70* (1961); *Yesterday, Today and Tomorrow* (1963); *Marriage, Italian Style* (1964);

Man of La Mancha (1972); and *The Fortunate Pilgrim* (1988). She has worked with a host of outstanding directors: notably Vittorio De Sica, Stanley Kramer, Delbert Mann, Martin Ritt, Sidney Lumet, George Cukor, Peter Ustinov, Stanley Donen, Charlie Chaplin, Arthur Hiller, Ettore Scola, and Lina Wertmüller. She has also appeared alongside an extraordinary roster of actors, including Robert Taylor, MARCELLO MASTROIANNI [95], Anthony Quinn, Charles Boyer, Cary Grant, FRANK SINATRA [84], Alan Ladd, John Wayne, Rosanno Brazzi, Anthony Perkins, Burl Ives, William Holden, Maurice Chevalier, Peter Sellers, Charlton Heston, Anthony Perkins, Alec Guinness, James Mason, Omar Sharif, Paul Newman, Gregory Peck, Marlon Brando, David Niven, Peter O'Toole, Richard Burton, Richard Harris, John Huston, Max Von Sydow, Robert Vaughn, Billy Dee Williams, Hector Elizondo, and O. J. Simpson.

Loren won an Academy Award for Vittorio De Sica's *Two Women* in 1961. This powerful and heart-wrenching film tells the story of an Italian mother fleeing Rome during World War II with her thirteen-year-old daughter. During their sojourn, they are both raped by Allied Moroccan soldiers, but ultimately they find sanctuary in the mother's native village. Universally praised when it was first released, *Two Women* (based on a novel by Alberto Moravio) went on to win Loren the Best Actress Award at the Cannes Film Festival, as well as the aforementioned Oscar. (Loren remade *Two Women* in 1989 as a two-part movie for Italian television.) She was awarded a special Oscar in 1991, and has been the recipient of the New York Film Critics award, the Gold Palm at the Cannes Film Festival, and Italy's Golden Donatello Award. In recent years Loren has stretched her talents by taking roles that deliberately diminished her glamour and sex appeal, most notably the 1986 film *Courage*, in which she was superb as a Hispanic mother.

In 1957, Loren married producer Carlo Ponti, a man twenty-two years her senior. The marriage caused the couple great problems in Italy, since the Italian government did not recognize the validity of Ponti's prior divorce. In 1962, Italian authorities forced Loren and Ponti to have their marriage annulled. Shortly thereafter, the couple moved to France, renounced their Italian citizenship, became French citizens, and remarried in 1966. Loren and Ponti had two children, Carlo and Edoardo.

Camille Paglia
1947–

The women's movement is rooted in the belief that we don't even need men. All it will take is one natural disaster to prove how wrong that is. Then, the only thing holding this culture together will be masculine men of the working class. The cultural elite—women and men—will be pleading for the plumbers and the construction workers.

— CAMILLE PAGLIA
from *Playboy* MAGAZINE, May 1995

In the introduction to his May 1995 *Playboy* interview with Camille Paglia, David Sheff made a bold statement: "[Paglia] may be the most famous social philosopher in the country." This remark followed his account of how much effort it took first to contact her and then set up an appointment for lunch, which she only agreed to after setting out a lengthy series of conditions. Some of Paglia's more provocative statements (as delineated in Sheff's introduction to the published interview) have included the following:

- "Anita Hill was not harassed."

- "Pornography is sexual reality."

- "Rape is what used to be called 'unbridled love.' "

- "Lesbianism is increasing since unmasculine men have little to offer."

- "Prostitutes like their work."

- "Bisexuality should be the universal norm."

- "Legalize all drugs."

- "Stripping is 'a sacred dance of pagan origins' and the bills men put into the strippers' g-strings are a 'ritual offering.' "

Statements such as these have made Paglia both a bestselling author and a world-famous personality. She is a rare combination of qualities and ambitions. On the one hand, she is a pure academic whose opinions (even when they verge on linguistic bombast) are obviously informed by a stunningly fierce intellect and a vast body of knowledge. She also happens to be a smooth, glib, and naturally telegenic personality who comes across so vividly and with such power on television that viewers cannot take their eyes off her.

In the arena of ideas, Paglia's views and writings have been called "guerrilla scholarship." She shows no ideological mercy and takes no prisoners. Viewing human endeavor as a struggle between nature and the artificial psychosexual constructs of society, she emphasizes the biological differences between men and women and infuriates many feminists by claiming that the refusal to acknowledge this difference lies at the root of sexism, homophobia, and other destructive attitudes.

The espousal of these combustible ideas has made Paglia a star, and it has also made her wealthy. In her second book, *Sex, Art, and American Culture*, she mused on the making of her own celebrity:

> What has happened is not my doing but that of the zeitgeist. At the end of the century and millennium, the culture has suddenly changed. There is a hunger for new ways of seeing and thinking. Anti-establishment mavericks

like me are back in fashion. It's a classically American story, the loner riding out of the desert to shoot up the saloon and run the rats out of town.

Paglia has also been enormously influenced by her Italian American (and, of course, Catholic) upbringing. Regarding her philosophical views, she says in her second book, "I sometimes call my new system, 'Italian pagan Catholicism,' but it could more accurately be called 'pragmatic liberalism,' with roots in Enlightenment political philosophy. It is a synthesis of the enduring dual elements in our culture, pagan and Judeo-Christian, Romantic and Classic."

Camille Paglia was born in 1947 in Endicott, New York, the child of conservative (yet remarkably tolerant) Italian parents. Her father taught Romance languages at Le Moyne College, and her mother worked in a bank. Paglia earned a Ph.D. in English at Yale and for a time taught at Bennington College in Vermont. For the past couple of decades, she has been a teacher at the University of the Arts in Philadelphia. Her first book, *Sexual Personae: Art and Decadence from Nefertiti to Emily Dickinson*, began life as a doctoral dissertation. After it was completed in 1981 she began submitting it to publishers, but the manuscript was rejected repeatedly for nine years until Yale University Press agreed to publish it in 1990.

When *Sexual Personae* was issued as a paperback by Vintage Books in 1991, it became an immediate bestseller. No less a literary luminary than Anthony Burgess said, "[*Sexual Personae* is a] fine, disturbing book. It seeks to attack the reader's emotions as well as his/her prejudices. It is very learned. Each sentence jabs like a needle."

In addition to *Sexual Personae*, Paglia has published extensively in magazines, journals, and newspapers. She has written astute (and often combustible) essays on MADONNA [100], Elizabeth Taylor, date rape, cross-dressing, "Rock as Art," the Clarence Thomas–Anita Hill controversy, homosexuality, the photographs of Robert Mapplethorpe, and the career of Marlon Brando. Several of her most important essays were collected in the 1992 book, *Sex, Art, and American Culture*.

Paglia has also appeared on many radio and television talk shows, both in the United States and abroad, and has lectured widely at academic institutions and in popular forums. She has also been profiled in magazines ranging from *New York* and *Harper's* to the *Harvard Crimson* and Taiwan's *Unitas: A Literary Monthly*.

Camille Paglia is included in *The Italian 100* because she is the most vocal and controversial feminist to emerge since Betty Friedan wrote her groundbreaking book *The Feminine Mystique* in 1963. Paglia's intellectual influence extends beyond academia and into popular culture. Her thinking will continue to stimulate—and infuriate—for years to come.

98

Franco Zeffirelli

1923–

> Despite all the evidence to the contrary I am loath to accept
> the fact that one day I will die: like most people I hold to the
> possibility of a vague immortality.
>
> —FRANCO ZEFFIRELLI

It can be reasonably argued that Italian writer and director Franco
Zeffirelli brought William Shakespeare and grand opera to the
masses of the twentieth century. That may sound like a lofty claim,
but it cannot be denied that Zeffirelli's film versions of classic works
captured audiences not typically inclined to attend the theater or
the opera. Most notably, with his 1968 version of *Romeo and Juliet,*

Zeffirelli proved that an "art" film can also be a moneymaker; in addition to winning an Academy Award nomination for best picture, *Romeo and Juliet* was among the highest-grossing films of the year and has since earned over $60 million worldwide.

Zeffirelli's best work includes huge projects that were often deemed overly ambitious (and guaranteed financial losers) when first considered: *Hamlet, Otello, The Taming of the Shrew,* a film biography of Arturo Toscanini (1988's *Young Toscanini*), a biography of ST. FRANCIS OF ASSISI [40] (*Brother Sun, Sister Moon,* 1972), and his most ambitious project to date, the 1977 six-hour television miniseries, *Jesus of Nazareth.*

Like many artists who enjoy large-scale commercial success, Zeffirelli has come under fire from critics. Pauline Kael once wrote that Zeffirelli directed *The Champ* "as if he had never met a human being." And there were few positive reviews of *Endless Love,* his 1980 film starring Brooke Shields. (Zeffirelli himself said that directing Shields was "like cracking a whip at a limping horse.") On the other hand, Zeffirelli has a fervent coterie of fans who adamantly insist that his films move them deeply. Zeffirelli's films may be big and splashy, but his personal love for and engagement with the source material is evident in every detail, and he is responsible for some of the finest film adaptations of classic literature ever produced.

Franco Zeffirelli was born on February 12, 1923, in Florence, Italy. He was an only child and was sent off to live with an aunt at the age of six, after his parents divorced. Franco's parents were Ottorino Corsi and Alaide Cipriani. His baptismal surname, Zeffirelli-Corsi, came from an artistic whim of his mother's. In his 1986 autobiography, Zeffirelli reveals that his mother was very fond of an aria in Mozart's *Così fan tutte* in which the *zeffiretti*—little breezes—are mentioned: "Apparently she intended to name me 'Zeffiretti,' but this was misspelled in the register and came out as the previously unheard-of Zeffirelli."

As a young man Zeffirelli studied architecture at the University of Florence, but his studies were interrupted by World War II. When the Allies invaded Italy in 1943, Zeffirelli joined a British detachment and fought against the Fascists and the Germans.

After the war, when he was twenty-three, Zeffirelli met the man whom he would later claim taught him everything he knew, the great Italian director Luchino Visconti. Zeffirelli had been working as an actor, in Florence, but Visconti saw that he was clearly meant to do more and gave him an opportunity to design sets for a number of stage productions, including *The Three Sisters* and *A Streetcar Named Desire*. Zeffirelli embraced this new craft with a passion. He moved on to design stage sets for operas at La Scala in Milan and then to actually direct performances in that legendary theater.

Zeffirelli made his debut as a feature film director in 1966 with *The Taming of the Shrew*, an adaptation of the Shakespeare play that starred Elizabeth Taylor and Richard Burton. (Zeffirelli also wrote the screenplay.) The film was universally praised, nominated for three Academy Awards, and named one of the ten best films of the year by the National Board of Review. Close to ten films have followed, with adaptations of Shakespeare among the highlights, notably the 1990 version of *Hamlet*, starring Mel Gibson and Glenn Close.

Zeffirelli has also staged operas at the Metropolitan Opera in New York, beginning with *Falstaff* in 1964. Zeffirelli's opera productions are invariably lavish and spectacular; though some critics complain that he overdoes it, audiences always get their money's worth. Zeffirelli's 1985 staging of the ballet *Swan Lake* also raised eyebrows, as he used *two* ballerinas (one each for the roles of Odette and Odile) instead of the traditional single star.

At the conclusion of his autobiography, Zeffirelli explains the motivating force behind his influential career:

> I don't want to claim a sense of mission, as if I have singlemindedly been striving all my life to give opera back to the people, but now that the chance has come, I am happy to have done it. I have always been a popularizer and have always regretted that after Puccini the mass audience has been neglected, even on occasions despised, by modern composers. I have found it an irritating irony that those who espouse populist political views often want art to be "difficult"; and the supposedly *avant garde*, while being politically left-wing, has often proved culturally élitist. Yet I, who favour the Right in our democracy, believe passionately in a broad culture made accessible to as many as possible. I am wary of critics who think it smart to pour scorn on my productions because, as they put it, they are aesthetically self-indulgent. In all honesty, I don't believe that millions of young people throughout the world wept over my film of *Romeo and Juliet* just because the costumes were splendid.

99

Frank Capra

1897–1991

When Jimmy Stewart walked the halls of the Capitol building, I walked with him. When he stood in awe of that great man at the Lincoln Memorial, I bowed my head too. When he stood in the Senate chamber and refused to knuckle under to the vested interests, I began to realize, through the power of motion pictures, one man can make a difference.
— RONALD REAGAN, talking about Frank Capra's *Mr. Smith Goes to Washington*

In addition to creating an annual Christmas tradition with his now classic film *It's a Wonderful Life*, Frank Capra virtually created an entire genre of filmmaking with a series of comedy-dramas in which an idealistic young hero faces the powers of an evil and mercenary foe and ends up the triumphant winner after a battle of wits and morals. Capra essentially created the archetype of the "happy end-ing" movie, and his work spawned generations of filmmakers who mimicked his warm and sincere style. Capra's style and directorial voice were so unique that today, when someone describes a film, a book, or even a real-life event as "Capraesque," we all know exactly what the speaker means.

Frank (Francesco) Capra was born in Bisaquino, Sicily, on May 18, 1897, and emigrated to the United States with his parents when he was three years old. His family settled in California, where his father picked fruit in the San Fernando Valley to support his family. Capra had six brothers and sisters; when the Capra children were growing up, they all worked in the fruit fields while attending school. In 1915, at the age of eighteen, Capra entered the California Institute of Technology in Pasadena, ultimately graduat-ing with a degree in chemical engineering. After a period of wan-dering around trying to find work, he ended up with a job writing gags for Hal Roach and Mack Sennett, after which he went to work for Columbia Studios. His first film for Columbia was the 1928 com-edy *That Certain Thing*. The studio was pleased with the results, and in the same year Capra turned out a string of low-budget flicks, including *So This Is Love, The Matinee Idol, The Way of the Strong, Say It With Sables, Submarine*, and *The Power of the Press*.

Capra's break-out success came in 1933 with *Lady for a Day*, which featured the character of "Apple Annie" and foreshadowed many of the ideas and themes that would characterize his later, more mature works. In 1934, Capra turned to screwball comedy with *It Happened One Night*, which starred Clark Gable and Claudette Colbert. *It Happened One Night* has consistently been ranked as one of the best screen comedies of all time, and *Entertainment Weekly* notes that "Frank Capra gives [Gable and Colbert's] strange coupling emotional pull—something that few imitators have achieved."

The first truly Capraesque film came in 1936 with the stirring *Mr. Deeds Goes to Town*. In the film, Gary Cooper's character, Mr. Deeds, inherits $20 million and immediately gives it away. He falls in love with a beautiful reporter played by Jean Arthur, who tries diligently to figure out this unlikely philanthropist's motives. Based on Clarence Buddington Kelland's play *Opera Hut*, this simplistic morality tale about honesty and corruption struck a chord with a nation struggling through the Great Depression, and it made Capra famous.

Lost Horizon and *You Can't Take It With You* (based on the play) followed *Mr. Deeds* and then, in 1939 (the year that also saw the release of *Gone With the Wind* and *The Wizard of Oz*), Capra hit a huge homerun with the thematic sequel to *Mr. Deeds, Mr. Smith Goes to Washington.* The film scholar Leland Poague has described the essence of this film in *The Cinema of Frank Capra:*

> *Mr. Smith Goes to Washington* . . . is Capra's most successful attempt at dealing with politics within the comic framework. He achieves a level of moral sophistication that does full duty to the political reality without attempting the kind of detailed political analysis that would obstruct the essential comic movement. Capra was clearly aware that he had excelled himself, for the film evidences a stylistic confidence far beyond the low-key perfection of . . . *It Happened One Night* . . . which was concerned very much with minute observations of personal, emotional reality. Accordingly, Capra could let his camera dwell longer on a single mood or gesture. In *Mr. Smith,* on the other hand, Capra expands his field of vision. We see a greater use of long shot and montage, and a higher editing frequency, all calculated to present a larger world with the same sense of acute observation that has always been Capra's forte.
>
> And it is this stylistic precision that makes the film the masterpiece it is.

Mr. Smith Goes to Washington tells the story of a naive scoutmaster (James Stewart) who is picked by his state's praetorian governor to fill out the term of a dead senator. When he arrives in Washington he quickly realizes that he is beset by corruption. With the help of a hard-as-nails reporter (Jean Arthur) who is won over by Smith's dedication and faith in America, he speaks out in a day-long filibuster on the Senate floor that is one of the most emotionally powerful scenes ever filmed. *Mr. Smith* illustrates the "David vs. Goliath" theme Capra revisited many times throughout his career: Good ultimately prevails against the powerful and corrupt, as long as the ideals of America—liberty, decency, and courage—are ardently applied. This cinematic expression of the eternal struggle between good and evil is one of the notable hallmarks of a "Frank Capra" film.

In 1946, after producing the *Why We Fight* series of films for the War Department, Capra released the film that to this day is his most beloved, *It's a Wonderful Life.* This uplifting classic has become part of the Christmas tradition in America. George Bailey and his trials still mesmerize new generations of viewers, and filmmakers continue to pay homage to its influence with references in a wide range of films, notably Steven Spielberg's *Gremlins* (1984).

Frank Capra died in 1991 at the age of ninety-four. During his life he and his films won a number of Academy Awards, including Best Director Oscars for *It Happened One Night, Mr. Deeds Goes to Town*, and *You Can't Take It With You*. It is safe to say that as long as films are made in the United States, some of them will inevitably be described as Capraesque.

Madonna

1958–

I have the same goal I've had since I was a little girl: I want to
rule the world!

—MADONNA

In September 1987, Madonna performed in Turin, Italy, for a
crowd of 65,000 fans. Toward the end of the show, she drove the
audience wild by shouting out, "*Io sono fiera di essere italiana!*" which
means, "I am proud to be an Italian!" Madonna's ethnic pride
notwithstanding, there are many Italians and Italian Americans
who are reluctant to acknowledge her as one of their own. Her blatant sexuality and no-holds-barred style offends many people who
have conservative religious and social views or who simply grew up
in a time when women were expected to display considerably more
modesty. However much opposition she arouses, there is no deny-

ing that Madonna has had a gigantic impact on contemporary music, fashion, and popular culture. In *Madonna Unauthorized*, Christopher Andersen noted that "*NBC Nightly News* deemed her a 'growth industry' " while "no less an authority than *Forbes* magazine proclaimed her 'the Smartest Business Woman in America.' " He also observed:

> There has never been anyone like her. On top of the show business Everest since 1984, Madonna is, quite simply, the most famous woman in the world today. She is not just the planet's number one female pop star with over 50 million albums sold and more consecutive top hit singles than The Beatles, but more: a self-made icon. She has held the public's attention by repeatedly shocking and offending it. "Hate this!" seems to be her credo, as she smashes one taboo after another. Like a stinging slap in the face from an angry lover, Madonna is often painful to take but also impossible to ignore.

Some fans become so obsessive about Madonna that they will endure hours in the rain or the cold just to get a glimpse of her. At the other end of the spectrum, her detractors sometimes go to extremes of rhetorical overkill, as did Boston University president John Silber when he said, "Madonna has no more right to set this example for our kids than Adolf Hitler did or than Saddam Hussein does."

Madonna Louise Ciccone was born on August 16, 1958, in Bay City, Michigan. She was named after her mother, whom she adored. To this day, the defining event in her life was her mother's tragic death from breast cancer at the age of thirty. "My mother's death left me with a certain kind of loneliness, an incredible longing for something," Madonna has said. "If I hadn't had that emptiness, I wouldn't have been so driven." As a teenager, she became rebellious and sexually precocious. After high school she moved to New York, where she attended the Alvin Ailey Dance School, made the underground film *A Certain Sacrifice*, posed nude, christened herself "Boy Toy" (a name she immortalized in Magic Marker graffiti all over town) and hit the clubs every night, hoping for her big break as a singer.

In 1980, after working as lead singer with the New York dance band Breakfast Club, Madonna left the group and formed the band Emmy with Stephen Bray. Madonna and Bray made some demo dance tracks without the other band members, and after one of the tapes was heard by an executive at Sire Records, the label signed Madonna to a recording contract.

Madonna's first single, "Everybody," became a huge club hit in 1982. Her second single, "Physical Attraction," enjoyed equal success with clubgoers. She followed these two tracks with "Holiday" (penned by Jellybean Benitzez)—her first top-forty hit—in the summer of 1983. In September 1983, Madonna released her first album, *Madonna*. This recording included the track "Borderline," which became her first top-ten hit in March of 1984. *Madonna* ultimately went triple platinum and started the age of the music video.

Since 1984, Madonna has starred (and done cameos) in movies (*Desperately Seeking Susan, Vision Quest, Shanghai Surprise, Who's That Girl?, Bloodhounds of Broadway, Dick Tracy, Truth or Dare, A League of Their Own, Body of Evidence, Shadows and Fog,* and *Evita,* for which she won a Golden Globe award in 1997); produced a controversial bestseller, the soft-core pornographic book of photos and erotic writings entitled *Sex;* released videos for all of her singles; acted on Broadway in David Mamet's *Speed-the-Plow,* traveled the world with her massive Blonde Ambition concert tour; and had a baby (Lourdes Maria).

Madonna's musical output has also been prodigious, including such notable albums as *Madonna* (1983): *Like a Virgin* (1984); *True Blue* (1986); *Vogue* (1990); *Truth or Dare* (1991); *Erotica* (1992); *Bedtime Stories* (1994); and *Human Nature* (1995). Important Madonna singles include "Everybody" and "Holiday" (1983); "Material Girl" and "Crazy For You" (1985); "Papa Don't Preach" (1986); "Open Your Heart" and "La Isla Bonita" (1987); "Express Yourself" and "Cherish" (1989); "Justify My Love" (1990); "Erotica" and "This Used to Be My Playground" (1994).

Madonna has had a wide-reaching impact on larger cultural issues, including the debate over feminism and the widespread sociocultural unfamiliarity with art and history.

One of Madonna's biggest fans and staunchest defenders is writer Camille Paglia (see CAMILLE PAGLIA [97]). In her 1992 book, *Sex, Art and American Culture*, Paglia champions Madonna in two essays, "Madonna I: Animality and Artifice"; and "Madonna II: Venus of the Radio Waves." In the first, Paglia responds to those who believe Madonna has set feminism back years with her "Boy Toy" persona and sensibility:

> Madonna is the true feminist. She exposes the puritanism
> and suffocating ideology of American feminism, which is

stuck in an adolescent whining mode. Madonna has taught young women to be fully female and sexual while still exercising control over their lives. She shows girls how to be attractive, sensual, energetic, ambitious, aggressive, and funny—all at the same time.

In the second essay, Paglia convincingly cites Madonna's historical and artistic sources (including peep shows, Marlene Dietrich, "Italian Catholic paganism," European art films of the fifties and sixties, the Whore of Babylon, and the high-glamour photographs of Hurrell) and boldly proclaims to those who would denounce the megastar, "Most people who denigrate Madonna do so out of ignorance."

Madonna changed popular culture with her recordings, concerts, videos, and fashion statements. Her influence can be felt in many aspects of today's music, dance, and video, and she has left her mark on everything from magazine photography to TV commercials.

PICTURE ACKNOWLEDGMENTS

Every effort has been made to locate the copyright holder of the photos used in *The Italian 100*. Some illustrations and photos are in the public domain.

© The Nobel Foundation: Enrico Fermi, Rita Levi-Montalcini, Salvador Edward Luria.

Courtesy Bank of America: A. P. Giannini.

Courtesy Bettmann Archives: Dante Alighieri, St. Thomas Aquinas, Giovanni Boccaccio, John Cabot, Christopher Columbus, Leonardo Fibonacci ("page from Italian arithmetic book, ca. 1491"), St. Francis of Assisi, Galileo Galilei, Lorenzo de' Medici, Michelangelo, Petrarch, Giacomo Puccini, Raphael, Gioacchino Rossini, Alessandro Scarlatti, Domenico Scarlatti, Titian, Evangelista Torricelli, Leonardo da Vinci, Antonio Vivaldi, Alessandro Volta, Giovanni da Verrazano, Amerigo Vespucci.

Courtesy Brown Brothers: Amadeo Avogadro, Al "Scarface" Capone, Enrico Caruso, Giotto, Maria Montessori, Niccola Sacco and Bartolomeo Vanzetti.

Courtesy Culver Pictures, Inc.: Leon Battista Alberti, Filippo Brunelleschi, Giulio Caccini (frontespiece from the opera "Euridice" with music by Caccini), Benvenuto Cellini, Cimabue, Camillo Golgi, Niccolò Tartaglia.

Courtesy Iacocca & Associates, Inc.: Lee Iacocca.

Courtesy Metropolitan Museum of Art, The Crosby Brown Collection of Musical Instruments, 1889. (89.4.1219): picture of grand pianoforte, ca. 1720, built by Bartolommeo Cristofori.

Courtesy New York Public Library: Vincenzo Bellini, Boethius, Donatello, Gaetano Donizetti, Gabriel Fallopius, Girolamo Fracastoro, Luigi Galvani, Giuseppe Garibaldi, Francesco Maria Grimaldi, Guido of Arezzo, Niccolò Machiavelli, Marcello Malpighi, Aldo Manuzio (Aldus Manutius), Alessandro Manzoni, Masaccio, Giuseppe Mazzini, Claudio Monteverdi, Giovanni Battista Morgagni, Niccolò Paganini, Marco Polo, Francesco Redi, Ascanio Sobrero, Lazzaro Spallanzani, Antonio Stradivari, Gasparo Tagliacozzi, Giorgio Vasari, Giuseppe Verdi.

Courtesy Photofest: Bernardo Bertolucci, Frank Capra, Francis Ford Coppola, Robert De Niro, Vittorio De Sica, Joe DiMaggio, Federico Fellini, Sophia Loren, Madonna, Marcello Mastrioanni, Benito Mussolini, Al Pacino, Luciano Pavarotti, Martin Scorsese, Frank Sinatra, Arturo Toscanini, Luchino Visconti, Franco Zeffirelli.

Courtesy New York Times Pictures: Italo Calvino (photo by Fred R. Conrad).

Courtesy Salk Institute: Renato Dulbecco.

Courtesy Time Magazine Syndication: Camille Paglia (photo by Mario Ruiz).

Courtesy Wide World Photos: Charles "Lucky" Luciano.

350

BIBLIOGRAPHY

Abodaher, David. *Iacocca.* New York: Zebra Books, 1982.

Acton, Harold. *The Last Medici.* London: Methuen, 1973.

Allen, Woody. *Four Films of Woody Allen: Annie Hall, Interiors, Manhattan, Stardust Memories.* New York: Random House, 1982.

Allsop, Kenneth. *The Bootleggers and Their Era.* Garden City, N.Y.: Doubleday, 1961.

Alpert, Hollis. *Fellini: A Life.* New York: Atheneum, 1986.

Andersen, Christopher. *Madonnna Unauthorized.* New York: Dell, 1991.

Attenborough, David. *Life on Earth: A Natural History.* Boston, Mass.: Little, Brown, 1979.

Augarde, Tony, ed. *The Oxford Dictionary of Modern Quotations.* New York: Oxford University Press, 1991.

Aylesworth, Thomas G., and John S. Bowman. *The World Almanac Who's Who of Film.* New York: Pharos Books, 1987.

Barone, Arturo. *Italians First! An A to Z of Everything Achieved First by Italians.* Kent, England: Renaissance Books, 1994.

Barzini, Luigi. *The Italians.* New York: Atheneum, 1964.

Beckett, Wendy (in association with the National Gallery of Art, Washington, D. C.). *The Story of Painting: The Essential Guide to the History of Western Art.* New York: Dorling Kindersley, 1994.

Belford, Ros, Martin Dunford, and Celia Woolfrey. *Italy: The Rough Guide.* London: Rough Guides, 1993.

Bergin, Thomas G. *Dante.* New York: Orion Press, 1965.

Berra, Yogi (with Tom Horton). *Yogi: It Ain't Over . . .* New York: McGraw-Hill, 1989.

Betti, Liliana. *Fellini.* Boston, Mass.: Little, Brown, 1979.

Blackwell, Earl. *Earl Blackwell's Entertainment Celebrity Register.* New York: Visible Ink Press, 1991.

Boccaccio, Giovanni. *The Decameron.* Translated by Mark Musa and Peter E. Bondanella. New York: Norton, 1977.

Bolander, Donald O., comp. *Instant Quotation Dictionary.* New York: Dell, 1972.

Boorstin, Daniel J. *The Creators.* New York: Random House, 1992.

———. *The Discoverers.* New York: Random House, 1983.

Bramley, Serge. *Leonardo: Discovering the Life of Leonard da Vinci.* Translated by Siân Reynolds. New York: HarperCollins, 1991.

Browning, Frank, and John Gerassi. *The American Way of Crime: From Salem to Watergate.* New York: Putnam's, 1980.

Calvino, Italo. *If on a Winter's Night a Traveler.* Translated by William Weaver. New York: Harcourt Brace Jovanovich, 1981.

———. *Mr. Palomar.* Translated by William Weaver. New York: Harcourt Brace

Jovanovich, 1985.
———. *The Uses of Literature.* Translated by Patrick Creagh. New York: Harcourt Brace Jovanovich, 1986.
Cellini, Benvenuto. *Autobiography.* Translated by George Bull. New York: Penguin, 1956.
Chotzinoff, Samuel. *Toscanini: An Intimate Portrait.* New York: Knopf, 1956.
Clark, Ronald W. *Einstein: The Life and Times.* New York: World Publishing, 1971.
Closson, Ernest. *History of the Piano.* Translated by Delano Ames. New York: St. Martin's Press, 1974.
Colón, Ferdinand. *The Life of the Admiral Christopher Columbus by His Son Ferdinand.* Translated by Benjamin Keen. New Brunswick, N.J.: Rutgers University Press, 1959.
Conati, Marcello, and Mario Medici, eds. *The Verdi-Boito Correspondence.* Chicago, Ill.: University of Chicago Press, 1994.
Connors, Martin, and Julia Furtaw, eds. *Videohound's Golden Movie Retriever.* Detroit, Mich.: Visible Ink Press, 1995.
Cowie, Peter, ed. *50 Major Film-Makers.* London: Tantivy Press, 1975.
Debus, Allen G., ed. *World Who's Who in Science: A Biographical Dictionary of Notable Scientists from Antiquity to the Present.* Chicago, Ill.: Marquis Who's Who, 1988.
Delaney, John J. *Pocket Dictionary of the Saints.* New York: Doubleday, 1980.
Delzell, Charles F., ed. *The Unification of Italy, 1859–1861: Cavour, Mazzini, or Garibaldi?* New York: Holt, Rinehart and Winston, 1965.
Dibner, Bern. *Galvani-Volta: A Controversy That Led to the Discovery of Useful Electricity.* Norwalk, Conn.: Burndy Library, 1952.
———. *Luigi Galvani.* Norwalk, Conn.: Burndy Library, 1971.
Donadio, Stephen, Joan Smith, Susan Mesner, and Rebecca Davison. *The New York Public Library Book of 20th-Century American Quotations.* New York: Warner Books, 1992.
Durant, Will. *The Renaissance: A History of Civilization in Italy from 1304–1576 A.D.* New York: MJF Books, 1953.
Durso, Joseph. *DiMaggio: The Last American Knight.* Boston, Mass.: Little, Brown, 1995.
Earl of Harewood, The, ed. *The Portable Kobbe's Opera Guide.* New York: Perigee Books, 1919.
Fargis, Paul, and Sheree Bykofsky, ed. dirs. *The New York Public Library Desk Reference.* New York: Simon & Schuster, 1989.
Fellini, Federico. *Fellini on Fellini.* Translated by Isabel Quigley. New York: Delacorte, 1976.
Fritzsch, Harald. *The Creation of Matter: The Universe from Beginning to End.* Translated by Jean Steinberg. New York: Basic Books, 1984.
Garraty, John A., and Peter Gay, eds. *The Columbia History of the World.* New York: Harper & Row, 1972.
George, Leonard. *Alternative Realities: The Paranormal, the Mystic and the Transcendent in Human Experience.* New York: Facts on File, 1995.
Gies, Joseph, and Frances Gies. *Leonard of Pisa and the New Mathematics of the Middle Ages.* New York: Crowell, 1969.
Gipe, George. *The Great American Sports Book: A Casual but Voluminous Look at American Spectator Sports from the Civil War to the Present Time.* Garden City, N.Y.: Doubleday, 1978.
Gore, Al. *Earth in the Balance: Ecology and the Human Spirit.* Boston, Mass.: Houghton Mifflin, 1992.
Gosch, Martin A., and Richard Hammer. *The Last Testament of Lucky Luciano.* Boston, Mass.: Little, Brown, 1974.
Green, Julien. *God's Fool: The Life and Times of Francis of Assisi.* New York: Harper &

Row, 1985.

Greenfield, Howard. *Caruso*. New York: Putnam's, 1983.

Hale, John. *The Civilization of Europe in the Renaissance*. New York: Atheneum, 1994.

Hales, E. E. Y. *Mazzini and the Secret Societies: The Making of a Myth*. New York: Kenedy & Sons, 1956.

Halliwell, Leslie. *Halliwell's Filmgoer's and Video Viewer's Companion*. 9th ed. New York: Harper & Row, 1988.

Hart, Michael H. *The 100: A Ranking of the Most Influential Persons in History*. New York: Citadel Press, 1995.

Hibbert, Christopher. *The House of Medici: Its Rise and Fall*. New York: William Morrow, 1975.

Hotchner, A. E. *Sophia, Living and Loving: Her Own Story*. New York: William Morrow, 1979

Howells, John G., M. D. *World History of Psychiatry*. New York: Brunner/Mazel, Publishers, 1975.

Humble, Richard. *Marco Polo*. New York: Putnam's, 1975.

Iacocca, Lee (with William Novak). *Iacocca: An Autobiography*. New York: Bantam Books, 1984.

James, Marquis, and Bessie Rowland James. *Biography of a Bank: The Story of Bank of America*. New York: Harper & Brothers, 1954.

Janson, H. W. *History of Art: A Survey of the Major Visual Arts from the Dawn of History to the Present Day*. Englewood Cliffs, N.J.: Prentice-Hall, and New York: Abrams, 1970.

Jones, Judy, and William Wilson. *An Incomplete Education*. New York: Ballantine Books, 1987.

Kael, Pauline. *State of the Art*. New York: Dutton, 1985.

———. *Taking It All In*. New York: Holt, Rinehart and Winston, 1980.

Katsaros, Thomas, and George J. Schiro. *A Brief History of the Western World*. Washington, D. C.: University Press of America, 1978.

Kelley, Kitty. *His Way: The Unauthorized Biography of Frank Sinatra*. New York: Bantam Books, 1986.

Kelly, Mary Pat. *Martin Scorsese: A Journey*. New York: Thunder's Mouth Press, 1991.

———. *Martin Scorsese: The First Decade*. Pleasantville, N.Y.: Redgrave Publishing, 1980.

King, Norman. *Madonna: The Book*. New York: William Morrow, 1991.

Kobler, John. *Capone: The Life and World of Al Capone*. New York: Putnam's, 1971.

Kolneder, Walter. *Antonio Vivaldi: His Life and Work*. Translated by Bill Hopkins. Berkeley, Calif.: University of California Press, 1970.

Kramer, Rita. *Maria Montessori: A Biography*. New York: Putnam's, 1976.

Kuiper, Kathleen, ed. *Merriam-Webster's Encyclopedia of Literature*. Springfield, Mass.: Merrian-Webster, Inc., Publishers, 1995.

Leff, Leonard J. *Film Plots: Scene-by-Scene Narrative Outlines for Feature Film Study*. Ann Arbor, Mich.: Pierian Press, 1983.

Lesberg, Sandy. *A Picture History of Crime*. New York: Haddington House, 1976.

Lewis, R. W. B. *The City of Florence: Historical Vistas and Personal Sightings*. New York: Farrar, Straus and Giroux, 1995.

Lloyd, Ann. *The Illustrated History of the Cinema*. New York: Macmillan, 1986.

Lomask, Milton. *The Biographer's Craft*. New York: Harper & Row, Publishers, 1986.

McClelland, Doug. *Hollywood Talks Turkey: The Screen's Biggest Flops*. Boston, Mass.: Faber and Faber, 1989.

Mangione, Jerre, and Ben Morreale. *La Storia: Five Centuries of the Italian American Experience*. New York: HarperPerennial, 1992.

Manzoni, Alessandro. *I Promessi Spose* (*The Betrothed*). New York: Collier & Son, 1909.

Marek, George R. *Toscanini*. New York: Atheneum, 1975.

Martin, George. *Verdi: His Music, Life and Times*. New York: Dodd, Mead, 1983.

Messadié, Gerald. *Great Inventions Through History*. New York: Chambers, 1991.

———. *Great Scientific Discoveries*. New York: Chambers, 1991.

Montessori, Maria. *Education and Peace*. Chicago, Ill.: Henry Regnery Company, 1972.

Morison, Samuel Eliot. *The Great Explorers: The European Discovery of America*. New York: Oxford University Press, 1978.

Ness, Eliot. *The Untouchables*. New York: Julian Messner, 1957.

Nicholls, Peter. *The Science in Science Fiction*. New York: Knopf, 1983.

Norwich, John Julius. *The Italians: History, Art, and the Genius of a People*. New York: Abrams, 1983.

Nowell, Charles E. *The Great Discoveries and the First Colonial Empires*. Ithaca, N.Y.: Cornell University Press, 1954.

Nuland, Sherwin B. *Doctors: The Biography of Medicine*. New York: Knopf, 1988.

Ochoa, George, and Melinda Corey. *The Timeline Book of Science*. New York: Ballantine Books, 1995.

———. *The Timeline Book of the Arts*. New York: Ballantine Books, 1995.

Osborne, Charles, ed. *The Dictionary of Composers*. New York: Barnes & Noble Books, 1995.

Oxford Dictionary of Quotations, The. 3d ed. New York: Oxford University Press, 1980.

Paglia, Camille. *Sex, Art, and American Culture*. New York: Vintage Books, 1992.

———. *Sexual Personae: Art and Decadence from Nefertiti to Emily Dickinson*. New York: Vintage Books, 1991.

———. *Vamps and Tramps*. New York: Vintage Books, 1994.

Panati, Charles. *Panati's Browser's Book of Beginnings*. Boston, Mass.: Hoghton Mifflin, 1984.

———. *Panati's Extraordinary Endings of Practically Everything and Everybody*. New York: Harper & Row, 1989.

———. *Panati's Parade of Fads, Follies, and Manias: The Origins of Our Most Cherished Obsessions*. New York: HarperPerennial, 1991.

Parry, J. H. *The Age of Reconnaissance*. Cleveland, Ohio: World Publishing, 1963.

Pavarotti, Luciano, with William Wright. *Pavarotti: My Own Story*. Garden City, N.Y.: Doubleday, 1981.

Pelikan, Jarislov, ed. *The World Treasury of Modern Religious Thought*. Boston, Mass.: Little, Brown, 1990.

Penrose, Boies. *Travel and Discovery in the Renaissance 1420–1620*. New York: Atheneum, 1975.

Phillips-Matz, Mary Jane. *Verdi: A Biography*. New York: Oxford University Press, 1993.

Plumb, J. H. *The Italian Renaissance: A Concise History of Its History and Culture*. New York: Harper & Row, 1961.

Poague, Leland A. *The Cinema of Frank Capra: An Approach to Film Comedy*. London: Tantivy Press, 1975.

Polo, Marco. *The Travels of Marco Polo*. New York: Modern Library, 1953.

Pottle, Frederick A. *James Boswell: The Earlier Years, 1740–1769*. New York: McGraw-Hill, 1966.

Pugnetti, Gino. *Portraits of Greatness: Verdi*. New York: Elite Publishing, 1984.

Raeburn, Michael, and Alan Kendall, eds. *Heritage of Music, Volume I: Classical Music and Its Origins*. New York: Oxford University Press, 1989.

———. *Heritage of Music, Volume II: The Romantic Era*. New York: Oxford University Press, 1989.

———. *Heritage of Music, Volume III: The Nineteenth-Century Legacy*. New York: Oxford University Press, 1989.

_____. *Heritage of Music, Volume IV: Music in the Twentieth-Century*. New York: Oxford University Press, 1989.

Raphael, Frederic, and Kenneth McLeish. *The List of Books*. New York: Harmony, 1981.

Ridley, Jasper. *Garibaldi*. New York: Viking, 1976.

Ridolfi, Roberto. *The Life of Niccolò Machiavelli*. Translated by Cecil Grayson. Chicago, Ill.: The University of Chicago Press, 1963.

Ringgold, Gene, and Clifford McCarty. *The Films of Frank Sinatra*. New York: Citadel Press, 1993.

Ripley, Elizabeth. *Botticelli: A Biography*. Philadelphia, Penn.: Lippincott, 1960.

Rowling, Marjorie. *Life in Medieval Times*. New York: Perigee Books, 1968.

Rudman, Harry W. *Italian Nationalism and English Letters: Figures of the Risorgimento and Victorian Men of Letters*. New York: AMS Press, 1966.

Russell, Paul. *The Gay 100: A Ranking of the Most Influential Gay Men and Lesbians, Past and Present*. New York: Citadel Press, 1995.

Sabatier, Paul. *Life of St. Francis of Assisi*. New York: Scribner's, 1894.

Sackett, Susan. *The Hollywood Reporter Book of Box Office Hits*. New York: Billboard Books, 1990.

Salachas, Gilbert. *Federico Fellini*. New York: Crown, 1963.

Salvemini, Gaetano. *Mazzini*. Translated by I. M. Rawson. New York: Collier Books, 1962.

Scorsese, Martin. *Scorsese on Scorsese*. Edited by David Thompson and Ian Christie. London: Faber and Faber, 1989.

Seldes, George, compiler. *The Great Quotations*. New York: Pocket Books, 1967.

Sennett, Ted. *Laughing in the Dark: Movie Comedy from Groucho to Woody*. New York: St. Martin's Press, 1992.

Servadio, Gaia. *Luchino Visconti: A Biography*. New York: Franklin Watts, 1983.

Seymore, James W., Jr., managing ed. *The Entertainment Weekly Guide to the Greatest Movies Ever Made*. New York: Warner Books, 1994.

Seymour-Smith, Martin, ed. *Novels and Novelists: A Guide to the World of Fiction*. London: Windward, 1980.

Shapiro, Andrew L. *We're Number One!: Where America Stands—and Falls—in the New World Order*. New York: Vintage Books, 1992.

Shepherd, William R. *Historical Atlas*. New York: Hammond, 1929.

Sigerist, Henry E. *A History of Medicine, Volume I: Primitive and Archaic Medicine*. New York: Oxford University Press, 1951.

_____. *A History of Medicine, Volume II: Early Greek, Hindu, and Persian Medicine*. New York: Oxford University Press, 1961.

Slonimsky, Nicolas, ed. *Baker's Biographical Dictionary of Musicians*. New York: Schirmer Books, 1984.

Smith, Dennis Mack. *Mussolini's Roman Empire*. New York: Viking, 1976.

Smith, Huston. *The Religions of Man*. New York: Harper & Row, 1958.

Smith, John Holland. *Francis of Assisi*. New York: Scribner's, 1972.

Smith, Robert. *Baseball in the Afternoon: Tales from a Bygone Era*. New York: Simon & Schuster, 1993.

Smith, Roger. *Catastrophes and Disasters*. New York: Chambers, 1992.

Spignesi, Stephen J. *The Odd Index: The Ultimate Compendium of Bizarre and Unusual Facts*. New York: Plume, 1994.

Stempel, Tom. *Framework: A History of Screenwriting in the American Film*. New York: Continuum, 1988.

Stern, Jane, and Michael Stern. *Jane & Michael Stern's Encyclopedia of Pop Culture: An A to Z Guide of Who's Who and What's What, From Aerobics and Bubble Gum to Valley of the Dolls and Moon Unit Zappa*. New York: HarperPerennial, 1992.

Stirling, Monica. *A Screen of Time: A Study of Luchino Visconti*. New York: Harcourt

Brace Jovanovich, 1979.

Stokstad, Marilyn. *Art History*. New York: Abrams, 1995.

Sullivan, Jack, ed. *The Penguin Encyclopedia of Horror and the Supernatural*. New York: Viking Penguin, 1986.

Took, Barry. *Comedy Greats: A Celebration of Comic Genius Past and Present*. Wellinborough, England: Equation, 1989.

Trager, James. *The People's Chronology: A Year-by-Year Record of Human Events from Prehistory to the Present*. New York: Holt, 1992.

Trefil, James. *1001 Things Everyone Should Know About Science*. New York: Doubleday, 1992.

Vasari, Giorgi. *The Great Masters: Giotto, Botticelli, Leonardo, Raphael, Michelangelo, Titian*. Translated by Gaston Du C. de Vere. Beaux Arts Editions, 1986.

_____. *The Lives of the Artists*. Translated by Julia Conaway Bondanella and Peter Bondanella. New York: Oxford University Press, 1991.

Walker, Frank. *The Man Verdi*. Chicago, Ill.: University of Chicago Press, 1982.

Wallace, Irving, David Wallechinsky, Amy Wallace, and Sylvia Wallace. *The People's Almanac Presents the Book of Lists #2*. New York: Bantam, 1980.

Weaver, William. *Verdi: A Documentary Study*. New York: Thames and Hudson, 1977.

White, John. *The Meeting of Science and Spirit: Guidelines for a New Age*. New York: Paragon House, 1990.

Whitfield, J. H. *A Short History of Italian Literature*. Middlesex, England: Penguin, 1960.

Who's Who in America, the Editors of. *The Celebrity Who's Who*. New York: Pharos Books, 1986.

Wilkins, Ernest Hatch. *A History of Italian Literature*. Cambridge, Mass.: Harvard University Press, 1954.

World Resources Institute. *The 1993 Information Please Environmental Almanac*. Boston, Mass.: Houghton Mifflin, 1993.

Wyden, Peter. *The Unknown Iacocca: An Unauthorized Biography*. New York: William Morrow, 1987.

Yanak, Ted, and Pam Cornelison. *The Great American History Fact-Finder*. New York: Houghton Mifflin, 1993.

Young, Colonel G. F. *The Medici*. New York: Modern Library, 1930.

Youngson, Robert M., and the Diagram Group. *The Surgery Book: An Illustrated Guide to 73 of the Most Common Operations*. New York: St. Martin's Press, 1993.

Yule, Andrew. *Life on the Wire: The Life and Art of Al Pacino*. New York: Donald I. Fine, 1991.

Zampaglione, Gerardo. *Italy*. London: Ernest Benn Limited, 1956.

Zeffirelli, Franco. *Zeffirelli: The Autobiography of Franco Zeffirelli*. New York: Weidenfeld & Nicolson, 1986.

INDEX

ABOUT THE AUTHOR

Stephen J. Spignesi is a writer who specializes in topics of popular culture, including television, film, contemporary fiction, and historical biography. He has written several authorized entertainment books and has worked with Stephen King, Turner Entertainment, the Margaret Mitchell Estate, Andy Griffith, Viacom, and other entertainment industry personalities and entities on a wide range of projects. Mr. Spignesi has also contributed essays, chapters, articles, and introductions to a wide range of books.

In addition to writing, Mr. Spignesi also lectures on a variety of popular culture subjects; has taught courses on writing and publishing; and is the founder and editor-in-chief of the small press publishing company, **The Stephen John Press**. He is a graduate of the University of New Haven and lives in New Haven with his wife, Pam.

Spignesi's books include: *Mayberry, My Hometown* (Popular Culture, Ink); *The Complete Stephen King Encyclopedia* (Popular Culture, Ink; Contemporary Books); *The Stephen King Quiz Book* (Signet); *The Second Stephen King Quiz Book* (Signet); *The Woody Allen Companion* (Andrews and McMeel; Plexus London; Popular Culture, Ink); *The Official "Gone With the Wind" Companion* (Plume); *The V. C. Andrews Trivia and Quiz Book* (Signet); *The Odd Index: The Ultimate Compendium of Bizarre and Unusual Facts* (Plume); *What's Your "Mad About You" IQ?* (Citadel Press); *The Gore Galore Video Quiz Book* (Signet); *What's Your "Friends" IQ?* (Citadel Press); *The Celebrity Baby Name Book* (Signet); *The "ER" Companion* (Citadel Press); *The J.F.K. Jr. Scrapbook* (Citadel Press); *Stephen King A to Z* (forthcoming, Popular Culture, Ink); *The Robin Williams Scrapbook* (forthcoming, Citadel Press).